D1112567

THE SPECTRE OF DEMOCRACY

The Spectre of Democracy

The Rise of Modern Democracy as Seen by its Critics

Michael Levin

Senior Lecturer in Politics
Goldsmiths' College, University of London

NEW YORK UNIVERSITY PRESS
Washington Square, New York

321.8
L665a

© Michael Levin 1992

All rights reserved

First published in the U. S. A. in 1992 by
NEW YORK UNIVERSITY PRESS
Washington Square
New York, N.Y. 10003

Printed in Hong Kong

Library of Congress Cataloging-in-Publication Data
Levin, Michael, 1940–
The spectre of democracy : the rise of modern democracy as seen by
its critics / Michael Levin.
p.   cm.
Includes bibliographical references and index.
ISBN 0–8147–5060–5
1. Democracy—History.   2. Suffrage—History.   3. Conservatism–
–History.   I. Title.
JC421.L48   1992
321.8'09—dc20   91–30645
                                                       CIP

For Patricia

University Libraries
Carnegie Mellon University
Pittsburgh, Pennsylvania 15213

Contents

A Spectre is haunting Europe – the spectre of Communism. All the Powers of old Europe have entered into a holy alliance to exorcise this spectre: Pope and Czar, Metternich and Guizot, French radicals and German police-spies.

Marx and Engels

Today's chaos hides behind one word, 'democracy'. This word is sovereign, universal. All parties seek to appropriate it . . . It is the revolutionary and despotic idea *par excellence*. It is this idea that must be extirpated.

Guizot

Whence comes it, this universal, big, black Democracy; whither tends it; what is the meaning of it?

Carlyle

Preface

'A Spectre is haunting Europe.' On that point Marx and Engels were certainly correct. However, that spectre was not so much of communism as of democracy. Today these phenomena are regarded as mutually exclusive. A century-and-a-half ago they could be taken as identical. Communism was merely the most extreme form of the wider democratic tendency. Before the 1848–9 revolutions the main radical currents, whether liberal, socialist or anarchist, saw themselves as on the same side and engaged in the same struggle against the forces of restoration. At the time the *Communist Manifesto* was written, the Communist League, from whom it was commissioned, represented no more than a minor clique. It was a form of self-important special pleading to imagine that the established powers of Europe feared this as-yet fringe group of mainly German artisans and intellectuals. Thus Marx and Engels drew on to themselves an antipathy that really applied to the much broader radical movement of which they were but a small part.

It is the fear of this wider movement which is the theme of this book. My interest in the subject developed out of my study on *Marx, Engels and Liberal Democracy* (Macmillan, 1989). A number of themes mentioned briefly in Chapter 1 of that work are given more extended treatment here. In a sense the two books are complementary. The first considered a left-wing analysis of emerging liberal democracy while the second looks at the same phenomenon from the viewpoints of certain right-wing thinkers.

The first chapter of the present book provides a history of franchise extensions in the United States of America, France, Germany and the United Kingdom. It is, admittedly, too brief for students primarily interested in that process but is intended just to present in outline the milestones along the road of political democratisation. It should, additionally, provide some background and context for the four thinkers from those four countries who will be considered in Part II (Chapters 3 to 6).

The second chapter provides an overview of the main themes used by opponents of franchise extension. They tended to regard the *status quo* as satisfactory and hence judged proposals for change as unnecessary. They also emphasised that stability should be given priority, that experience and expertise were basic necessities and that the soundest judgements were most likely to come from those possessed of property and rationality.

We now turn from the general to the particular and look at four key thinkers in the debate on democratic government. Chapter 3 considers John Adams, the first Vice-President and second President of the United States of America. Adams had supported the American Revolution of 1776 but the consequences of the French Revolution and fears for the stability of his own country made him suspicious of the democratic movement.

In Chapter 4 we turn to Hegel, who accepted the liberatory ideas of the French Revolution, but regarded the attempts at implementation as incapable of creating the cohesion that modern societies required.

Alexis de Tocqueville, who is the subject of Chapter 5, visited the United States of America to see democracy in action. He viewed the victory of democracy as inevitable but feared for the survival of liberty alongside it.

In Chapter 6 we consider Thomas Carlyle, a right-wing radical critic of aristocratic regimes both in pre-revolutionary France and in nineteenth-century England. In his view democracy dealt negligent aristocracies their just deserts, but was in itself incapable of producing the true and worthy aristocracy that society required.

Two groups were relatively late in achieving citizenship rights. Their disqualifications were genetically based. In Chapter 7 we examine the ideology of black subordination as found in the United States of America. The southern states' pro-slavery literature drew on the Bible, the ancient Greeks and the hardships of the modern 'free' worker in the attempt to justify continuing black slavery. The ideology of black subordination survived emancipation from slavery and helped delay the political enfranchisement of American blacks until the 1960s.

Women, whose political integration is the subject of Chapter 8, were the last major grouping to achieve political rights. In addition to particular alleged disqualifications, such as being suited by nature for domestic life, they shared the deficiencies attributed to other subordinate groups. Thus they were seen by men as being irrational, relatively uneducated and, for most of the nineteenth century, unpropertied.

In the Conclusion we shall take an overview of the anti-democratic arguments and consider which of them appear most prescient and insightful, and whether any have survived as factors in modern liberal democratic politics.

To an extent I am here telling a story because I happen to be interested in it. Beyond that, however, I hope this account has a certain educational value. I wish to counter the inclination which too easily accepts present values as eternal norms by showing that the prevailing ideological status of democracy is relatively new. Before the First World War the case for franchise extension had to contend with an entrenched antipathy to democratic ideas. As history is so often biased towards the winners this is something of which we easily lose sight. Consequently, only if we resurrect expressions of this antipathy are we able to understand the victories that the democratic cause has won, for that requires us to know what it was won against.

There remains much that my focus leaves out. Other western countries can also lay claim to an absorbing franchise history and I am also interested in them as well as in the later fate of democracy in the 'Third' and communist worlds. Some of these concerns I now hope to investigate. However, the restricted scope of this work is as much as I can cope with at one go.

Whatever merits this study possesses have been much enhanced by the help of friends and colleagues who agreed to look through earlier drafts. Shirley Hyde and Barbara Ballis Lal have each read and commented on nearly the whole work. I am very grateful for their help and encouragement as also for that of Frances Heidensohn, David Lazar, Josep Llobera, Howard Williams and Jim Wood. Thanks are also due to Joy Seaton both for her typing and for stylistic improvements. My wife has taught me not to write 'America' when I mean merely the United States of America. That is the least of my reasons for dedicating this book to her.

Michael Levin
Forest Hill, London

Acknowledgements

Chapter 4 includes sections drawn from my part of 'Inherited Power and Popular Representation: A Tension in Hegel's Political Theory', co-authored with Howard Williams. The article appeared in *Political Studies*, Vol. xxxv, no. 1 (1987) and I am grateful to the publishers, Basil Blackwell Ltd, for permission to make use of it.

PART I Facts and Theories

1 The Legislative Background

I THE UNITED STATES OF AMERICA

In the last quarter of the eighteenth century two mighty revolutions shook the supposedly solid foundations of the European *anciens régimes*. In 1776 the thirteen American colonies opted out of the British Empire by asserting their independence. Thirteen years later the French overthrew the Bourbon monarchy and attempted to establish government on the basis of liberty and rationality. The latter upheaval has left a deeper imprint upon the historical memory. Its excesses, as much as its successes, have been a constant source of fascination. The French overthrew an indigenous ruling class. Theirs was truly a social revolution. The Americans, in contrast, despatched their external rulers from whence they came. Theirs was the first major colonial independence movement. Though no great internal social revolution took place, we may say that theirs was also the first modern political revolution. The constitution of 1787 outlined a form of government that claimed no ecclesiastical basis and was without hereditary offices. Furthermore, in contrast to the various constitutions of the French Revolution, the United States Constitution remains the sole survivor of such early attempts at the rational construction of governmental systems.

For over two hundred years the United States of America has been a potent symbol of the modern. The very phrase 'the new world' encapsulates the perceived distinction between the old world of Europe with its medieval encumbrances, class distinctions and ossified political arrangements, and the virgin territories of America where land was plenty and mankind had the opportunity to begin afresh on the basis of rationality, equality and human rights. In many ways the modern age begins with 1776 as what Seymour M. Lipset calls 'The First New Nation' shook off colonial subservience and adopted a pioneer stance, not just in terms of westward exploration but, even more significantly, in terms of political arrangements. Some saw the American experiment as the powder-keg that led to the explosion in France in 1789 and whose ineluctable task was still to be completed. From a European perspective the United States was the

3

first democracy, scrutinised from afar with a fascination that has not yet abated. For some it was a warning experiment best avoided; for others a model for imitation. In 1831 the French aristocrat Alexis de Tocqueville travelled to America to observe democracy in its most advanced form. In 1847 Engels referred to America 'where a democratic constitution has been introduced'.[1] An image of America as born free, unencumbered and thereby in the vanguard of modernisation, has continued into our own time. Thus the aforementioned Professor Lipset found 'universal suffrage in America long before it came in other nations', and the first President, George Washington, 'set a precedent as the first head of a modern state to turn over office to a duly elected successor'.[2]

Here we shall not deny America's trendsetting achievements, although the simple corollary of their deriving from a cultural *tabula rasa* must be rejected. The 'Founding Fathers' were not the Romulus and Remus of the new republic, orphaned, unsocialised, juvenile, and, apart from the company of wolves, alone. Rather were they cultivated, civilised white men who carried their Bibles under their arms and were imbued with Anglo-Saxon social and political assumptions.[3] America's advanced role, then, stems not from the absence of a European culture, but, more precisely, from the absence of the entrenched power structures that European radicals struggled to overcome. Thus, in respect of the class disqualifications from political participation, the United States could modernise without generating the full counter-movements that impeded political change in Europe. However, in terms of overcoming the sex disqualification, the United States moved in accord with the pace of European developments; in terms of race barriers the country had acute problems of its own, as we shall see in Chapter 7. Whether, in Lipset's imprecise phrase, the United States actually had universal suffrage *'long before . . .* other nations' (emphasis added) is a matter I hope the rest of this chapter will illuminate.[4]

The absence of entrenched aristocratic and ecclesiastical power gave the United States a propitious basis from which to move towards modern democracy. This, however, was certainly not a path the founders intended to explore. Although they would in principle have opposed the British House of Lords for its basis in inheritance, they would have accepted the consequence that the landed interest had a veto-right on all legislation. In contrast to more modern assumptions, they regarded politics as an activity important enough to require certain qualifications. It was rightfully the preserve of white, Anglo-

Saxon, educated, propertied, Protestant, adult males; in fact of people just like themselves. Furthermore, in accord with British assumptions of the same period, 'party' was a term of abuse; a threat to the common interest not far removed from treason. In number fourteen of *The Federalist Papers*, Alexander Hamilton referred to 'the diseases of faction'.[5] Thus the vote was used to choose individuals rather than groups, and was prudently confined to those who could be trusted to secure stability and respect for the sanctity of property. It is one of history's ironies that such people found themselves in a revolutionary situation, for they were demanding little more than the alleged rights of Englishmen to be represented in a parliament of their own choosing. The medieval notion of 'virtual representation', by which all the estates of the Realm were presumed to be represented in the British parliament, carried no conviction to the colonists. 'No taxation without representation' implied the latter to involve delegates elected by the colonists themselves. The different assumptions here separate the medieval notions that still pervaded Britain's *ancien régime* from the modern belief that representation can only be a product of actual election. Direct election for a parliament that met on the other side of a vast ocean was clearly implausible. To be able to determine their own affairs, the settlers had to throw off colonial status and accord full sovereignty to their pre-existent councils and assemblies.

During the period of the revolution, eleven of the thirteen states drew up new constitutions. Connecticut and Rhode Island continued to use the colonial charters of 1662 and 1663, merely deleting all references to the British crown. In the context of the independence struggle the perceived need was to guard against the authoritarian tendencies of government. Thus, by and large, the states settled for a weak chief executive, a strong legislature and frequent elections.

In terms of suffrage requirements, Connecticut, Rhode Island, Virginia and Delaware made no alterations at this time. However, a significant general shift away from the real-estate requirement is evident. Before the revolutionary war four states stipulated an acreage requirement; after, only two. For the first time there were states that had no landed qualification at all. New Jersey demanded 50 pounds proclamation money; Georgia, property of ten pounds value; and Pennsylvania merely that public taxes had been paid. The Pennsylvania constitution of 1776, influenced by the British reform movements, was the most radical of all. It had a unicameral legislature, and also allowed adult sons of freeholders to vote even if they had not paid taxes themselves. In the context of the revolutionary war all the states disfranchised those who took the British side, or else required oaths of allegiance from them. With just one exception they confined the vote to men over 21 years of age. Georgia, South Carolina and Virginia explicitly excluded blacks. Of the ten bicameral states the general tendency was to set a higher voting qualification for the upper house, which was intended to represent and, hence, defend the large property holders. Thus in Massachusetts all free, white, male taxpayers could vote for the Governor and members of the House of Representatives, but only those worth 60 pounds were eligible to vote for members of the Senate.

In response to colonial grievances against the British crown and government the ideology of independence had emphasised anti-authoritarianism. Financial instability and debtors' riots in the ensuing decade produced a different mood when the Constitutional Convention met in Philadelphia in 1787. The perceived need now was for central organisation, unity and control over improper and threatening pressures from below. Thus the President and Senate were to be indirectly elected and the judiciary appointed for life. Only the House of Representatives was to be chosen by the people. No explicit mention of franchise requirements was written into the Constitution, which thus appeared to come under the control of the separate states almost by default. In fact members of the convention were acutely aware of how jealously the separate states guarded their control of this issue. A general franchise stipulation would have rendered the prospects for constitutional ratification even more difficult than they already were. The issue was best left off the agenda. As a consequence the franchise history of the United States does not present the simple developmental outlines found within unitary state systems. Nevertheless, within the patchwork-quilt history of United States federalism certain broad tendencies can be discerned.

Generally speaking, property qualifications were the first to be overcome, followed later by those based on taxpaying, race and sex. At the 1787 Federal Convention, James Madison declared 'the right of suffrage . . . one of the fundamental articles of republican Government. . . . Viewing the subject in its merits alone, the freeholders of the country would be the safest depositories of Republican liberty.'[6] From this perspective the farming interest provided the backbone of the body politic. In practice the property requirement proved far from onerous. Easy availability of land meant that a real-estate qualification could produce a relatively broad suffrage. Rather than dividing the rich from the poor, it separated one form of wealth from another; the landed wealth of the countryside from the new commercial and then industrial wealth of the towns. Thus transcendence of the property qualification can be seen as a concession serving urban interests. New Hampshire abandoned its property qualification in 1784. Georgia did the same five years later. In 1791 Vermont came into the union without either property or taxpaying qualifications. The only requirements were to be male, resident for one year, and 'quiet and peaceable behaviour'. A year later Kentucky became a full state also with white manhood suffrage, as did Indiana in 1816. From this time existing property qualifications were gradually removed, as in Connecticut in 1818, Massachusetts and New York in 1821, Tennessee in 1834, Michigan in 1835 and Arkansas in 1836. A property qualification was never introduced west of Tennessee, which was, in fact, the only state outside the original thirteen, where one had ever been introduced. The last state to keep a property test was North Carolina, where it survived until 1856.

In most cases a taxpaying requirement survived once the property-holding qualification was abolished. At face value this appears as a new mode for operating an old practice – confining the franchise to the wealthy. In fact, however, both the real-estate and the taxpaying franchises were undermined by an unintended inbuilt democratic drift. Inflation overcame the hurdle of the latter restriction just as land availability had reduced the former. According to Chilton Williamson: 'With taxation of adult males almost universal, a taxpaying suffrage was almost universal suffrage', at least so far as adult, white males were concerned. He gives the example of Pennsylvania 'where a taxpaying qualification was effected in 1776' and 'taxables comprised about 90 per cent of the adult males'.[7] In 1809 Maryland abolished all tax and property qualifications. The vote was explicitly restricted to white, adult male citizens with one year's residence in the state. A year later South Carolina extended the vote to all free, white male adult citizens who had lived in the state for two years. Maine removed the taxpaying restriction for state elections in 1819 but retained it for town meetings. In New York the taxpaying requirement proved difficult to operate and gave rise to considerable abuse. In 1826 it was abandoned on grounds of convenience as much as of principle. In 1832 Mississippi granted the vote to all white, male citizens, as did Michigan in 1835 and Arkansas in 1836; all modified by a short residence requirement. In the southern states removal of the tax divide was a means of welding all adult white males into one composite political bloc, the better thereby to enforce the race divide. A 'white male democracy' was taken to be the best guarantee of continuing black slavery.

The issue of black disqualification and citizenship is dealt with in Chapter 7. We shall here just note the main outlines of the situation. Six New England states never excluded blacks from the franchise. Six other states soon altered their constitutions explicitly to exclude them.[8] Prior to the Civil War most northern states had excluded blacks from voting. In many mid-western and western states blacks were, from the start, excluded by law. In the south most of them were slaves and thus, as the phrase went, not independent nor in possession of a will of their own. In the aftermath of the Civil War, the fifteenth amendment in 1870 was the first constitutional attempt to interfere in the franchise issue as a state's right. It granted blacks the right to vote, but literacy and other voting tests were introduced by the states to replace the explicit colour bar. In 1965 the Voting Rights Act suspended such tests and authorised federal supervision as a means of facilitating black voting. In 1940 there were only 149 000 registered black voters in the eleven southern states. By 1967 this figure had risen to 2.8 million.[9] It thus took nearly two centuries from the Declaration of Independence, and nearly one from the constitutional guarantee of black voting rights, for black political participation to become a normal aspect of American politics.

The other main racial exclusion was of the country's original inhabitants. They were excluded, firstly, as 'another nation', and later, when they were hemmed into reservations, as in effect permanent children, and thus incapable of reaching the requisite maturity. In 1844 Josiah C. Nott, from whom more will be heard in Chapter 7, informed an audience in Mobile that: 'The Indian is by nature a savage, and a beast of the forest like the Buffalo – can exist in no other state, and is exterminated by the approach of civilization'.[10]

In 1776 the redoubtable Abigail Adams wrote to her husband, a member of the committee that drafted the Declaration of Independence, asking him to 'remember the ladies'. He didn't, so in time women had to campaign for their own interests. The first women's rights convention was held at Senaca Falls, New York, in 1848. When Colorado came into the union in 1876 its constitution allowed women to vote in school elections, a level at which they were assumed to have the requisite competence. The same provision was made by Montana, North Dakota, and South Dakota, when they came into the union in 1889 and by Washington in 1896. Full female suffrage was granted by Wyoming in 1890 and Utah in 1896, when these states first came into the union. Colorado altered its constitution to allow female suffrage in 1898, as did a number of western states prior to being joined by New York in 1917. The issue was finally taken up at federal level in 1920, when the nineteenth amendment, adapting the wording on race in the fifteenth, decreed that 'the rights of citizens of the United States to vote shall not be denied or abridged by the United States or by any state on account of sex'.

In the last century certain states excluded from the vote those who denied the existence of God. Jews did not gain political rights until 1842 in Rhode Island, 1868 in North Carolina and 1877 in New Hampshire. The vote has also been denied to students, soldiers and sailors, on grounds of temporary residence; to the criminal and insane, and to minors. The most recent change was in 1971 when the twenty-sixth amendment of the Constitution lowered the voting age to 18 in all elections.

II FRANCE

From a perspective that was commonplace in the nineteenth century, the United States and France embodied the alternative faces of democracy. The American experiment, however one judged its results, was carried out in a relatively planned and rational manner. The democratic movement had been carefully controlled by the recognised elites. Such was not the case in France, where democracy appeared to have run wild. In an orgy of bloodletting, the fury of the mob had destroyed the power and culture of Europe's most cultivated aristocracy. Which, then, was the manner in which the democratic movement would impose itself elsewhere? The spectre of 'the Terror' haunted the imagination of countries which, as had France of the *ancien régime*, contained established landed aristocracies. The threat, however, was not to that class alone, for the history of the French Revolution had shown that democratic fury strikes against enemies as much imagined as real.

Who could have foreseen the democratic whirlwind when Louis XVI inherited the French throne in 1774? Through marriage to Marie-Antoinette four years earlier, the alliance with Catholic Austria had been strengthened. Through its support for the American rebel colonies four years later, France had won the friendship of the 'First New Nation' and extracted some revenge against the British for defeats in previous decades.

Louis XVI had inherited not just a throne but a system most famously embodied in the statement of Louis XIV: '*L'état c'est moi*'. The monarchy claimed to rule by divine right and authority descended from the king down through his appointed agents, ministers and magistrates. The obligation of such state functionaries was thus not downward to those over whom they ruled but upward to him who had appointed them. The Ministers of State in the highest of his Councils, the *Conseil d'état*, were appointed by the king and could be dismissed by him also. There was a certain clarity and consistency in such a system, but adaptability and administrative efficiency were not its strongest features. A key weakness was in the area of finance. The wealthiest citizens were exempt from taxation, and state regulation and internal customs barriers curtailed the development of trade and industry. The Treasury was burdened both by its own cumbersome organisation and by a few decades of rather unsuccessful imperial warfare. Support for the American colonists had reduced it to near-bankruptcy.

In medieval Europe it was common for monarchs to summon councils or parliaments when they were in financial difficulties. In his study of medieval parliaments and Estates, A.R. Myers notes the 'German saying that *Landtage sind Geldtage*' – 'Representative assemblies are financial assemblies'.[11] In 1788 the French were in financial difficulties and so in August Louis XVI summoned the Estates General to meet the following year. It had previously convened as long ago as 1614 and so there was understandable confusion on some of the finer points of its organisation. That it contained three houses – the clergy, the nobility and the so-called Third Estate – was beyond dispute. What now proved contentious was whether voting should be by Estate, in which case the two privileged orders would always outvote the Third Estate by two to one, or whether voting by head would be allowed. The King wanted the old traditions followed, but he gave way to pressure from the Third Estate in allowing them to double their traditional number of deputies to 600, leaving the other two Estates with 300 deputies each. Thus, unwittingly or otherwise, he conceded the principle that was to undermine the *ancien régime*, that numbers were to be granted political weight. The right to vote for deputies to sit in the Third Estate was open to all men over 25 who paid direct taxes, which nearly all of them did.

Something very near to universal male suffrage produced a Third Estate in which two-thirds of the deputies were lawyers and in which an overwhelmingly rural electorate sent only one peasant to sit in the 600-strong assembly.

The still-unresolved problem of whether the Estates voted separately or together was pre-empted by the Third Estate which, on 17 June 1789, proclaimed itself a National Assembly and called upon members of the other two Estates to join it in reforming France. In a famous pamphlet the Abbé Sieyes declared that the Third Estate was more than just one Estate among three, for it alone constituted the nation. The weight of numbers gave strength to his claim. Out of a total population of about 25 million, the First Estate, the clergy, numbered about 130 000, and the Second, the nobility, about 200 000. This left about 98 per cent of the population to be represented by the Third Estate. The force of their claim was acknowledged even by members of the two privileged orders, for 170 clergy and 50 aristocratic representatives accepted the invitation to join the Third Estate.

With hindsight we can see that the calling of the Estates General was the beginning of the end of the *ancien régime*, but the precise moment of transition occurred when the Third Estate re-categorised itself as a National Assembly, for in that change of terminology is encapsulated the polarity between the medieval and the modern understanding of politics. From that decision most of the later democratic developments logically flow.

In place of prescription and divine right the revolutionary National Assembly drew up its 'Declaration of the Rights of Man and of the Citizen'. Men, they announced, 'are born and remain free and equal in rights. . . . These rights are liberty, property, security and resistance to oppression. . . . The source of all sovereignty is essentially in the nation; no body, no individual can exercise authority that does not proceed from it in plain terms.' Here, clearly, the 'descending thesis' of monarchical sovereignty is reversed and replaced by the 'ascending thesis' by which sovereignty is seen to derive from the people. Declarations of broad principle, however, rarely provide a reliable guide to the small print of constitutional practice. The key concept of the 'Declaration' was 'Man', but within that category the prime qualification for the suffrage was property.

The Constitution of 1791 divided the adult male citizens into two groups, passive and active, on the basis of their economic standing. Active citizens were those men over 25 years of age who paid an annual direct tax of the value of three days' wages, and who were not domestic servants, bankrupt, nor awaiting trial. They had to be in the National Guard, have lived in the same canton for a year and have taken an oath of loyalty. These onerous qualifications meant that in Paris, for example, only 9.5 per cent of the population qualified as active citizens. In wealthier areas the percentage was, of course, higher, but overall revolutionary France initially imposed a more restricted franchise than that used for the elections to the Estates General early in 1789. Furthermore the elections for the unicameral legislative assembly were indirect, in that the active citizens only chose delegates who then elected the deputies of the Legislative Assembly. The delegates themselves had to be of even higher economic standing than the active citizens, but could then choose any active citizen as a deputy. Whatever else was endangered by the revolution, such stringent electoral requirements were meant to ensure that at least non-aristocratic property was safe. Robespierre had unsuccessfully proposed female enfranchisement, but this was disliked on the basis of women's presumed conservative predispositions. The king became, for a short time, a constitutional monarch, 'King of the French' rather than 'the King of France'. As for the other vestiges of the *ancien régime*, the Preamble to the Constitution declared that 'Nobility no longer exists, nor peerage, nor hereditary distinctions of orders, nor feudal régime, nor patrimonial courts.'[12]

The following year the Convention abolished the distinction between active and passive citizenship and broadened the franchise to include all men over 21 with a year's residence qualification, but excluded household servants. Following his failed attempt to escape from France, the powers of the King were suspended and in September 1792 the Convention declared monarchy abolished. Monarchists were also debarred from voting and four months later the King was executed. Force, intimidation, fear and reluctance to sacrifice a day's wages whilst going to vote meant that under 10 per cent of those eligible to vote for the Convention actually did so. The Society of Revolutionary Republican Women, founded in May 1793, was closed down in October. In slight compensation a decree passed in December allowed women to attend sittings of the Revolutionary Tribunal 'with their husbands and knit'.[13]

With the fall of Robespierre in July 1794, the Terror came to an end. The Constitution of the following year, III in the new revolutionary calendar, gave France a bicameral legislature for the first time. The franchise qualification for the Directory was much the same as under the Convention, but the decision as to whether members should sit in the Council of Ancients or the Council of Five Hundred was determined by the drawing of lots. The choice of the electorate was significantly restricted by the decree that two-thirds of the members of the new parliament should be drawn from those who had sat in the displaced Convention.

The Constitution of the Year III was, for what it is worth, the most durable of the revolutionary constitutions. However, among its 'most impressive errors', as one historian has noted, 'was the omission of provision for adequate legal settlement of disputes between Executive and Legislature, an error which left force as the only expedient on such occasions'.[14] In 1799 Napoleon, with the aid of his brother Lucien and a number of armed guards, drove the Council of Five Hundred out of their Assembly. Thus parliamentary government came to a temporary end and the rule of the Bonaparte family began.

The Constitution of the Year VIII (1799) preserved some of the surface forms of a parliamentary system but in fact real power was exercised by the First Consul, Napoleon himself. This virtual dictatorship was ratified by plebiscite with over three million in favour and only 1500 against. In 1802, following the Treaty of Amiens, a further plebiscite made Napoleon Consul for life. Bourbon monarchy had gone, but a new dynasty, based on monarchy by acclamation, was achieved on the swell of patriotic pride by the General who, in a few years, had made France the leading power and ruler of much of the European continent. In 1804 Napoleon crowned himself King of France. In the following years he looked after his brothers, appointing Jerome as King of Westphalia, Louis as King of Holland, Joseph as King of Spain, and reserving for himself the Kingdom of Italy. With the appointment of a new court and aristocracy, Napoleon 'the heir of the Revolution', became, in the words of one historian, 'something more like the restorer of a pseudo-*ancien régime*'.[15]

Having risen to power and glory by military means the Bonaparte dynasty eventually fell from the same cause. *Ersatz* monarchy was replaced by the return of the Bourbons in 1814, in the person of Louis XVIII. His Constitutional Charter of 1814 hoped 'to blot out from history, all the evils which have afflicted the fatherland during our absence'. 'Divine Providence' was declared the basis of the return of the 'King of France and Navarre' in whom 'all authority in France' was held to reside.[16] The Electoral Law of 1817 abolished the system of indirect elections, but reduced the electorate to men over 25 years of age, who paid 300 francs a year in direct tax. It is estimated that this produced an electorate of a mere 90 000 voters in a country of 26 million people. Those eligible for election as deputies had to be over 40 years old and pay at least 1000 francs in direct tax. Only about 15 000 people in all France met this requirement.

After the revolution of July 1830 the electoral qualification was lowered to include all men over 25 who paid 200 francs in direct tax annually. This raised the French electorate to 166 000 in 1831. Franchise extension could be achieved through the spread of wealth, as the government often reminded the reformers, and by 1846, 241 000 men had the vote, yet this figure still only represented 2.8 per cent of men over the age of 21. Individual constituency electorates could thus be quite small. When Alexis de Tocqueville was first elected for Valognes in 1839 only 627 men had votes. Five hundred and forty of them lined up in alphabetical order, 318 of whom voted for him. The July Monarchy lasted until 1848 and is said by Peter Campbell to have the considerable claim of displaying 'the most extensive electoral corruption that France has known'.[17]

At this point history repeated itself, the second time as farce according to Marx. Revolution brought down the monarchy, presumably for the last time, and a few years later replaced it by a Bonapartist Empire. In February 1848 Louis Philippe had been forced to abdicate. In a welter of decrees the left-wing provisional government granted the vote to all men over the age of 21. At a stroke the electorate increased 36-fold, to nine million, without there being any organisational or party developments to cope with the new situation. The left had introduced this dramatic change, but in an overwhelmingly peasant country it was inevitable that the right should benefit, and in elections in April about half the deputies elected were monarchists. Later in the same year a new Constitution was adopted, establishing a single-chamber parliament to be elected every three years by a universal male suffrage. Executive power was granted to a President directly elected for a four-year period. It was, said Marx, the firm conviction of the peasantry 'that a man named Napoleon would bring all the glory back to them', and so, trained to a career of 'adventurous vagabondage',[18] the nephew of the great Napoleon duly emerged to take up his 'destined' role.

Napoleon achieved a landslide victory in the Presidential election of 1848. With nearly five-and-a-half million votes he was nearly four million ahead of his nearest rival. The only limitation on his ambition was the four-year term prescribed by article 45 of the Constitution. This was overcome on 2 December 1851, when Louis Napoleon dissolved the National Assembly, and arrested its members for a few days, along with about 25 000 other people throughout France, during which period several hundred people were killed. In general the coup met little resistance and had considerable support. Universal male suffrage, restricted the year before, was reintroduced, and two plebiscites overwhelmingly ratified the coup and supported the establishment of the second Bonapartist Empire. As before, a revolutionary period came to an end with a Napoleon in power, and the 'establishment of dictatorship was justified by an appeal to popular sovereignty'.[19]

The Constitution of 1852 established a lower house which met for only three months each year, and which had no power over ministerial appointments or decisions. Control of elections and electoral boundaries and a restriction in press freedom ensured that little vitality or opposition could emerge from what remained of parliamentary life. Louis Napoleon himself appointed members of the Senate, thus following the example set by his uncle. From about 1860 some of the restrictions on political activity were eased, and the third plebiscite of the Empire, in May 1870, approved further moves in a liberal direction. These were of little consequence, for in September military defeat by the rising might of Prussia brought the Second Empire to an end after a period of nearly twenty years.

The Third Republic emerged from the ignominy of military defeat and almost by default, in that most of its founders wanted a monarchy but failed to agree on a suitable candidate. According to the Constitution of 1875 the lower house, the Chamber of Deputies, was to be elected by universal male suffrage. A third of the Senators were elected for life by a National Assembly composed of both houses, the remaining Senators being elected for nine years by the French departments and colonies. The President, no longer directly elected by the people, was to be chosen for a seven-year term by a majority of the National Assembly. The Presidentialism of the previous system was clearly abandoned and a key centre of power was now hard to locate. The governments, in the words of Eric Hobsbawm, 'often came and went like tourist parties in hotels'[20] as 108 distinct ministries were appointed during its existence.[21] This, however, was the most durable of France's modern political systems, lasting nearly seventy years until, like its predecessor, it fell through military defeat by the Germans, and was replaced for four years by their puppet regime.

Austria, Canada, Denmark, Germany, the Netherlands, Sweden,

the United Kingdom and the United States had all enfranchised women during or soon after the First World War. France, which had declared, but not implemented, universal male suffrage in 1793, stood back from this trend. A feminist movement had emerged in the 1860s and a bill for female enfranchisement came before parliament in 1901, but it was not until 1944 that women were granted the vote. This more than doubled the electorate, although in the early elections of the Fourth Republic the men proved the more likely to vote. The upper chamber was granted only consultative status, so that, in contrast to the Third Republic, sovereignty was clearly placed with the directly-elected National Assembly. This was based on proportional representation, which made it chronically difficult to ensure a stable majority. The demise of this system followed from its own *immobilisme* and clear inability to resolve the colonial problems of Indo-China and Algeria. General de Gaulle, whose intention was to see his country 'liberated from the stranglehold of the parties',[22] rescued the Republic from its impasse, and reasserted the pattern of having a directly-elected President to whom the parliamentary assemblies were subservient.

In September 1958 a referendum once again gave overwhelming support (79 per cent) to a change of regime. Under the Fifth Republic, which has endured to this day, the President obtained enhanced power. He appoints the Prime Minister and can call a referendum. In a time of crisis he can, after consultation, dissolve the National Assembly, declare a state of emergency and take 'the measures required by the circumstances'. In December 1958 General de Gaulle, with 78.5 per cent of the vote, was swept to power as President of a system which so markedly bore the stamp of his own political ideas. There were early doubts as to whether the Republic could survive the departure of its progenitor or the election of a President belonging to a party without majority support in the National Assembly. Both these challenges have been successfully met, and France, the country which, it is said, loves ideological battles and holds the world record for constitution-making,[23] has now kept its present system for over thirty years.

Of the four countries whose electoral history we are briefly surveying, France was the first to introduce universal male suffrage and the last to give women the vote. It has had the most constitutions and here the contrast with the USA, which still operates its 1787 Constitution, is particularly striking. At times fanatically committed to democracy, the prestige of parliament has nevertheless often been low. France was the first of our countries to have a directly-elected head of state and has made the most use of referenda. It has appeared the least stable, as each new system appeared as an attempt to nullify the one before, although underlying administrative continuity may have made the swings of the constitutional pendulum less disruptive.

III GERMANY

The United States and France were the foremost centres of the breakthrough to modern liberal democratic politics, and thus far our account of the process has been able to concentrate on the issue of representation in parliamentary assemblies. However, in terms of Germany we must broaden our concerns, for there, for most of the period we are covering, certain historically and logically prior issues were still unresolved. Behind the franchise movement lies the primary conflict between aristocracy and democracy. In the former, basic power is inherited, with those in the favoured line of succession able to appoint whom they wish to certain other positions. The democratic principle, in contrast, allocates power on the basis of election from below. One aspect of this is the process whereby the elected assemblies come to represent the whole adult population; another is that by which the power of such assemblies overcomes that of inherited rule. In these developments Germany lay a long way behind the two countries already considered. In the United States of America indigenous inherited political power hardly existed. Through the American War of Independence externally imposed hereditary power was shaken off. In France the monarchical and aristocratical principle was (in spite of Napoleonic setbacks) largely destroyed at one revolutionary blow. In the German territories though, even at the beginning of this century, the very notion of a meaningful parliamentary assembly still had to be fought for. Thus, shortly before the First World War, we find a conservative leader, Herr von Oldenburg auf Januschau, able to declare that 'The King of Prussia and the German Emperor must always be in a position to say to any lieutenant: "Take ten men and shoot the Reichstag"'.[24] Clearly, for such people the primacy of the elected assembly was not an axiomatic principle. The context behind the above assertion is that into the period of the First World War Germany and Austria both had monarchs who claimed authoritarian powers derived from God, to whom alone they were thus ultimately answerable.

Further, in contrast to France and the United Kingdom, we do not find a settled nation-state with relatively agreed and permanent frontiers. The United States of America already from 1787 formed one united state, even though federal and expanding. In Germany, however, our period begins with a plethora of dukedoms, principalities, and archbishoprics. The nation, if it existed at all at that time, did so more in a cultural than a political sense.

In 1789 Germany consisted of over 300 states. The largest included the monarchies of Austria, Prussia, Bavaria and Saxony. Some states were ruled by ecclesiastical and lay princes, some by counts and prelates, while there were also the 51 Free Towns. In terms of population the part of Austria within the Reich had over nine million inhabitants whereas, at the other extreme, some of the Free Towns contained a population of between 1000 and 5000 people.[25] The largest states were absolute monarchies, but in a more general sense bureaucratic autocracy was the dominant political form. In some of the medium-sized states, autocracy was modified by limited representation in a Diet consisting of three Estates. Forms of rule in the self-governing cities varied considerably. Lübeck was governed by 16 senators and four burgomasters, whose power was absolute and for life. Vacancies were filled by co-option. In contrast Frankfurt had a senate of 51 members and two burgomasters who were elected by the 14 000 burgers.

What little unity existed between these various states and principalities was provided by the loose confederation of the Holy Roman Empire. Its Reichstag sat in three Colleges, the Colleges of Electors, of the Princes and of the towns and cities. But by the end of the eighteenth century its power had diminished and the most consequential political relationship was that between the large and powerful monarchies of Prussia and Austria. In terms of distance from modern citizenship norms we should note that feudalism still existed in large parts of eastern Germany, and that the College of Princes contained religious authorities exercising virtually independent political power over two-and-a-quarter million people.

This quaint, decentralised and medieval patchwork proved strong enough to withstand all internal opposition during the revolutionary era but had no chance against the military might of France itself. In 1795 Prussia lost to France her possessions on the left bank of the Rhine. In 1803 Napoleonic reorganisation effectively abolished the ecclesiastical principalities and greatly reduced the number of Free

Cities. In 1806 the Holy Roman Empire came to an ignoble end. It was partially succeeded by the Confederation of the Rhine, a union initially of sixteen south and west German states that came under Napoleonic protectorate. As a consequence reforms on the French revolutionary pattern were introduced: the loss of church and aristocratic privileges, the abolition of serfdom, the introduction of equality before the law and the inviolability of property. A parliament was to meet in Frankfurt but never did, in fact, meet.

Later in 1806 Napoleon's armies defeated the Prussians at Jena and Auerstädt. Out of this débâcle emerged a reforming spirit that was to lay the foundations for Prussian preeminence later in the century. An edict of 1807 provided for the abolition of serfdom and of forced domestic service. The privileges of the trade guilds were abolished, thus granting open access to all occupations. Important reforms were also implemented in the army and education. In terms of political power the only significant changes were at the level of local and provincial government where, in a limited way, classes other than the nobility gained access to the assemblies. Nothing comparable occurred at the highest level, where, in December 1806, the king appointed a new council composed of ministers for war, foreign affairs and the interior. Two years later this was reorganised as the Council of State, composed of ministers of the crown, royal princes and certain privy councillors nominated by the king. In effect the Prussian reforms were implemented by a benevolent despotism that removed most elements of feudalism, but, given the strong bureaucratic tradition, believed in government by a combination of hereditary power and administrative expertise. Elsewhere, the Bavarian constitution of 1808 provided for a single-chamber legislative assembly, but it never met. In Frankfurt the constitution provided for an assembly that met in 1810 but not thereafter. In Westphalia a parliament was established but with severely limited powers, and chosen by electoral colleges nominated by the king. This was characteristic in that alterations or extensions of political power were only allowed within the context of uncontested monarchical sovereignty.

Following Napoleon's downfall and the Congress of Vienna the German states formed into a loose confederation of 34 independent states and four Free Cities. No overall executive or judicial authority was created. In Prussia and Austria absolute monarchy remained much as before, but in some of the south and mid-German states constitutions were introduced which slightly increased citizen participation in political affairs.

In 1818 Bavaria introduced a constitution providing for a bicameral parliament with a lower house elected on a narrow franchise and in the following year a bicameral parliament was introduced in Württemberg. Parliamentary constitutions were also established in Nassau (1814) Saxe-Weimar (1816) Baden (1818) and Hesse-Darmstadt (1820). The elected chamber of the latter had only fifty members. Such parliaments had little power of their own but 'were simply the channel for advice and criticism'.[26] In all cases the upper house was organised on the Estates system and included members appointed by the monarch. In Prussia a Provincial Estate Law of 1823 divided the country into eight provinces, each to have its own single-chamber assembly based on Estates representation. The nobility was given about half the seats, the farmers one-sixth and the towns one-third. In the towns only the very highest taxpayers could vote. Thus in Solingen six per cent of the inhabitants had the franchise, and in Düsseldorf only one per cent. Slight representation, where granted, had the purpose of increasing social cohesion but without intending any concession to liberal, let alone revolutionary, ideas. Of this period Agatha Ramm has concluded that 'Vormärz Germany was a country where to have a political opinion was difficult, to express it almost impossible and to join with others to promote it, conspiracy punishable by the heaviest prison sentences. It was a society of classes and privileges based on subjection at every level. Subjection was confirmed by the opening of letters, arbitrary arrest and a secret judicial procedure.'[27]

This repressive atmosphere appeared to be swept away by the revolutionary explosions which, in accord with what was now becoming a tradition, received their prime impetus from France, but spread outward to affect much of Europe. In February 1848 revolutionary unrest in Paris had forced the abdication of King Louis Philippe. In March uprisings in Vienna led to the resignation of Metternich. Riots occurred in Berlin and the King appointed the Liberals Camphausen and Hansemann to the Prussian ministry. In this heady atmosphere of apparently boundless liberal opportunity a preliminary parliament met in the Frankfurt *Paulskirche* to undertake the establishment of a German national assembly. They decreed that in each German state independent adult men were to be granted the vote. This was not the uniform franchise it appeared to be, as the definition of independence was left for each state to determine. In Austria domestic servants were excluded, in Bavaria those who did not pay a direct tax, in Prussia all who received public charity, in

Saxony and Baden servants and farmhands who lived with their masters, and in Württemberg and Hanover even workers receiving wages were declared non-independent. Clearly German liberalism stood for balanced and moderate assemblies that curbed hereditary power without succumbing to mob rule from below. Furthermore, most of the states introduced elections that were only indirect, i.e. the voters chose merely an intermediate stratum who then chose the actual parliamentary representatives.

Unsurprisingly, therefore, of the 596 members of the Frankfurt Assembly, there were only four artisans, one peasant and no workers. Nevertheless a single elected parliament representing all of Germany and claiming sovereignty over the princes had been achieved. Only one basic difficulty remained; it had no army and hence no power. The beginning of the end came when Frederick William IV of Prussia rejected the assembly's offer of the Imperial Crown. To an upholder of divine right the Crown could not be regarded as theirs to give. Shortly thereafter the monarchs of Bavaria, Saxony and Hanover joined him in rejecting the Frankfurt constitution. The brief liberal moment had passed and the impetus behind Germany's development now moved from Frankfurt to Berlin, the capital of Prussia.

In May 1849 a new Prussian electoral law dispensed with explicit property qualifications and granted the vote to all men over 25 who were independent, without a criminal record, not in receipt of 'poor relief from public funds' and could claim six months' residence in the constituency. This looks almost akin to universal male suffrage, but what was granted with one hand was taken back by the other, for the votes of the rich were weighted to outnumber those of the poor. One-third of the seats in the Prussian lower house went to the top 4 per cent of taxpayers, the second third of seats to the next 14 per cent of taxpayers, leaving approximately the lowest 82 per cent of taxpayers to elect the final third of the representatives. In the words of Theodore Hamerow: 'It was an ingenious arrangement for safeguarding the interests of the propertied without disfranchising the propertyless.'[28] The system was reinforced by indirect and public voting, was copied in Saxony in 1896 and survived, in spite of Social Democratic agitation against it, until the end of the German Reich in 1918.

After the Prussian defeat of Austria in the 'Seven Weeks' War' (1866), Bismarck established the North German Confederation of Prussia and seventeen smaller German states. Its lower house was elected on a universal male suffrage with secret and direct voting but had severely limited powers. Bismarck, as Chancellor, was responsible not to the elected parliament but solely to the hereditary King of Prussia. The first and only elections to the North German Confederation took place in 1867, but its political arrangements formed the basis for the German Reich founded four years later.

The German Reich was a federation of twenty-two monarchies, three Free Cities and the 'Reichland' of Alsace-Lorraine. This nominal diversity or even possible pluralism of the various parts conceals the dominant role that Prussia had over the whole Empire. Over half the Empire's population and about two-thirds of its territory were Prussian. The Prussian King was simultaneously the German Emperor, and the Prussian Chancellor was, likewise, Chancellor of the Empire. The Emperor was commander of the army, could appoint and dismiss the Chancellor and Imperial Civil Servants, and, with the consent of the Bundesrat, could declare war. However, the Prussian voting system was not adopted for the Reichstag, which instead granted universal suffrage by a secret ballot for all men over the age of 25. The inequality of the Prussian three-tier franchise was not reproduced at the Reich level, and thus a more representative lower house was achieved. This benefit was more than somewhat offset by the limited real power available to it. Although its consent was necessary for legislation and expenditure, it could not introduce legislation nor appoint and dismiss the Chancellor, who was responsible to the Emperor alone. No one could be simultaneously a minister and a member of the lower house, as was commonplace in Britain. There was not even a pretence at a parliamentary system, and one can include the Reich Bundestag in the comments Max Weber made on the various German state parliaments: 'The parliaments have been impotent. The result has been that no man with the qualities of a leader would enter Parliament permanently. If one wished to enter Parliament, what could one achieve there?'[29] It was a forum less of initiative than of either acclamation or criticism – but either way without significant consequences for the executive. In fact, members of the Bundestag were not granted the level of access to government and civil service information that would have enabled full scrutiny and grounded criticism of the executive to take place.

The fear of the traditional authorities in the nineteenth century was that an extended franchise would place legislation under the deleterious influence of the working men and their demagogic leaders. The Reich gave the German Social Democrats representation without influence, a form of subordinate partial incorporation into what H-U. Wehler has described as 'a Bonapartist dictatorship based on plebiscitary support and operating within the framework of a semi-absolutist, pseudo-constitutional military monarchy'.[30] Even this seemed beyond the bounds of safety to Chancellor Bismarck, and thus, on a flimsy pretext, he had the Social Democratic Party banned between 1878 and 1890. On its return in the 1890 election it gained more votes (but not seats) than any other party. Thereafter its strength further increased until in 1912 it became the largest party in the lower house, probably the first time for any socialist party anywhere. This was in spite of fixed constituency boundaries, settled in 1874, which, as time and population drift proceeded, increasingly disadvantaged the cities and the working-class suburbs.[31] Absurd paradoxes could emerge in the contrast between Reich and state representation, as under the three-tier system the Social Democratic Party obtained 18.79 per cent of the Prussian vote in 1903, but no seats in its parliament.

The upper house, the Bundesrat, was dominated by Prussia and presided over by the Federal Chancellor. Its members were appointed by the governments of the various federal states and, with the consent of the Emperor, it could dissolve the lower house. The German Empire was one in which military prestige and values overrode any democratic impulses. Founded on the basis of military victory over France in 1871, it foundered from the defeat of its army in the First World War, following which Kaiser Wilhelm II went into exile in Holland in November 1918, and abdicated a few weeks later.

Thus arose the opportunity for the re-emergence of the more liberal and democratic tendencies that had lain more or less subdued since 1848–9. The Constitution of the Weimar Republic established a political system where the focus of politics lay in the lower house more than ever before and where the political parties had direct influence on the executive. The Reichstag was elected on the basis of universal suffrage and proportional representation, with women given the vote on the same terms as men – that is, at the age of 21. Female participation in politics had been illegal in most of Germany between 1851 and 1908, and the first female suffrage society had been founded in 1902. In 1914, by which time there were three separate and mutually antagonistic female suffrage societies, it would have been almost impossible to imagine that within a few years their basic aims would have achieved fruition.

Instead of the hereditary Emperor, the Weimar Republic had a

President directly elected for seven years by all Germans over the age of 35. The President could appoint and dismiss the Chancellor, who determined policy and appointed cabinet ministers and was dependent upon the support of the Bundestag. Thus, in marked contrast to the Empire, legislative and executive were bound together in interdependence. Certain 'basic rights and basic duties' were outlined (articles 109–65), as was the possibility of a referendum.

If, as many nineteenth-century optimists had believed, history was a one-way process of improvement, our account might have ended here. Germany, in spite of its incongruous combination of an industrial economy emerging alongside a semi-feudal polity, had, fortuitously or otherwise, arrived at a political system that placed it firmly alongside other western liberal states and indeed in many respects made it the most democratic European power. However, our century has belied the optimism of the previous one. The historical path cannot match the straightness of a Roman road. Germany's democratic achievement was grounded neither in historical legitimacy nor economic stability. The ravages of depression created, first, rule by emergency decree and then, in effect, emergency as permanent, as the Nazi seizure of power in 1933 led to the irrelevance of the Weimar constitution, the centralisation of previous regional powers, the destruction of parliamentarism, the banning of all non-Nazi political parties, the abolition of human and civil rights, and, for twelve years, the imposition of totalitarian rule under the leadership of a Chancellor-Kaiser merged into the absurd yet terrible figure of Adolf Hitler, the *Führer*.

One of the Weimar Republic's many disabilities lay in its origins as a system externally imposed following military defeat. A comparable process occurred after the Second World War, but this time, as a consequence of growing disunity amongst the erstwhile wartime allies, Germany's postwar occupied sectors formed into western and eastern blocs, and remained divided for forty years. The Federal Republic of Germany has been fully integrated into the western capitalist system, with membership of both the European Economic Community and the North Atlantic Treaty Organisation. Its lower house is elected by universal suffrage on the basis of a modified system of proportional representation. The small upper house is chosen by the federal *Länder*. In contrast to the Weimar system the President has a mainly figurehead role and is chosen by the two houses of parliament, rather than directly by the people. A further indication of the Federal Republic's lingering distrust of the people, is the institution as articles 1 to 20 of the Basic Law, of human and civil rights which are totally inviolable, that is, not subject to constitutional amendment or removal.

In the former eastern sector of Germany the German Democratic Republic was established according to the norms of communist practice. Here, in spite of the democratic label, the people were trusted even less. Elections took place on the basis of universal suffrage but, as only one party was in non-contention for actual office, the consequences for the executive were minimal. This apparent totalitarianism collapsed with astonishing speed in the *annus mirabilis* of 1989, when genuine multi-party elections took place for the first time in this area since the early 1930s. The German Democratic Republic came to an end when the two German states were reunited on 3 October 1990. A united and democratic Republic of Germany, only achieved before from 1919 to 1933, has now appeared again. Friends of political democracy will wish it a longer and less stormy life than its predecessor.

IV THE UNITED KINGDOM

Unlike the United States, the United Kingdom did not have a colonial overlord to overthrow, nor, in contrast with the German provinces, was it overrun and reorganised by French revolutionary forces. Casting an eye upon the French, the British remained proud of their ability to avoid periodic revolutionary upheavals. In the eighteenth century Montesquieu and Voltaire had visited England and judged it an admirable example of free institutions. The historian R.R. Palmer has noted that even during 'the disputes that arose between King George's subjects in Britain and America after 1763 . . . scarcely anyone denied that the British constitution was the most remarkable constitution in the history of the world'.[32] One explanation for Britain's stability, which depends heavily on Tocqueville, notes that in France the aristocracy were a closed caste, drawn into Versailles at the expense of their everyday local functions, exempt from taxation, and thus appearing increasingly parasitic. In the United Kingdom by contrast the aristocracy, integrated with the middle class, engaged in commerce and industry, maintained key local functions in a relatively decentralised state, and were not exempt from taxation. Steering clear of internal revolution, the United Kingdom, helped by its island position, also managed to resist conquest from abroad. As a result the United Kingdom was the last of our countries to alter its medieval franchise, and today remains the only one with both a monarchy and a hereditary element in the upper house. In these senses, among others, it is unique among major states in the extent to which it still bears the marks of an *ancien régime*.

The United Kingdom, then, which took the pioneer role in creating a modern industrial society, felt no great need to follow the political paths of the United States or France. Instead it took itself to be the model of liberty that other countries would do well to imitate. However, even in the late eighteenth century, pressures did exist to redress the imbalance between constituency and population distribution. There was also a concern about the chaotic franchise qualifications. Pitt unsuccessfully introduced reform bills in 1782, 1783, and 1785. Nevertheless, one effect of the French Revolution was to delay the British reform movement for some decades. The defeat of aristocracy in France had led to chaos and violence. Its survival in the United Kingdom could consequently be seen as a prerequisite of order and liberty. Both before 1832 and, to some extent, after, the House of Commons was, again in the words of R.R. Palmer, 'socially continuous so to speak with the Lords'.[33] Most government ministers sat in the Lords; the upper house, as the representative of landed property, owned many of the constituencies represented in the Commons. A parliamentary seat was consequently seen as a piece of property, held either for the younger sons of aristocrats or sold to the newly wealthy as a business transaction.

In the boroughs a variety of electoral qualifications existed. For example, the vote was granted to freeholders, to all householders paying poor rates, or to those owning property in the borough. The basic county franchise remained as established by a statute of 1430 which gave the vote to forty-shilling freeholders; that is, owners of land worth that amount per year either in income or in rental values. Inflation served gradually to increase the size of the electorate but in 1831 only about five per cent of the adult population was entitled to vote. Elections could, therefore, be decided by a very small number of voters. In 1812, to take just one example, the four candidates standing in the Totnes constituency polled 36, 32, 29 and 23 votes; this represented a total of only 120 votes but only 60 voters, each elector being allowed to vote twice. Before 1872 when the secret ballot was introduced, corruption was rife, because the purchase of relatively few votes could swing the result. But in many constituencies there were no contests at all: 'often two of the leading families would agree to share the representation and avoid the ruinous costs of a contested election'.[34] In Yorkshire no election was held between 1760 and 1800. In the Northamptonshire borough of Higham Ferrers there were no elections held between 1702 and 1832 when the borough was abolished. The notorious constituency of Old Sarum matched no elections with virtually no electors. Prior to its abolition in 1832 'its eleven electors had last been called upon actually to vote in the election of 1715'.[35] Meanwhile the growing industrial cities of Sheffield, Leeds, Birmingham and Manchester remained unrepresented.

In 1830 a revolution in Paris led to the abdication of Charles X and a series of violent disorders in other European capitals. In Britain there were riots among both agricultural labourers and industrial workers in the years 1830 and 1831. British public opinion had previously viewed the likelihood of revolution as demonstrating the need to resist reform. This view was now inverted: now reform came to be seen as the only way to avoid revolution. The real extent of the revolutionary threat in Britain has been a matter of lively but fairly inconclusive debate. For our purposes what matters is that a *perceived threat* was one of the factors that led the Whig government of Earl Grey to commence what in retrospect we see as the long process of parliamentary reform.

The Reform Act of 1832 reduced some of the most glaring anomalies in the distribution of seats. Fifty-six rotten boroughs, returning 111 members, lost their parliamentary representation, and thirty boroughs with less than 4000 inhabitants each lost one Member of Parliament. Of the 143 seats made available for redistribution, 65 went to the counties, and 44 to 22 large towns, which included Birmingham, Manchester, Leeds and Sheffield. Twenty-one smaller towns were given one member each. The franchise qualification in the boroughs was simplified with the vote given to all householders paying an annual rental of ten pounds, provided that they had been in residence for a year and had paid their taxes and rates. In the counties the franchise was made more complex. The old forty-shilling freehold was retained and in addition, the vote was given to ten-pound copyholders, ten-pound long-leaseholders, fifty-pound medium-leaseholders and fifty-pound tenants. The main beneficiaries of these changes were the English county seats, the northern industrial towns, and Ireland, Scotland and Wales. The electorate rose from 478 000 to 813 000, but still comprised only about seven per cent of the adult population. The vote had been granted to a sizeable section of the middle class, who showed their deference by electing parliaments that remained markedly aristocratic. In 1841, 342 of the 658 MPs were still linked to the aristocracy by either birth or marriage. In 1865 this figure had dropped by only 16, to 326. The 1832 Act was, in other ways also, more significant for what it began than for what it achieved. Norman Gash has noted that 'there was scarcely a feature of the old unreformed system that could not be found still in existence after 1832'.[36] He comments on the survival of small pocket boroughs, borough-mongers (who arranged for the purchase of parliamentary seats), and corrupt constituences, and also that only half of the constituencies were contested in the five general elections that took place between 1832 and 1847.[37] Property still remained the basic criterion for the franchise and, furthermore, MPs were still unpaid and as a result only those with sufficient money and time were likely to stand for election. As E.J. Evans has commented, 'parliament was still dominated by gentlemen of leisure'.[38]

In 1832 Earl Grey told the House of Commons that his Reform Bill was 'large enough to satisfy public opinion and to afford sure ground of resistance to further innovation'.[39] In 1837 Lord John Russell, the leader of the Whig Party, described the first Reform Act as the final point of Britain's constitutional development. He later renounced that view, for from the late 1850s reform again became a major issue. In 1864, the National Reform Union was founded in Lancashire, recommending a ratepayer franchise and triennial parliaments. The more radical Reform League was founded in London in 1865. It had many working-class members and campaigned for both universal suffrage and the secret ballot.

Gladstone had proposed a reform act in 1866 but was outmanoeuvred by Disraeli who, a year later, successfully carried through even more radical proposals. This was a source of astonishment and fear at the time. How had Disraeli, who in 1866 opposed reform, and in 1867 was Prime Minister heading the presumed reactionary party, arrived at such a *volte-face*? Michael Bentley has called it 'the strangest story in the modern history of party politics',[40] for Disraeli had attacked the 1866 bill as replacing the 'prescriptive spell [of] . . . families of historic lineage' by 'the sway of turbulent multitudes'.[41] The explanation lies in political opportunism. Once convinced that reform was inevitable, Disraeli was determined that the Conservatives should reap the benefit of introducing it, thereby dividing the Liberals and demonstrating their own ability to move with the times. The 1867 Act provided for a further redistribution of constituencies. It gave the borough vote to all householders paying rates, and to lodgers paying a rental of ten pounds and also having one year's residence. This last qualification proved more important than was at first realised. As the electoral register did not come into force until half a year after its compilation, the minimum residence requirement was effectively eighteen months. In the counties the reform was less generous, extending the vote to owners of land worth five pounds per year and to occupiers of property rated at twelve pounds a year (fourteen pounds in Scotland). The electorate almost doubled, from 1 300 000 to 2 500 000, and now comprised 16 per cent of the adult population. In Great Britain one adult male in three was now permitted to vote. Large urban working-class constituencies were created with, for example, the electorate of Merthyr Tydfil increasing ten times and that of Leeds four times. To critics who feared that his 'leap in the dark' would endanger property, Disraeli declared: 'I have always looked on the interests of the labouring classes as essentially the most conservative interests of the country'.[42] The vote was given to the respectable working man, who was thereby to be separated from the 'residuum' of that poorest, most vagrant, unskilled and dependent section of society whose sense of deference to the existing constitution could not be guaranteed. F.B. Smith has argued for the Act's centrality in British constitutional development. It marked, he said, 'the decisive moment in the transformation of the electorate from the exclusive, propertied constituency of 1850 to the unselective, inclusive, mass constituency of 1900'.[43]

The Reform Act of 1884 brought the county franchise into line with that of the boroughs, and so for the first time a uniform qualification existed throughout the United Kingdom. Now electoral participation was possible for a wide range of categories: men who were householders, provided that they had been in residence for a year and paid rates; lodgers whose lodgings were worth ten pounds a year, also subject to the one-year residence qualification; those who owned lands or tenements worth ten pounds annually. In Ireland the electorate increased by about half a million. Scotland and Wales benefited too from the redistribution of seats which took place in 1885 and which made all the county boroughs into single member constituencies. These reforms were long regarded as having introduced democracy into the United Kingdom in the sense that class (although not sex) barriers to participation were largely removed. Such a view is no longer accepted, for it has been established that even as late as 1911 about 40 per cent of adult males were still denied the vote.

According to one estimate the time period required for electoral registration, which disadvantaged those who moved home, annually disfranchised about one million voters.[44] Other groups did not fit into any of the franchise categories. Among the excluded were domestic servants who lived with their employers, sons living with their parents, policemen, soldiers living in barracks, and those who received Poor Law relief, not to mention such groups as criminals, aliens and the mentally ill. Policemen were granted the vote in 1887, but these diverse groups were unlikely to combine to advance their cause and their exclusion aroused little comment or interest. The party system was now in a phase of rapid development and part of the political game consisted in the attempt to get as many of one's own side as possible on to the electoral register, whilst simultaneously seeking to disqualify opponents. According to one account, 'if a man got drunk and was put in the cells for twenty-four hours he was objected to, and probably lost the franchise'.[45] Another undemocratic feature of the franchise was that others, on the basis of their property ownership, had more than one vote. For instance, the leading Liberal politician, Joseph Chamberlain, had six votes and it seems likely that in 1911 about seven per cent of the electorate, that is, over 500 000 men, were plural voters.[46]

The 1885 electorate totalled two-and-a-half million more people than it had two years earlier. This extension was only gradually reflected in the composition of the elected lower house, and it was not until 1906, when the Liberals gained an overall majority of 84, that a predominantly middle-class and non-landed parliament was elected.

Women remained excluded from the franchise. In 1867 John Stuart Mill unsuccessfully proposed an amendment to the Second Reform Bill which would have granted women the vote on the same terms as men. A comparable proposal also failed at the time of the 1884 bill. Political exclusion came to appear as more and more of an anomaly as other areas of female subordination were slowly overcome. In 1848 women were admitted to London University, in 1857 divorce courts were set up, and in 1870 the Married Women's Property Act allowed women to retain two hundred pounds per year of their own earnings. The National Union of Women's Suffrage Societies was founded in 1897, followed six years later by the Women's Social and Political Union. In 1869 Parliament had granted the right to vote in local elections to widows and single women who paid rates as heads of households. Pat Thane has noted that as female 'participation in local government grew, their exclusion from the national vote was ever more visibly absurd; their success in local government contributed to the growing woman suffrage movement'.[47] In 1918, as part of the more general western movement of female enfranchisement, women over thirty were granted the vote if they were ratepayers or the wives of ratepayers. At the same time the vote was given to all men over 21. Thereby the total number of voters more than doubled, and now included 74 per cent of the adult population. Ten years later women were granted the vote at 21 and achieved parity with men in this respect.

In 1948 plural voting, based either on the place of business or for graduates at their university, was abolished. Only from that date did the United Kingdom have one person, one vote, as the last vestiges were removed of the old notions that property and knowledge entitled their possessors to special political privileges. The last extension of the franchise took place in 1969 when the minimum age for voting was lowered to 18.

In the United Kingdom, like nineteenth-century Germany, consideration of elections to the lower house is an insufficient guide to the extent of political democracy. As traditionally understood, the British political system consists of the monarchy and the Houses of Lords and Commons. The United Kingdom is alone among the countries we have considered in retaining its monarchy, yet in a European context it shares this characteristic with Sweden, Norway, Denmark, the Netherlands, Belgium and Spain.

The British monarch remains part of the formal legislative process in that she has to ratify bills passed by the two houses of Parliament. This has long been a formality: it is over 250 years since a monarch last refused assent. There is no modern statute by which the decline of the monarch's political power can be verified, yet occasional shifts can be observed. For example, in 1830 the King had to accept Wellington's resignation and replacement by Earl Grey because of the wishes of a House of Commons majority. From that time the presumption that a Prime Minister chosen by the monarch would be automatically supported by the Commons was no longer true. For a time Queen Victoria was still able to reject minor ministers, but from 1867 Britain 'became more fully a constitutional monarchy . . . than it had been before'.[48] In the late 1860s Walter Bagehot categorised the monarchy as the 'dignified' part of the constitution, and since then it has been assumed that its functions are confined to the elaborate ceremonial that it has so carefully cultivated. It is hard to delineate the monarch's precise power and role in modern Britain. Judging by the extent of hostility that greets even the most muted criticism of the monarchy it must be presumed to matter greatly to many people. It is the least democratic and yet most popular part of our constitution, just as, conversely, the House of Commons is the most democratic and least popular part. S.M. Lipset has described the survival of the monarchy in some of the stable European democracies as an 'absurd fact', yet explains that the survival of monarchy, even as an empty husk, has helped democracies retain 'the loyalty of the aristocratic, traditionalist and clerical sectors of the population'.[49] This was an important factor in enabling modernisation to proceed without generating violent resistance from established elites.

In comparison with the Crown, the declining power of the House of Lords is more clearly demarcated. In 1909 their lordships threw out Prime Minister Lloyd George's budget because of their opposition to proposed land taxes. In consequence the Parliament Act of 1911 denied the Lords the right to reject a money bill and removed their power to delay other bills by more than two years. This curb was reduced to one year by the Parliament Act of 1949. Since then the dominance of the male aristocracy has been somewhat reduced by an act of 1958 by which life peers, including women, could be appointed. However, Britain remains unique among major western states in having an unelected and still predominantly hereditary upper house.

In the nineteenth century, when 'democracy' connoted mob rule or a controlled but dangerous experiment, the British saw it as either French or American. In this century, by which time it had been reclassified as a good thing, for which the Second World War was allegedly fought, the British decided that their own system provided the supreme example. In an influential textbook S.E. Finer declared that 'Britain provides an outstanding example of the liberal-democratic type of government' and that 'LIBERAL-DEMOCRACY is an English export'.[50] In the decolonising phase, to which the above extract presumably refers, democracy was granted as a farewell present to countries from whom it had been withheld so long as Britain ruled over them. Democracy as the thing Britain gave away was thus presumed to be what she had plenty of. This view was accepted not only by the home country but by many influential leaders in the former colonies. For example, Nelson Mandela, speaking at the Rivonia trial, declared that he regarded 'the British parliament as the most democratic institution in the world'.[51] Finer also regards Britain's constitution as a democratic one, 'but poured into an antique medieval mould'.[52] The metaphor is illuminating, for a mould surely shapes the content of what it contains, and thus in Britain, even in comparison with the other countries we have considered, democracy remains as 'unfinished business'.[53]

2 The Case Against Democracy

The franchise changes outlined in the last chapter clearly show the same general trend in the four countries under consideration. From being the preserve of the privileged male few, the chance to elect one's representative to parliament has come to be seen as a human right that should be available to all adults. This transition is, in part, a response to certain basic social changes in western societies, as well as an accompanying philosophical shift concerning notions of sovereignty, legitimacy and citizenship.

Turning first to the underlying social changes, we can see how medieval voting rights reflected the fact that in basically agricultural societies economic and social power were virtually monopolised by those who owned the land. There was, then, a certain congruity in that the narrow base of political rights was broadly in accord with that of other significant areas of power. The congruity lessened as first commerce and trade, and later industry, undermined the economic predominance of the landed interest. In time a new commercial middle class pressed ever more insistently for political rights commensurate with the importance they felt they had in the economic life of their societies. Then with the emergence of modern industry, a formerly dispersed population of rural labourers aggregated in the growing industrial cities to form the urban proletariat. Concentration facilitated organisation and from the late eighteenth century, but only with effective impact in the nineteenth, there emerged organisations at first mainly concerned to secure adequate wages and other rights in the workplace, but later to represent workers' interests in the political arena. We shall see that as each of these new groups sought to establish their claims they provoked a response from those who feared that disorder and inefficiency would result from upsetting established arrangements.

Certain shifts in terminology from medieval to modern times are indicative of the political changes we have discussed. In the United Kingdom, where there has been no basic crisis of the regime since 1688, some anachronistic political language still survives like fossil remains which serve as a reminder of the state of mind, and the society from which it derived. Thus the notion of 'Her Majesty's Government' is a relic from a time when the monarch owned, if not the land, then certainly the state. In the famous words attributed to Louis XIV of France: *L'état c'est moi*. The state was his instrument, and in some ways an extension of his household. In contrast certain states founded in this century have chosen to call themselves 'People's Republics', or, in one interesting instance (that of Algeria), a 'Popular and Democratic Republic'. Of course in the literal sense Her Majesty's Government is no longer owned and controlled by Her Majesty any more than the People's Republics have been controlled by the people. What the terminology provides is not so much a description of political reality as an indication of the varying modes of legitimacy. According to the medieval concept of politics, authority derived from above and could be diffused downwards at the discretion of each level of power. At its most pronounced this theory finds expression in the notion of the divine right of kings. Here authority is seen to come from God. The king's obligation was thus to God above, from whom his legitimacy was said to derive, rather than to the people below, over whom his power was exercised. This descending thesis of legitimate authority eventually gave way to the opposite 'ascending thesis' that dominates western liberal democracies today.[1] Now the legitimacy of government derives from the people below, who grant the right to one party or another to rule them for a limited period.

The French Revolution of 1789 provides the most sudden shift from the one conception of politics to the other. Its key moment is usually taken to be the storming of the Bastille on 14 July 1789. Certainly revolution as drama here found its most theatrical event as the symbol of tyranny was overrun and then destroyed by the lower classes of Paris. However, in terms of the shift in constitutional arrangements, we have already referred to that decisive moment when the Estates General recategorised itself as a National Assembly. Here we see emerging the notion of popular sovereignty rather than divine right, and of the conceptualisation of individuals as citizens rather than as members of a limited legal and social Estate. In its modern sense democracy may be seen as the movement which replaced the politics of the court by that of the masses, the subject by the citizen, and aristocratic by popular power.

DEMOCRACY AS GREEK

As a label descriptive of this transformation, 'democracy' was a term that had long been in the political vocabulary, though its existence was seen as mainly confined to the distant past. Democracy was understood as having existed at certain times among the city-states of ancient Greece, from which the concept derived. According to Aristotle, 'a democracy exists whenever those who are free and are not well-off, being in the majority, are in control of government'. It was thus not the rule of all, but rule by the poorest class of citizens. In Aristotle's fuller classification, democracy was distinguished from aristocracy or monarchy by involving the rule of the largest class of citizens rather than the few (an aristocracy), or one (a monarchy). Furthermore, of course, not all the inhabitants of a Greek city-state were citizens. Citizenship was, for Aristotle, indicated by 'participation in Judgement and Authority, that is, holding office, legal, political, administrative'.[2] This excluded many people. Sometimes as many as a quarter of the inhabitants of a Greek city-state were slaves, with no political rights at all. Another group, to which Aristotle himself belonged while resident in Athens, was the *metoikos*, resident aliens who were likewise devoid of political rights. Women were confined to the household and thereby excluded from public life. A further difference from modern notions is that the Greek system included forms of direct democracy, where those with the status of citizens directly participated in framing the laws by which they would be bound. They also used selection by lot as a means of avoiding the turmoil of elections.

Clearly, this idea of democracy does not bear a close resemblance to what is taken to be democracy today. The Greeks have first claims on the use of the word and from their perspective present usage constitutes a misnomer, for ancient and modern democracies are clearly two different things. If present possession is nine-tenths of the law, and we accept the current definition as paramount, then, on our criterion, the common tendency to describe the city-states of antiquity as democratic becomes just one more Greek myth.

Today 'democracy' is a label that virtually all state systems seek to appropriate for themselves. Thus, it would seem, the term is more an evaluative one of approval than a description of particular political arrangements. The current status of the term is so overwhelmingly positive that it is easy to forget how comparatively recent such approval is. Paul Corcoran has reminded us that

From the perspective of twenty-five hundred years of Western political thinking, almost no one, until very recently, thought democracy to be a very good way of structuring political life. . . . The great preponderance of political thinkers for two and a half millennia have insisted upon the perversity of democratic constitutions, the disorderliness of democratic politics and the moral depravity of the democratic character.[3]

We have many examples of how the image of ancient democracy was used as an argument against a modern variant. In the tenth of *The Federalist Papers*, James Madison noted that

democracies have ever been spectacles of turbulence and contention; have ever been found incompatible with personal security or the rights of property; and have in general been as short in their lives as they have been violent in their deaths.[4]

The same lesson was given by Chancellor James Kent of the New York Supreme Court opposing universal manhood suffrage in a debate in the New York Constitutional Convention in 1821:

That extreme democratic principle . . . has been regarded with terror by the wise men of every age because in every European republic ancient and modern, in which it has been tried, it has terminated disastrously and been productive of corruption, injustice, violence and tyranny.[5]

In April 1832, the month in which the British First Reform Bill passed its second reading in the House of Lords, *Fraser's Magazine* sought to make American democracy an exception while still upholding the general rule.

Against the single example of the United States we quote the whole history of democracy, the turbulence and destruction of the Greek states; the overthrow of the liberties of the Roman republic; the confusion of the Long Parliament, followed by the iron sway of Cromwell; the horrors of the French Revolution; the feebleness of the South American Republics; we read one convincing tale, the despotism of the many occasioning the misery of all, and terminated by the absolute power of the few. It is repeated from Athens to Bogota.[6]

Such was the low status of democracy even into the mid- and late nineteenth century that Disraeli, in his speech introducing the 1867

Reform Bill, assured fellow MPs that 'it will never be the fate of this country to live under a democracy' and that 'the propositions which I am going to make tonight certainly have no tendency in that direction'.[7] Gladstone, whose 1884 Reform Bill extended the vote to working men in the countryside, was deeply offended when an opponent described him as a 'democrat'.

So ancient democracy comes down to us through the literature as a political practice associated with mob rule and disorder which eventually finds itself replaced by tyranny. If, for most of western history, democracy has not had a good press, we must, as always in such instances, ask who were the journalists or writers. Mass literacy is a twentieth-century achievement. In all previous times the opportunity for education was largely confined to the better-off, for whom the political arrangements are likely to have been seen as predominantly satisfactory. The link made between education and political rights is one that will shortly occupy our attention. For anyone in western societies before the First World War with any pretentions to being educated, a prime sign of such education was knowledge of the classics, and from these was imbibed the distrust of democracy transmitted by the writers of antiquity, Plato and Aristotle among them.

In his seminal and lengthy attack on the French Revolution, Edmund Burke quoted Aristotle just once, and that in a significant way: 'If I recollect rightly, Aristotle observes, that a democracy has many striking points of resemblance with a tyranny.'[8]

In spite of what we have said about the basic differences between ancient and modern democracy, there were some points of limited similarity, in that political power was diffused downwards beyond the exclusive zone of the most educated, wealthy and propertied. These aspects provided the basis from which nineteenth-century authors drew on the points of criticism developed by the writers of antiquity. It is indeed fascinating to note the extent to which modern arguments against democracy replicated those that had already been made in Athens in the fifth century BC. A modern student of ancient Athens has summarised the outlook of the critics of democracy: 'Democracy . . . was the rule of the poor, base, uneducated, incapable and irresponsible masses for their own interest. It deprived the noble, wealthy, educated, capable, experienced and morally superior upper classes of their traditionally exclusive power in the polis. Democracy was unreasonable because it did not adequately use the existing capacities and it was unfair because it did not sufficiently reward existing merits.'[9]

DEMOCRACY AS MODERN

In this study we shall concentrate on the reaction to the democratic threat between the late eighteenth century and the end of the First World War, at which time women obtained the vote in a number of western countries. Before this period democracy was either far away in ancient history or 'pie-in-the-sky'.[10] However, with the American Revolution of 1776 and the French Revolution of 1789, democracy was believed to have re-emerged in a modern guise. These events were, of course, significantly different, but each in its own way was held by opponents to illuminate some of the disadvantages of democracy. Most clearly adverse was the image of the French Revolution, first presented in a lurid light by Burke in 1790, then by de Maistre in 1796 and later, at another time of economic and social unrest, by Carlyle in the 1830s. Democracy French-style was identified less with the attempt at constitutional monarchy in 1791 than with the Terror of 1793–4. It connoted the guillotine, dictatorship at home and conquest abroad, and provided the excuse for much repressive legislation in Britain in the early nineteenth century. Fewer people died during the Terror than were killed by the British in putting down the Fenian uprising in Ireland in the 1790s, but historical impact has less to do with the facts than with how they are propagated. Through to the middle of the nineteenth century, Jacobinism and democracy were often regarded as identical. Raymond Williams has noted that democrats 'at the end of the eighteenth and the beginning of the nineteenth centuries, were seen, commonly, as dangerous and subversive mob agitators'.[11] Occasionally the American system was held to have the same characteristics. Thus a Tory pamphlet of 1820 saw the source of current disorders as follows: 'It is America, it is Paine, it is democracy, it is Jacobinism.'[12]

The first volume of Tocqueville's *Democracy in America* appeared in 1835 and was soon translated into both German and English. It popularised the notion that democracy, which had proceeded farthest in North America, was also destined to rise in Europe. In the European countries whose franchise history we have outlined, newspapers often carried reports of political developments in North

America and travellers' reports also received widespread attention. European radicals were enthusiastic about American developments, whilst conservatives took them as a warning of threatening dangers. In the mid-nineteenth century the French conservative statesman Guizot declared that 'Today's chaos hides behind one word, "democracy". This word is sovereign, universal. All parties seek to appropriate it. . . . It is the revolutionary and despotic idea *par excellence*. It is this idea that must be extirpated.'[13]

EXPEDIENCY

One disability incurred by the nineteenth-century democratic movement arose from its proposing something that did not exist. To bring about radical aims required basic changes and thus involved a transition period of presumed inevitable instability. For many nineteenth-century thinkers order was primary. It had to be put first in both social and political affairs. The security of the state necessarily ranked above all other considerations. A consequence of this was the belief that access to state and political affairs should only be granted to those who would strengthen, or at least affirm, the traditional arrangements. On the other hand, it was also seen that the political structure might itself be fortified if it could successfully incorporate wider social groupings. A broadening of the basis of the state to the greatest extent compatible with its security came to be seen by some as the optimal position. Where this line should be drawn was, of course, a matter to be determined by an analysis of the temperament, morals, behaviour and education as well as the social, political and economic positions of the various contenders for political incorporation. Consequently, the line was a historical variable, as economic development brought new groupings into positions of prominence and responsibility. Movements of the dividing line that separated the included from the excluded are indicative both of changing relationships between different social forces and, in connection with that, a changing evaluation of the proper relationship between order and freedom.

The American and French revolutions brought to political prominence the notion of human rights, and virtually all written constitutions since then have included key articles that affirmed this priority. Such fine pronouncements can mislead us as to the nature of much of the actual debate which took place when political rights were being contested. The reasons we might give today to justify the franchise may be quite different from those for which particular groups demanded it and other groups eventually acceded to their requests. Those who make claims may use the language of rights, whilst those who resist them prefer to speak of order, duty and expediency. It is the views of the latter that are our subject here and for many nineteenth-century conservatives the language of the natural rights of man was not appealing. It was too reminiscent of Jacobinism. In May 1874 Prime Minister Disraeli addressed the British House of Commons on this theme: 'Now, Sir, what has surprised me most in the course of the remarks I have listened to closely, is that on the question of the conceding of political privileges to classes of our fellow-subjects, the expediency of such a course has been advocated on the plea that they are the rights of man.' This he dismissed as 'perilous', for 'The distribution of political power in the community is an affair of convention, and not an affair of moral or abstract right, and it is only in this sense that we can deal with it.'[14]

Franchise extension, when granted, was more likely to have occurred for reasons such as the following:

1. That through the exercise of diligence, sobriety and responsibility the social category under consideration had demonstrated their eligibility for political privileges. In 1884, the year of Britain's Third Reform Act, Arnold Toynbee was pleased to report that 'Those who have had the most in experience in manufacturing districts are of the opinion that the moral advance, as manifested, for example in temperance, in orderly behaviour, in personal appearance in dress has been very great . . . and the discussion of the newspaper is supplanting the old, foul language of the workshop'.[15] Clearly such a group could at last be allowed legitimate political activity. As late as 1913 Prime Minister Asquith declared that voting was a duty and a privilege, but not a right.[16]

2. A party in power might attempt to pre-empt its opponents by introducing a franchise extension which would give them particular advantage. We have seen that in 1867, once convinced that reform was inevitable, the British Conservatives determined that they should reap the advantage of introducing it. The belief that a newly-enfranchised group will always reward such a party does not always hold true, for the Conservatives lost the next, 1870, election. They had the consolation, however, of having carried out reform on a narrower basis, in the towns only, than the Liberals would have

done. In 1884 the Liberals hoped to break Conservative power in the countryside, gave the vote to the rural working class, and won the 1885 election.

After the American Civil War the victorious north imposed the fifteenth amendment and the right of black voting on the defeated south. This can hardly have been done out of a belief in racial equality or more general equal rights, for at that time few northern states allowed their own blacks the vote. Rather, the imposition of black suffrage in the south challenged the Democratic party in its heartland and was thus a means towards Republican hegemony. Similarly, the motive of political advantage and survival played its part in the women's suffrage campaign. Once it became clear that the battle was effectively over, former opponents who hoped to continue their political career suddenly 'espoused the women's cause with panic-stricken fervour'.[17]

3. In a rather broader sense than we have so far taken it, the general democratic movement was sometimes seen as inevitable, and so the only plausible course was to come to terms with it. This was the view of Tocqueville, as we shall see in Chapter 5.

4. Franchise extension came about not only through fear of one's parliamentary opponents, but also through fear of social violence from below. Advocates of reform have raised the prospect of revolution as a political threat, although such rhetoric does not prove that revolution was actually either likely or the only alternative. It merely shows that the threat can be made use of.

We can, then, agree with Kirk Porter that the 'philosophy of suffrage has always been more or less opportunistic. . . . Suffrage qualifications are determined for decidedly materialistic considerations and then a theory is evolved to suit the situation.'[18] We have seen that the momentum for a franchise extension can derive from tensions between two already-enfranchised sections, which lead them into competition for the support of a new group. Although such extensions are victories which point in a democratic direction, it should not be assumed that the right to vote has always been a primary human aspiration, nor that there was always an overwhelming desire to exercise that right once granted. In Paris in 1791, in what one might conceive to be a highly politicised situation, less than a quarter of the electors actually voted, and for the whole of France in the following year, only ten per cent made it to the polling booths. At another time of apparently heightened political fervour, the German revolution of

1848–9, Theodore Hamerow points out that 'the apathy of the electorate was the most effective guarantee against the dangers of a broad suffrage'. He notes that the electoral participation rate 'did not usually exceed 50 per cent, and often it was no more than 30'.[19] In Prussia we have seen how the three-tier voting system disadvantaged working-class men, so it will come as no surprise that the average participation-rate of voters in the third class was a mere 23.5 per cent.[20]

COMMON SENSE

As well as the primacy of order favouring the *status quo*, so too does 'common sense', which is usually attached more closely to what exists than to what is merely proposed. We too easily assume the democratic argument to be one of simple, natural justice and that the onus of justification lies more heavily upon its opponents. In reality, in most places at most times, there is a presumption in favour of the established order and thus suggestions for change are always at a disadvantage unless that order is in a state of evident collapse, or a strong case can be made against it on other grounds. One historian has declared that Britain's unreformed constitution based 'very largely on custom and precedent . . . was extremely hard to justify on rational grounds'.[21] Here custom and reason are counterposed as opposites, but to conservatives like Burke, the one incorporated the other. It was rational to follow custom, for what went under that name incorporated the accumulated wisdom of many generations forged through a continual process of interaction with actual experience. Thus custom, in spite of its often unsophisticated form, comprised a higher wisdom than the abstract rationality of one generation's *literati*. Such special pleading, easily labelled as the ideology of the possessing classes, certainly served their interests, but was equally certainly not confined to them alone. Theodore Hamerow notes that for 'the lower classes everywhere in Central Europe . . . public affairs were the province of the well-to-do, in the same way as material affluence or social respectability or higher learning'.[22] A settled society is often accepted as 'the natural order' by rich and poor alike.

REFORM UNNECESSARY

One constant argument against reform was that it was quite simply unnecessary when the optimal situation had already been achieved. To the members of 'certain societies' in London who recommended the French revolutionary example, Burke replied: 'I shall only say here, in justice to that old-fashioned constitution, under which we have long prospered, that our representation has been found perfectly adequate to all the purposes for which a representation of the people can be desired or devised.'[23] This was in reference to a situation where under two-and-a-half per cent of adults had the right to vote. Burke would not have claimed it as perfection, for, in contrast to the radicals, he did not believe that the affairs of men could reach such heights. He did, though, turn the tables on his opponents by recommending the British example to the French.

James Kent's speech to the New York Convention of 1821 encapsulates so much that is characteristic of the anti-democratic argument that it must frequently engage our attention. Chancellor Kent wished to defend a senate 'representative of the landed interest and exempted from the control of universal suffrage' on the grounds of its past achievements. During its 44-year existence under the prevailing constitution, New York State had, he said:

> wonderfully fulfilled all the great ends of civil government . . . we have enjoyed, in an eminent degree, the blessings of civil and religious liberty. We have had our lives, our privileges, and our property protected. We have had a succession of wise and temperate legislatures . . . a regular, stable, honest and enlightened administration of justice. . . . Our financial credit stands at an enviable height.

With such a record of benevolent government, Kent saw absolutely no case for 'the bold and hazardous experiment of remodelling the constitution'.[24]

During the debate on the British First Reform Bill, Sir Charles Wetherell, the member for Boroughbridge, referred to the previous century and a half 'during which the population had enjoyed greater happiness than was ever enjoyed by any population under Heaven'.[25] In such a situation how could any change be necessary? By the middle of the nineteenth century the increased productivity of British industry, the remarkable domination of world markets and the enlargement of an overseas Empire, could all be used to fortify the case that the British Constitution was beyond reproach. Two years after the Great Exhibition of 1851, through which Britain recognised itself as 'the Workshop of the World', *The Economist*, with characteristic understatement, told its readers that 'the reform of our representative system stands not very early on the list of topics of pressing or immediate importance'.[26]

Just two years before he engineered Britain's Second Reform Act, Benjamin Disraeli hoped the House of Commons would 'sanction no step that has a tendency to democracy, but that it will maintain the ordered state of free England in which we live'. Democracy was thus counterposed to an order and freedom from which Britain had

> created the greatest Empire of modern time. You have amassed a capital of fabulous amount. You have devised and sustained a system of credit still more marvellous. And, above all, you have established and maintained a scheme so vast and complicated of labour and industry, that the history of the world offers no parallel to it. . . . If you destroy that state of society, remember this – England cannot begin again.[27]

VIRTUAL REPRESENTATION

One argument still common into the first third of the nineteenth century sought to undercut the demand for franchise extension by asserting that, in a metaphysical sense at least, the whole population was already represented. This theory of 'virtual representation' can be traced at least as far back as thirteenth-century England when the magnates and prelates 'insisted on their role as virtual representatives of the rest of the nobility and the clergy and even of the community of the realm'. In the older European parliaments of the fourteenth and fifteenth centuries juridical theory conceived of the nobility who owned the land thereby representing the people who lived on it. A.R. Myers points out that 'in 1484 the Chancellor of France described the Estates-General at Tours as representing the whole of the French people'.[28] Modern democratic theory presumes that representation can only be achieved through explicit electoral choice by those deemed to be thereby represented. The older, paternalist theory asserts that a representative, like the father of a traditional household, acts on behalf of all those under his care, irrespective of whether the latter have made a choice or, if they have, how they have made it.

As the modern movement for franchise extension emerged, the old assumptions were employed against it. Edmund Burke regarded virtual representation as 'in many cases, even better than the actual. It possesses most of its advantages, and is free from many of its inconveniences.'[29] In writing for the 1820 *Encylopaedia Britannica*, James Mill explained the circumstances in which the vote of one individual could be taken as representing others with whom he was closely linked. 'One thing is pretty clear, that all those individuals whose interests are indisputably included in those of other individuals may be struck off [the electorate] without inconvenience.' In this light may be viewed all children, up to a certain age, whose interests are involved in those of their parents. In this light, also, 'women may be regarded, the interest of almost all of whom is involved either in that of their fathers or in that of their husbands'.[30]

In the 1760s and 1770s the attempt was made to apply this theory to the American colonies. Soame Jenyns in Britain, and some of the Tories in America, asserted that the British House of Commons did in fact represent the colonists. Americans were in the same position as Birmingham, Manchester and the other British cities which did not have their own MP, for after all, as Burke had famously argued in 1774, the MP represents not just his constituency but the whole nation. The people of the nation were thus represented, *wherever they might be*. This was challenged in America on the grounds that virtual representation was implausible. Similarity of interest did not exist, for, as one pamphleteer pointed out: 'There is not that intimate and inseparable Relation between the *Electors of Great-Britain* and the *Inhabitants of the Colonies*, which must inevitably involve both in the same Taxation; on the contrary, not a single *actual* elector in *England*, might be immediately affected by a Taxation in America.' Another pamphleteer quipped that 'Our *privileges* are all *virtual*' but 'our sufferings are *real*'.[31] A further counter-argument, which clearly implies the claim to full independence, denied the one-nation appeal by asserting that the Americans had become a *different* people. On this basis, of course, virtual representation might still make sense within an American context, in respect of, for example, women and children.

THIN END OF THE WEDGE

The critics of franchise extension looked at particular proposals not just in isolation but in the wider context of their long-term effect.

Any change validates the idea of change and so one extension, however modest, could roll the constitution down a slippery slope. The redoubtable Duke of Wellington warned their lordships of this in the debate on the British First Reform Bill. 'If we are to make a change, there can be no reason for not going the full length that the people wish . . . that is to say, Universal Suffrage, Vote by Ballot, and Annual Parliaments?'[32] Putting it this way, it hardly needs saying, was intended as an argument against making any change at all. Hegel, too, watching English developments from afar, shared the view that the 'reform of the franchise will bring in its train other reforms of substance . . . one instinctively suspects that more far-reaching changes will issue from this subversion of the formal basis of the existing order'.[33] Tocqueville, as we shall see in Chapter 5, gave a sophisticated analysis of the logic of incremental reform. He argued that the more the vote is extended, the greater the resentment of those without it. Demand increases, concessions follow, and 'no stop can be made short of universal suffrage'.[34]

Robert Lowe, perhaps the most formidable opponent of the Second Reform Bill, argued that its inherent tendency was democratic:

> It is trifling with the House to suggest that when you have passed this Bill you will have settled anything; all that you do is to unsettle everything, perhaps to lay the foundation of a real agitation, because people, when they find that so much will be gained with such little trouble, will be encouraged to ask for a great deal more.[35]

THE BALANCED CONSTITUTION

One objection to franchise extension that was common in the nineteenth century was that it would undermine 'the balanced constitution'. As with so much in western political thought, this idea can be traced back to ancient Greece. It can also be found in England during and after the period of the Civil War. The most prestigious legal commentary of the late eighteenth century was Sir William Blackstone's *Commentaries on the Laws of England*. Here we are told that 'the legislature of the kingdom is entrusted to three distinct powers entirely independent of each other'. Freedom was held to rest upon a balance between the monarchical, aristocratic and democratic elements of the constitution, for 'there can be no inconvenience be attempted by either of the three branches but will be withstood by one of the other two; each being armed with a negative power sufficient to repel any innovation which it shall think inexpedient or dangerous.' Now so long as the lower house directly represented only a section of the people it was held in check and could claim no preponderance over the other two elements. Blackstone had warned that 'nothing can endanger or hurt' the constitution 'but destroying the equilibrium of power between one branch of the legislature and the rest'.[36] This is precisely what some conservatives took to be happening in the nineteenth century. The more the franchise was extended, the more the House of Commons might claim to represent the whole people. It might then enforce its dominance over the House of Lords and the monarchy. The equilibrium which was held to protect freedom would then be disturbed and liberty would succumb to the changing fashions and temporary enthusiasms of the masses. Such views can be found through to the time of the First World War in the speeches of, for example, Canning, Peel, Disraeli, Salisbury and Lord Cecil.

IGNORANCE

A more widespread argument against franchise extension emphasised the ignorance and illiteracy of the lower classes. In his *Reflections on the Revolution in France*, Edmund Burke found consolation and support from *Ecclesiastes*:

> The wisdom of a learned man cometh by opportunity of leisure: and he that hath little business shall become wise. . . . How can he get wisdom that holdeth the plough and that glorieth in the goad; that driveth oxen; that is occupied in their labours; and whose talk is of bullocks?[37]

This extract seems to have been reasonably well-known in our period, for J.S. Mill, an agnostic and so presumably no Bible scholar, quoted it in an article for *The Examiner* in July 1832.[38] The French liberal Benjamin Constant believed that the qualification for political participation required 'a further condition in addition to those prescribed by the law of birth and age. This condition is the leisure indispensable for the acquisition of understanding and soundness of judgement'.[39] The southern slaveholder James Henry Hammond had also grasped the point: 'It will scarcely be disputed that the very poor have less leisure to prepare themselves for the proper discharge of public duties than the rich; and that the ignorant are wholly unfit for them at all.'[40] Likewise Walter Bagehot, writing just after the passage of Britain's Second Reform Act, observed that 'the average can only earn very scanty wages by coarse labour. They have no time to improve themselves, for they are labouring the whole day through.'[41] William Lecky, writing in 1896, over sixty years after Tocqueville's famous journey, also looked to the United States for evidence concerning the nature of democracy. 'The crudest, most ignorant, most disorderly elements of European life have been poured into America as into a great alembic.' From such unpromising material he felt able to conclude that 'modern democracy is not favourable to the higher forms of intellectual life. Democracy levels down quite as much as it levels up' and produces merely 'the apotheosis of the average judgement'.[42] The leader of the German National Liberals, Rudolf von Benningsen, had come to the same conclusion: 'To date I at least have discovered nothing about the educational virtues of universal suffrage, unless it be education to demagogy and general brutality.'[43]

We arrive, then, at two related propositions. Wealth allows leisure, which facilitates education, which produces fitness for public life. The negative corollary of this is that poverty necessitates full-time labouring, hence absence of learning and so a basic unfitness for political participation. These assumptions may well surprise or shock a modern democrat, but we have to remind ourselves of the context from which they emerged. First, the nineteenth-century critics still held to the now almost forgotten, but not intrinsically implausible, notion that certain qualifications are required for the important tasks involved in political life. Second, sentiments that might now seem snobbish or arrogant were perhaps less inappropriate in societies with much lower literacy levels than our own, and very little, or no, free state education. Furthermore, of course, we are dealing with a time when radio and television were not yet available as alternative or supplementary sources of political information and discussion.[44]

Let us, then, briefly consider the various levels of education available in the nineteenth century and into this one. Eric Hobsbawm has estimated that in 1850 illiteracy was over 50 per cent for non-whites in the USA, between 30 and 50 per cent in France and England, and below 30 per cent in Germany and among white North Americans.[45]

Prussia certainly led the way in educational attainment, concerning which Theodore Hamerow provides rather more precise figures than those of Hobsbawm. Hamerow mentions an estimate published in 1845 according to which the Prussian illiteracy rate was below ten per cent, as compared with 36 per cent in France and 93 per cent in Russia. However, taking the German Confederation as a whole, Hamerow comments on the political situation of the less educated:

> Both semi-literacy and illiteracy implied nonparticipation in public affairs. The men who could barely recognize the letters of the alphabet or sign his name may have had political convictions, but he was in effect deprived of the opportunity to influence state policy. His failure to acquire the basic tools of education con-demned him to ignorance of civic issues, to submissiveness and apathy. In other words, one German out of four could not take part in politics because he lacked the minimal learning essential for a comprehension of the problems of government.[46]

Attempts had been made, as in Saxony in 1769, to make school attendance compulsory, but its enforcement had proved impossible, especially when help was needed on the land. Prussia had been near to achieving universal elementary education before 1870, and in 1888 free schooling was introduced throughout Germany.

In the United Kingdom the 1833 Factory Act, which prohibited the employment of children under 9, required school attendance of two hours a day for children between 9 and 13 years of age. A govern-ment grant, quite inadequate in itself but a significant step for the future, was provided for school buildings. The first major Education Act was that of 1870. It increased the grants to the existing 20 000 voluntary schools, and allowed poorer parents to be excused the school fees of a few pence each week. Compulsory schooling for children between the ages of 5 and 10 was introduced in 1880, although this was not made free until 1891. There was no national secondary system before 1902 and not until 1918 was the school-leaving age raised to 14.

France, which moved early on franchise extension, was less for-ward in matters of education. A law of 1816 required the provision of a school in every commune and free education for the children of poor parents, but, as elsewhere, good intentions were not fully implemented. A major impetus towards education provision derived from the crushing military defeat of 1870, which 'was regarded as a victory for the German teacher'.[47] In 1879 Jules Ferry became Minis-ter of Education and, in the following years, introduced free edu-cation without religious instruction in the public primary schools. In

1882 this was made obligatory for all children between 6 and 13 years of age. However, attendance at secondary schools remained low. In 1910 less than three per cent of children between 12 and 19 attended secondary schools and only in 1936 was the school-leaving age raised to 14.

In the United States of America, a federal ordinance of 1785 stipulated that every township had to reserve land for a public school. Two years later the United States Constitution, which excluded franchise qualifications from its scope, likewise left matters of educational provision to the particular states. A wide variety of provisions was the inevitable result, particularly so as many states devolved education further down to the local authorities. In general, the United States was in advance of western Europe in the gradual raising of the school-leaving age, although it was not until 1920 that Mississippi made primary education compulsory, the last of the states to do so. There, as in other southern states, blacks and whites were educated separately until the famous 1954 Supreme Court decision declared 'separate but equal' schooling implausible and unconstitutional. It is estimated that in 1860 only about five per cent of the slave population could read and write, and for the United States as a whole, only about seven per cent of the relevant age group attended secondary schools in 1890. The enforcement of compulsory schooling has been less strict than in the United Kingdom, France and Germany, and the 1940 census showed that ten per cent of children between 6 and 15 years of age were not receiving any schooling at all, and that 10 million American adults were functionally illiterate.

According to conservative opinion, notions of popular sovereignty or the Rights of Man were producing political demands that threatened the quality of leadership. Passive categorisation of grounds for disqualification no longer seemed sufficient. Ignorance had to be kept firmly in its place.

In France the *doctrinaires* of the Restoration period developed the theory of the sovereignty of reason. Royer-Collard, Victor Cousin, Benjamin Constant and Destutte de Tracy produced a defence of the liberal middle classes who both feared popular sovereignty and rejected the political basis of the *ancien régime*. Against notions of the sovereignty of kings or peoples, Royer-Collard asserted 'the sovereignty of reason, the only true legislator of mankind'. Reason alone was held to provide political eligibility and this gave preference to the educated middle classes who were taken to represent the national interest. Above them, according to Royer-Collard, 'is a certain desire to dominate against which it is necessary to guard; below, ignorance . . . complete incapacity'.[48]

In England, too, we find concern that ignorance should be kept in its place. In his *Representative Government* (1861) John Stuart Mill advised that 'it is not useful, but hurtful, that the constitution of the country should declare ignorance to be entitled to as much political power as knowledge'.[49] The following year James Fitzjames Stephen recommended that 'the highest function which the general mass of mankind could ever be fitted to perform would be that of recognizing the moral and intellectual superiority of the few'. In a speech on the Second Reform Bill, Robert Lowe asked a series of rhetorical questions: 'If you want venality, if you want ignorance, if you want drunkenness and the facility for being intimidated, or if, on the other hand, you want impulsive, unreflecting and violent people, where do you look for them in constituencies? Do you go to the top or the bottom?'[50] After that Reform Bill had passed into law, Walter Bagehot voiced his fears of the consequences: 'But in all cases it must be remembered that a political combination of the lower classes, as such and for their own objects, is an evil of the first magnitude; that a permanent combination of them would make them supreme in the country; and that their supremacy, in the state they now are, means the supremacy of ignorance over instruction and of numbers over knowledge.'[51]

In Germany the ultra-royalist Baron Adolf Senfft von Pilsach was also perplexed and troubled by the new *Zeitgeist*:

> I cannot consider it just and reasonable that a simple workingman has as much voice as his employer who hires hundreds or thousands like him, gives them bread, and feeds their families. That employer and worker should be equal in this respect makes no sense. Furthermore, I cannot call it proper that the people who first of all do not understand anything about legislation and secondly do not really want to vote at all are designated as voters. I find that to make such people voters is not just, not fair, not reasonable.[52]

The historian Heinrich von Treitschke warned how universal suffrage threatened national values: 'Our idealism has always been our strongest national asset; and thus it is absolutely un-German to let stupidity and ignorance have the decisive voice.'[53]

If politics and ignorance were to be regarded as incompatible one arrived at two logical and opposite conclusions. The more conservative view, as we have seen, was that the uneducated should be excluded from politics. Many liberals, however, reasoned the other way, and said that the working classes should now be given the education that their new situation required. A member of the Frankfurt parliament, Gustav von Mevissen, unsurprisingly influenced by the recent revolution, declared in 1850 that 'the rule of the masses has begun in Europe although they have not been trained to rule. . . . These masses . . . must still acquire the education needed for government, they must still acquire the measure of self-control necessary for the achievement of social purposes.'[54] Robert Lowe eventually resigned himself to the new situation and concluded: 'We must educate our masters to compel our future masters to learn their letters.'[55]

There is, then, a link between the extension of political rights in the mid- and late nineteenth century and the emergence of provision for state education. Through education the working class might be made fit for democracy. For some, however, such reasoning was too confined. A political solution need not be a social one. A working class fit for politics might not remain fit to be a working class. Guizot, who had sponsored the French Education Law of 1833, which required every village to have a primary school, came to suspect that the spread of education might produce social unrest. At the end of the century the social psychologist Gustave le Bon feared that the French system of education 'recruits numerous disciples for the worst forms of socialism'. The system 'gives those who have been submitted to it a violent dislike to the state of life in which they were born. . . . The working man no longer wishes to remain a working man, or the peasant to continue a peasant.'[56]

The British Conservative MP Sir Charles Adderley maintained that 'It is clearly wrong to attempt to keep ordinary children of the working class at school after the age at which their proper work begins, and there are some kinds of work which must begin very early.'[57] A little education was useful for industrial life and thus, in the words of William Lecky, 'should be much more technical and industrial than literary'. Beyond that modest level the political value of education 'is often grossly overrated. The more dangerous forms of animosity and dissension are usually undiminished, and are often stimulated, by its influence . . . [for] the half-educated mind is peculiarly open to political utopias and fanaticisms.'[58] So, it seems the masses are dangerous in one way when they are ignorant, and dangerous in another when they receive education. Thus we must conclude it was not their level of learning that was feared so much as their existence. They were dangerous *per se*.

THE MOB

The democratic movement, then, had to overcome a traditional and intense fear of the lower orders, a 'swinish multitude' in Burke's infamous phrase or a 'vile multitude' in Thiers' variant.[59] It is note-worthy how easily such designations deny both individuality and humanity to the working classes. They could, it seems, only be considered in the mass, an 'uncultivated herd' as Mill put it,[60] thus both ignorant and subhuman. Guizot warned of the 'passions of the multitude', Bagehot of their lack of 'the *sense* of morality' and the German economist Hermann Schulze-Delitzsch warned that 'there is in human nature, in all of us as we are, in large and small, in the eminent and the humble, a dim boundary line where the bestial and the human meet, and woe to him . . . who wantonly and with a frivolous hand touches this boundary line! He unleashes the beast which will tear him to pieces with its lion's claws!'[61] This was a disturbing piece of psychology, but the usual conclusion was that the educated had acquired the means to give rationality preponderance over the passions. The historian Johann Gustav Droysen feared that 'the people are only to be won demagogically, whether the dema-gogues are political swindlers of the sort who were at the helm in 1848, or clerics, both Catholic and Lutheran. We must direct our activity at a much higher level.'[62] J.S. Mill felt that the masses were not yet ready for socialism, his ultimate aim. 'We were now much less democrats than I had been, because so long as education continued to be so wretchedly imperfect we dreaded the ignorance and espe-cially the selfishness and brutality of the mass.'[63] Here, as elsewhere, the mere mention of ignorance serves almost automatically and without any logical link being established, to bring selfishness, brut-ality and other undesirable traits in its train.

The poor and uneducated only became a mass when they aggre-gated and this is precisely what the process of commercial and industrial development produced. A middle class that pursued profit created the urban proletariat as the necessary means. The seemingly inexorable growth of London, Cobbett's 'all-devouring Wen'[64] had long been a source of unease, but now cities threatened to become the normal site of human habitation. In the new cities the poor were aggregated and uncontrolled. Their 'betters' did not know what they were getting up to and could not set the social and behavioural tone in the manner that had long prevailed in the villages. Even before the taking of the Bastille, the Gordon riots in London in 1780 and Shay's Rebellion in Massachusetts seven years later had revealed disturbing possibilities. In that same year of 1787, Thomas Jefferson drew what seemed to be the logical conclusion.

> I think our governments will remain virtuous for many centuries as long as they are chiefly agricultural; and this will be as long as there shall be vacant lands in any part of America. When they get piled upon one another in large cities, as in Europe, they will become corrupt as in Europe.[65]

The hope of rural virtue predominating for 'many centuries' seemed less plausible just 34 years later. Chancellor Kent noted that 'We are no longer to remain plain and simple republics of farmers. . . . The growth of the city of New York is enough to startle and awaken those who are pursuing the *ignis fatuus* of universal suffrage. It [New York] is rapidly swelling into the unwieldy population, and with the burdensome pauperism, of a European metropolis.'[66]

After the 1848–9 revolutions, the mob on the street appeared as a recurrent nightmare to the middle and upper classes. Social investigation of urban life, coupled with biological and psychological speculations, produced some disquieting conclusions. The mere ignorance of the urban poor was now combined with the theory of hereditary urban degeneration. In 1884, Alfred Marshall, following a line of thought already developed by Francis Galton in the 1860s, concluded that 'long life in the town is accompanied by more or less degeneration of the race', producing a characteristic alignment, 'those who are limp in body and mind'. It seemed that starting with the stout and sturdy countryman, each generation of urban living produced a progressive lowering of physical quality, and furthermore, according to an investigation published in 1887, a biological Gresham's Law seemed to operate as the bad drove out the good. 'Criminal and pauperised classes with low cerebral development renew their race more rapidly than those of higher nervous natures.' The Paris Commune of 1871 was seen to provide a generally applicable warning. 'This mighty mob of famished, diseased and filthy helots is getting dangerous, physically, morally, politically dangerous.'[67] In the nineteenth century, London was by far the largest city in the world, but Paris was the most revolutionary. So it is hardly surprising that the most outspoken analysis of mob psychology should have been written by a Frenchman. In *The Crowd* (1895) Gustave Le Bon explained that individuals suffer a psychological derangement when transposed into a mob. 'In the collective mind the intellectual aptitudes of the individuals, and in consequence, their individuality, are weakened . . . . In crowds it is stupidity and not mother-wit that is accumulated.' Personal responsibility now disappears and lower instincts seek unrestrained gratification. Such pessimism produced its characteristic intellectual theory – a cyclical view of history. The current stage was one where 'the populace is sovereign, and the tide of barbarism mounts'. Socialism would mark society's return to the barbarism from which it had once so strenuously emerged.

> Today the claims of the masses are becoming more and more sharply defined and amount to nothing less than a determination to destroy utterly society as it now exists, with a view to making it hark back to that primitive communism which was the normal condition of all human groups before the dawn of civilization.[68]

WEALTH AND PROPERTY

The only criteria held to match the significance of intelligence and rationality were those of wealth and property. The latter pairing, as we have noted, were prerequisites of the former. That those with leisure would *use* it to gain wisdom seems to have been taken as self-evident. The converse of the property/education/morality equation was noted by a speaker at the 1787 American Federal Convention. He referred to 'the dangerous influence of those multitudes without property and without principle', as if the lack of one necessarily excluded the other.[69] Boissy d'Anglas, the chief author of the French Constitution of the Year III (1795) was rather more self-conscious in drawing the same connection. 'We should be governed', he said, 'by the best, and the best are those best educated and most interested in upholding the laws. With very few exceptions you will only find such men among those who, possessing property, are attached to the country containing it and the laws which protect it.'[70] This alignment was also evident to Macaulay who counterposed to 'mere numbers' the belief that it is by 'property and intelligence, that the nation ought to be governed'.[71]

In 1793, the future Earl of Liverpool 'supposed every person would agree that the landed interest ought to have the preponderant weight [in parliament]. The landed interest was, in fact, the *stamina* of the country.'[72] In the nineteenth century this proposition was less self-evident, and property had to demonstrate its presumed intelligence with a more reasoned presentation. Chancellor Kent argued in Lock-ean manner that 'Society is an association for the protection of property as well as of life, and the individual who contributes only one cent to the common stock ought not to have the same power and influence in directing the property concerns of the partnership as he who contributes his thousands.'[73]

Those with property had the most to lose and so were taken to be the most reliable guarantors of stability. Physical and mental stability were often taken to be conterminous. Possession of land keeps a man in one place. Such a person could be relied upon. Conversely, to be unsettled in one sense was to be unsettled in all. In the United States to 'Go West, Young Man' was to be a pioneer and to grasp the opportunities that a new and expanding country offered. Yet the same society viewed the vagrant poor with intense suspicion. A speaker at the 1837 Pennsylvania Convention was determined to cling to the residence qualifications that were such a normal part of the franchise requirements.

> But, Sir, what does the delegate propose? To place the vicious vagrant, the wandering Arabs, the Tartar hordes of our large cities on a level with the virtuous and good man? . . . These Arabs steeped in crime and in vice, to be placed on a level with the industrious population is insulting and degrading to the community . . . I hold up my hands against a proceeding which confers on the idle, vicious, degraded vagabond a right at the expense of the poor and industrious portion of this common-wealth.[74]

Not even Disraeli was given to quite such colourful language, but he believed 'society has a right to ask that the person who exercises the suffrage is not a migratory pauper' and that 'if you see a man without a coat, you would hardly say he should have the franchise'.[75]

A further argument against the propertyless was that their economic condition left them necessarily dependent upon others. Thus they had no will of their own. Their vote, if permitted, would merely express the choice of those to whom they were beholden. Benjamin Constant explained that 'Only he who possesses the necessary revenue to subsist independently of any external will can exercise the rights of citizenship.'[76] The minds of those without property 'are naturally and almost necessarily governed by the minds of those who have', thought James Mill.[77] Mill's emphasis here seems to be on cultural hegemony. More common, under the system of open voting, was the effective political coercion that employers and landlords could exercise over employees and tenants. In 1843 Friedrich Engels referred to the situation of the English agricultural population which had

> taken no interest in public affairs; dependent on the landowners who can put an end to the lease agreement any year, the farmers, phlegmatic and ignorant, have sent only Tories to parliament year after year. . . . If an individual farmer wanted to come out against this traditional vote, he found no support among his fellow farmers and the landlord could easily give him notice.[78]

If such a man's vote was not really his own, the simple solution lay in introducing secret voting. This reform was brought about in England in 1872. Now, presumably, the real will of the poor could gain unimpeded expression. Some opponents of democracy, however, merely shifted on to higher ground. According to William Beveridge, writing in 1906, those 'who through general defects' are unemployable and hence dependent on the state, should suffer 'a complete and permanent loss of all citizen rights including not only the franchise, but civil freedom and fatherhood'.[79] Dicey, writing eight years later, also thought that receipt of an old age pension was incompatible with possession of the franchise.[80] The justification of such exclusions could range broadly over the various reasons outlined previously, but, in terms of non-taxpayers dependent upon state provision, the argument considered to be the most apposite was that those who do not contribute to public wealth should not be trusted with decisions on its use. They had no motive for care and frugality and every incentive for irresponsible extravagance. The obverse of 'No taxation without representation' was 'No representation without taxation'. Political rights should be granted according to a man's economic contribution. Even Tom Paine, often represented as a radical democrat, stipulated financial qualifications for political rights.[81] We saw in Chapter 1 that from 1849 to 1918 the vote for the Prussian parliament was weighted according to levels of taxation. One defender of that arrangement pointed out that 'the ability to pay taxes occupies a pre-eminent position' in securing the existence and prosperity of society. 'It provides the most general measure of individual contribution to the public welfare. It therefore seems reasonable to regulate voting power according to the tax situation.'[82]

Levels of taxation were, of course, a partial measure of levels of wealth, but did not indicate what for some was the significant distinction of particular sources of wealth. In Coleridge, and as we shall see, Carlyle, and to an extent in Constant, we find a defence of traditional landed wealth against *nouveau riche* industrial capitalists. The former were held to operate within a traditional community where accepted responsibilities of *noblesse oblige* fitted and prepared the aristocracy for exercising leadership over society as a whole. The new 'millocracy' of commerce and industry, on the other hand, were viewed as narrow and philistine profit-maximisers who were devoid of wider social responsibilities and obligations.

So property could be regarded either as one homologous substance, or else separated into different components of varying quality according to one's particular political purpose. The same also applied to the aggregation of land, property and education as qualifications for the suffrage. Although each criterion might tend to give broadly the same people the vote, the particular emphasis tends to shift pre-eminence to a different social group. The landed qualification most clearly suits the traditional aristocracy, or, as in the United States of America, the landed interest; the property and taxpaying qualifications exalt both them and the commercial wealth of the towns; but reason, and the emphasis on educational prerequisites, best serve professional groupings. It is the ideal criterion for a middle-class *juste milieu*, for it extends political rights beyond the aristocracy while simultaneously denying their extension to the allegedly emotional and ignorant masses. John Stuart Mill was quite explicit in disaggregating the usual franchise qualifications. In his *Thoughts on Parliamentary Reform*, he recommended 'a plurality of votes, to be given, not to property, but to proved superiority of education'.[83] As against land and property, the educational barrier was the lowest hurdle. The masses might become more educated without obviously threatening the educational levels of the middle and upper classes, but for the lower classes to gain property, or, even more conclusively, land, was a different matter. Would not lower-class acquisition in fact be an expropriation at the expense of the current possessors? It was property more than anything else which determined the basic social divide, and it was property which democracy was held most to endanger.

THE THREAT TO PROPERTY

In France, Benjamin Constant warned that 'the necessary aim of those without property is to obtain some'. If given the vote, 'these rights, in the hands of the greatest number, will inevitably serve to encroach upon property'.[84] Chancellor Kent of New York warned that 'the tendency of universal suffrage is to jeopardize the rights of property'.[85] After the turmoil of 1848, the Rhineland industrialist David Hansemann advised Prince William that manhood suffrage was 'the most dangerous experiment in the world'.[86] Robert Lowe in the 1860s, echoing the views of the Duke of Wellington and Lord Macaulay a few decades earlier, warned that once working men have political rights 'the machinery is ready to launch those votes in one compact mass upon the institutions and property of this country'.[87]

Nevertheless the vote was precisely what working men were getting. Even so, all was not lost. 'One man – One vote' did not equalise political power, for a series of more or less subtle devices ensured that the seemingly less worthy vote was subdued, filtered or channelled into safe reservoirs. The debate on such procedures was particularly acute in Germany, for, in Prussia at least, universal male suffrage was introduced in 1849, and not so long afterwards, in 1863, an organised socialist party threatened to facilitate the feared alignment of (male) universal suffrage and socialism. The Prussian three-tier taxpayer franchise might seem sufficient to allay unease, but for some German conservatives, for whom even Bismarck was too modern, this was still insufficient. They wanted a return to the medieval system of Estates, or *Stände*, which replaced 'individualistic' voting with an 'organic' organisation based on occupational groupings. This suggestion was the most frequently mentioned device for curbing universal male franchise, having been proposed by Adolf Stöcker in the 1880s and in 1906 by Oertzen, who sought thereby to prevent the dictatorship of the proletariat.

If, in the words of deputy von Gerlach in 1866, 'every election is a misfortune'[88] the obvious policy was to minimise them. In 1878 there were two assassination attempts on Kaiser Wilhelm I. In debating the consequent anti-socialist laws the conservative deputy Otto Heinrich von Helldorf called for less frequent elections so that a proper sense of authority might be re-established. Another device (as noted in the previous chapter) was the use of indirect elections so that the will of the people might be 'purified', an effect further enhanced by leaving deputies unpaid, for then only men of independent standing could become legislators. For the Prussian liberal diarist and gossip Theodor von Bernhardi 'the daily allowance of three talers which the members of the legislature receive is a misfortune for our country. Thereby the sort of people enter the chamber who certainly do not belong there.'[89]

The most effective means of electoral control was, of course, open voting. This had the prestigious support of Montesquieu, who thought the 'lower class ought to be directed by those of higher rank, and restrained within the bounds by the gravity of eminent personages'.[90] An estate-owner in Silesia no doubt bore the philosopher's injunction in mind when issuing the following threat on the eve of the 1863 elections:

> To the royal Prussian voters of the manor Meffersdorf, Schweta, and Volkersdorf. His Majesty our most gracious king and sovereign has commanded that on the 20th of this month the election should take place, and has pronounced that the election will be free only if the choice falls on such persons who will vote in accordance with the disposition and will of his Majesty and his ministers. . . . I have commanded that those voters who act to the contrary shall, if they are workers in the forest or on the estates, be dismissed, and that the same procedure shall be followed in the brickworks, the peat banks, and the factory for ovenware and pottery.[91]

SOCIALISTS AND DEMOCRACY

If the popular vote were so dangerous to political conservatism and the propertied interests it could be presumed to favour socialism and the working classes. Indeed, for this reason Friedrich Engels aligned himself with the British Chartists, their parliamentary orientation notwithstanding. In 1844 he thought the Chartist 'six points which are all limited to the reconstitution of the House of Commons, harmless as they seem, are sufficient to overthrow the whole English Constitution, Queen and Lords included'.[92] The social position of the proletariat seemed to guarantee a political response opposed to the power of private property. This materialism – the view that generally opinion is a function of social position rather than an independent, intellectual variable – is often taken to be a distinctive feature of Marxism. However, we have heard enough to know that this analysis had already been developed by the political right, and was merely taken over by the left, for whom it was a source of hope.

A contemporary socialist has declared that 'Democracy is what working people have made it; neither more nor less'.[93] That the right was against democracy and the left for it may have some plausibility as a broad generalisation. For some people it would be axiomatic. Yet this simple dichotomy has many exceptions and so is unhelpful and rather misleading, for in some strands of socialist thought we can trace a mistrust of universal suffrage. In terms of Marxism, for example, the failures of the 1848–9 revolutions undermined simple faith in the unaided revolutionary potential of the working class. In *Capital*, Marx wrote that 'the advance of capitalist production develops a working class which by education, tradition and habit looks upon the requirements of that mode of production as self-evident natural laws'.[94] Guidance from those with knowledge, that is, the party, was now needed. This analysis was given greater prominence by Kautsky and Lenin at the beginning of this century. For them socialist consciousness could only come to the working class from the outside. Correct understanding was transmitted to them by those possessed of it, the radical intelligentsia. We see, then, that the link between political understanding and general educational level can be found at many points along the political spectrum. All sides hoped that the ignorant working class could be made receptive to their respective notions of truth and justice.

In France, the anarchist Pierre-Joseph Proudhon voiced his disillusionment with a 'universal' suffrage that had 'absolved [Louis] Bonaparte of his *coup d'état*'. He concluded that 'Universal suffrage given to a people of so neglected an education as ours, far from being the instrument of progress, is only the stumbling-block of liberty.'[95] In 1848 his compatriot Louis-August Blanqui had wanted elections postponed until the electorate could be properly educated. The French experience taught socialists throughout Europe that democratisation would not serve their purposes in a predominantly rural society. E.S. Beesly, writing in the English socialist newspaper *The Bee-Hive*, noted that 'the dogma of universal suffrage cannot be applied in France without subordinating the intelligent and energetic populations of the large towns to an ignorant and narrow peasantry'.[96] In the late nineteenth century, English Fabian thought was as much influenced by the positivism of August Comte as by that of Marx, and mistrusted urban ignorance almost as much as 'the idiocy of rural life'. In her autobiography, Beatrice Webb looked back on the 'priggish . . . anti-democratic and anti-collectivist bias' with which her investigations began. 'I do not quite understand', she had written in 1884, 'the democratic theory that by multiplying ignorant opinions indefinitely you produce wisdom.'[97] Her fellow-Fabian H.G. Wells went much further in developing a rejection of democracy that contains echoes both of Saint-Simon's Council of Newton and of Carlyle's contempt for mass opinion. Wells knew 'of no case for the elective Democratic government of modern States that cannot be knocked to pieces in five minutes'. Government, he thought, should ideally be carried out by the best-qualified rather than the most numerous. This, he believed, fortunately, was evidently destined to happen. Democracy, though part of an inevitable process, was merely 'a transitory confusion' bound to pass away 'as the twilight passes, as the embryonic confusion of the cocoon creature passes into the higher state, into the higher organism, the world-state of the coming years.'[98]

Wells represents the highpoint of a Fabian theoretical elitism that, perhaps, found its institutional apotheosis in the centralised nationalised industries created by the 1945–51 British Labour governments. Otherwise his kind of elitism was most pronounced in communist regimes where the self-proclaimed correctness of the party was taken to render unnecessary the test of actual working-class opinion. The attack on private property, so feared by conservative critics of democracy, has come about mainly in countries where parliamentary democracy was absent. Thus democracy and expropriation have not gone together. The image of socialism conjured up by its opponents has derived from revolution in France from 1789 to the Paris Commune of 1871, and later, from communism in Russia and eastern Europe. To apply this image to socialist parties in parliamentary contexts is, wilfully or otherwise, misleading. More characteristic of western socialist democracy has been the stance of bending over backwards to appear respectable and constitutionalist. What little bark remained has proved rather devoid of bite. Whereas eastern communism has, until recently, been able to place itself above democratic opinion, western socialism has done the opposite. It has renounced, as Bagehot said of the British parliament as a whole, the task of enlightened educator, and made itself subservient to what it thought the electorate could stand.

TORY DEMOCRACY

Returning to our broader concerns, we see that the political group-ings, of whatever colour, have looked at democracy primarily in terms of its consequences for them. Would democracy undermine or fortify their policies? Was it their gravedigger or their gravy-train? We have suggested that most nineteenth-century conservatives feared the former. But, just as actual events forced a reappraisal on the left, so too did they on the right. To both sides came a slow dawning realisation that parliamentary democracy might have less devastating consequences than they had either hoped or feared. Alexis de Tocqueville wrote as follows of the changing political scene in France in 1849:

> The Conservatives, who for six months had seen all the by-elections going in their favour, and who filled and dominated almost all the local councils, had come to put unlimited confidence in the system of universal franchise, which had formerly filled them with unlimited mistrust.[99]

Louis Napoleon had reinstated universal male suffrage after his coup in 1851, and the electorate overwhelmingly supported the new ar-rangements. The Emperor had not forgotten his Saint-Simonian youth and had made some attempts at social legislation, including the legalisation of unions and strikes in 1864, to hold working-class support. The rest of Europe watched with interest this demonstration of how universal male franchise and even the referendum – that most democratic of electoral procedures – could produce conservative results.

In Prussia the idea of collaboration between crown and proletariat against the liberal bourgeoisie emerged in the 1840s. The conserva-tive tactic was to gain support from the workers by offering to reintroduce corporate regulation of production as preferable to the insecure free-for-all of *laissez-faire* economics. A key spokesman for this policy was General Joseph von Radowitz, whose *Gespräche aus der Gegenwart über Staat und Kirche* was published in 1846. He advised Frederick William IV that the socialist movement could be rescued from radicalism by regulation of industry, a progressive income tax and a system of poor relief. It would 'provide new and large resources for the monarchical principle'.[100] Such a policy of welfare from one side and obedience from the other was intended to squeeze liberalism out of contention for either power or support. In 1854 Bismarck had been pleased to observe that those excluded from voting were 'better royalists than the rest of the bourgeoisie and upper classes'[101] and more committed to preserving state order. His tactic of a cross-class alliance against liberalism survived through the 1860s but foundered due to left-wing support for the Paris Commune in 1871.

In Britain, extensions of the franchise took place in 1867 and 1884, without property and privilege being endangered. The assumption that the working class would destroy the hierarchical order was shown to be mistaken. Already in 1847 Disraeli had declared that 'liberal opinions are very convenient opinions for the rich and powerful'.[102] Thus emerged 'Tory Democracy', defined by one wit as a democracy that votes Tory. This is the conservatism that derives from the discovery of the deference voter, the working man attached to the symbolism of the monarchy, Lords and Commons, and not disturbing prevailing social distinctions. The other side of this tacit alliance is an upper class which declares its responsibilities to society as a whole. It is the Toryism of *noblesse oblige* and 'One Nation'. As in Germany, such responsible conservatism derided liberalism as the selfish ideology of a narrow stratum of factory-owners and merchants. Clearly, in North America, where liberalism was hegemonic and where no remnants of a feudal ruling class existed, a similar political strategy had no basis. After Disraeli, Tory Democracy is associated with Lord Randolph Churchill and Lord Cecil at the end of the nineteenth century, and continues through to the present day, although currently somewhat eclipsed. Early in this century Dicey noted that 'Democracy in modern England has shown a singular tolerance, not to say admiration, for the kind of social inequalities involved in the existence of the Crown, and of an hereditary and titled peerage.'[103]

This was the politics that Marx and Engels derided as 'feudal socialism'. In the *Communist Manifesto* they observed that 'The aristocracy, in order to rally the people to them, waved the proletarian alms-bag in front for a banner.' This self-interested attempt at survival was doomed, for 'the people, so often as it joined them saw on their hindquarters the old feudal coats of arms and deserted them with loud and irreverent laughter'.[104] Nearly a century-and-a-half later it is far from clear who should be having the last laugh. Aristocracies in Europe have survived better, and the left in parliamentary elections have done worse, than either side expected. Democracy has shown itself to be safe. Rather than undermining the upper classes it tends to incorporate the lower.

Our account of characteristic suspicions of democracy has thus far not mentioned that at the start of this century well over half the adult population in the countries we have considered did not have the vote. By far the largest excluded grouping were women, who were the last of the major categories to be granted the franchise. Various objections to their participation in politics will be discussed in Chapter 8. One disqualification, that of supposed insufficient rationality, had also been levelled at working-class men, but in this argument there had always lurked an element of ambiguity. What, for example, was to be taken as a sign of rationality? If it were formal education, then of course the poor were unable to obtain it in the days before free state schooling. Here it was lack of money that was more self-evident than lack of reason. If, alternatively, rationality was signified by an ability to identify self-interest, as was often held to be the case, then some noteworthy conclusions emerge. Through lack of reason the poor were held to be unable to perceive their interest in maintaining the prevailing order. An obvious response to this is that the prevailing order most suited those who did best out of it and that what was really feared about the working class was that their rational interest was different from that of the upper classes, and thus that they might pursue it by changing the social order.

The end of the nineteenth century witnessed the growth of a social psychology which purported to fear the irrationalism of the masses. This need not, as was once supposed, have threatening social and political consequences, for it could be turned to conservative account. The masses could be appealed to at the emotional, rather than the materialistic, level. Arno Mayer has noted how in the surviving monarchies 'King, emperor, and tsar remained the focus of dazzling and minutely choreographed public rituals that rekindled deep-seated royalist sentiments while simultaneously exalting and relegitimating the old order as a whole.' It is clear that during the nineteenth century most conservatives saw class as a necessary yet dangerous divide, the crossing of which spelt disaster for all sides. Class privilege, then, had to be kept in place against the threatening political onslaught. The means thereto were the connected cults of racism, nationalism and war.[105] The rise of Social Darwinism and ethnic pseudo-science pulled together the various social classes in common hostility to alleged 'natural' (because biological) inferiors and so the exaltation of the nation against the foreigner has taken much of the pressure off inequities of class.

In the nineteenth century, appeals to class politics had seemed the most likely source of fanaticism and instability. Now class remains, but calls to class struggle are the stale and weary echo of a bygone age. Yet the era of mass education has not produced a society of utilitarian rationalists. On the contrary, the emotional appeals of ethnicity, nationality and religious fundamentalism have been the most potent sources of political antagonism.

These reflections have drawn us into viewing emergent democracy from our late-twentieth-century vantage-point. Our overview has also necessarily taken a rather broad span of the subject. For closer particulars we must now return to the beginning and see how emergent democracy appeared to a few concerned and acute observers who looked, not back, but around at what appeared to be occurring, and forward to the imagined consequences.

PART II Thinkers

3 John Adams

Of the major figures of the American Revolution, John Adams remains the least glamorous and least known. George Washington is renowned for his leadership qualities and as the first President; Thomas Jefferson as the author of the Declaration of Independence; Hamilton, Madison and Jay as the authors of what has become a political theory classic, *The Federalist Papers*. In what follows we shall see that John Adams also deserves a place of honour among the leading figures of the foundation of the American republic.

As a resident of Massachusetts he was engaged in that state's resistance to British attempts to tax goods coming into the port of Boston. In a number of articles in the Boston *Gazette* Adams voiced his opposition to the 1765 Stamp Act. He was a delegate to the first and second Continental Congresses (1774–8), helped draft a petition to the King of England, and recommended George Washington as commander of the army. He was also part of a delegation that met Lord Howe on Staten Island in June 1776, as the British made a last-ditch attempt at reconciliation. Once convinced that the British tie was untenable Adams became a zealous advocate of independence. He thus argued for the Declaration of Independence in its passage through Congress and was principal author of the 1780 Massachusetts state constitution. His foreign policy objectives were that the new republic gain full diplomatic recognition and acceptance from other states, but that she keep clear of too close entanglement with the European powers. In 1783 he joined Franklin and Jay in negotiating the Paris peace treaty that ended hostilities with Great Britain. Two years later he was appointed American Plenipotentiary in London. (The states did not yet appoint Ambassadors). This he did not greatly enjoy. The British Court had not yet forgiven the former colony for its effrontery. Of the city in which this essay is written Adams remarked:

> The Smoke and Damp of the City is ominous to me. London boasts of its Trottoir, but there is a space between it and the House through which all the Air from Kitchens, Cellars, Stables and Servants Appartments ascends into the Street and pours directly on the Passenger on Foot. Such whiffs and puffs assault you every few Steps as are enough to breed the Plague if they do not suffocate you on the Spot.[1]

For most of the 1780s Adams was in Europe. Thus he watched from afar as the rather loose confederation of former colonies increasingly appeared in need of a 'more perfect Union'. The further consolidation produced by the 1787 constitution won his general approval. When Washington became President in 1789 Adams became the first Vice-President, not a position that he found very rewarding. 'I have been too ill-used in the office to be fond of it', he wrote to his friend Benjamin Rush,[2] yet he stayed in it for a second term. In 1797 Adams won the Presidency for a four-year term and thus completed twelve continuous years at the centre of national power. His defeat in the 1801 Presidential election left him rather embittered, and at the age of 65 he retired to the family home in Braintree, Massachusetts, where he lived quietly for another quarter of a century, dying on the same day as his distinguished friend and former opponent, Thomas Jefferson, on the fiftieth anniversary of the Declaration of Independence.

Thus far we have outlined what was clearly a prominent political career. Our enquiry, however, is of Adams as a political thinker. If not a great writer he was certainly a dilligent scholar. His method was well demonstrated in his *Defense of the Constitutions of the Governments of the United States*, the first of whose three volumes alone takes up over three hundred pages. Gordon S. Wood once described this work as 'the only comprehensive description of American constitutionalism that the period produced – the first fruit of the American Enlightenment', but also as a 'bulky, disorganised conglomeration of political glosses on a single theme'.[3] On his favourite topic of the advantages of multi-cameralism over single-chamber parliaments he ransacked world history in an astonishing display of erudition. Covering alleged democracies, Adams's investigations included San Marino and Zug among the moderns; Carthage, Corinth and Thebes among the ancients; with Franklin, Montesquieu, Harrington, Polybius and Plato among the philosophers and historians. Adams's stamina was staggering; whether the reader can survive it is another question. We have here not the quick rapier thrusts of the despised Rousseau, but rather the persistent, heavy onward plod of an almost endless artillery of historical facts.[4]

In an illuminating account of Adams's attitude to the major Enlightenment philosophers, Zoltan Haraszti has drawn on the critical notes, jibes and exclamations Adams placed in the conveniently wide margins provided by eighteenth-century publishers.[5] The comments are fascinating in themselves, but also produce the realisation that

Adams's 'real' books are of the same type; sometimes not much more than marginal comments on other authors. Thus his *Works* contain quite enormous chunks of Nedham, Turgot, Henrico Davila and other such opponents whom he painstakingly copied down in order to highlight their errors. By the standards of modern scholarship Adams was none too careful in inserting the appropriate quotation marks, a failing only partially remedied by his grandson, Charles Francis Adams, who brought out ten volumes of the *Works* in the 1850s.

John Adams was in fact aware of the structural weaknesses of his writings, and once commented that he would have made his works shorter if he had had more time! Let us, however, conclude these preliminaries by acknowledging that Adams displayed a depth of historical knowledge and philosophical concern that none of his recent presidential successors could begin to match.

As younger nations have learnt to their cost, the heady moments of independence can produce hopes that are hard to fulfil. Opposition to external rule can weld together a disparate coalition that soon fragments once the common opponent is vanquished. The art of decolonisation is to manage an external disturbance without generating an uncontrollable internal one. The eleven years from the 1776 Declaration of Independence to the 1787 federal constitution marked a long journey towards political self-understanding. The Declaration is a radical and optimistic document couched in the language of natural rights; the Constitution, in contrast, has been regarded by one school of thought as a conservative attempt by the class of property-owners to defend their privileges against the masses.[6] This change of emphasis to a more conservative mood is found in the writings of John Adams too, and is but a reflection of changing circumstances in the fledgling republic itself.[7]

The Declaration seemed to Adams thoroughly justified. From the time of the Stamp Act the colonists had come to realise that the British King, Lords and Commons had declared war against them. The implicit contract by which rule carried with it the obligation of protection had been broken. The colonists were of British stock, entitled to British rights, and thus in the irony of prevailing circumstances, were forced into self-government as a means of retaining them.[8] For some time thereafter Adams shared the mood of national self-congratulation. Whereas Eastern despotism had claimed 'their emperors and nobles being all descended from their gods', the Americans, by contrast, 'were universally too enlightened to be imposed on by artifice'. They had produced 'perhaps, the first example of governments erected on the simple principles of nature . . . without a pretence of miracle or mystery'. Thus was 'a great point gained in favor of the rights of mankind. The experiment is made and has completely succeeded.'[9]

Nevertheless, through the 1780s conditions arose which served to subdue the initial enthusiasm. Prior to independence the thirteen colonies already possessed well-established social and political systems, and were now wary of creating a central power which might gradually push them into subservience. Thus one of the crucial weaknesses of the newly-created Congress was its lack of financial control. From 1781 a debt crisis emerged that began to highlight threatening social divisions and was accompanied by talk, from both north and south, of secession. The intellectual postulates of the 'Founding Fathers' included the notion that a republic can survive only in a condition of relative equality. Hence the Jeffersonian emphasis on the yeoman farmer and the suspicion of cities, trade and large manufacture. Yet suddenly a social chasm emerged between wealthy creditors on the one hand, and, on the other, farmers and storekeepers who were falling increasingly into debt. Pressure arose from the latter for relief by means of paper money legislation, and riots ensued among debtors in eight of the thirteen states. The most serious outbreak occured in Adams's own state of Massachusetts in 1786, when Daniel Shays led western farmers in closing the judicial courts so that debts could not be collected. 'I . . . am much affected with the disagreeable state of things in the Massachusetts', wrote Adams from London. 'Mobs will never do to govern States or command armies.'[10] Returning from Europe keenly aware of the dangerous social divisions he had left behind him, Adams now found a similar prospect facing him at home. To hold down this threat became one of his main reasons for supporting the Federalists in their advocacy of a strengthened central government as achieved with the Constitution of the following year.

Then at the end of the decade came news of the revolution in France, a particularly disturbing upheaval because it occurred in Europe's most cultivated and populous country, whose language was that of aristocracies throughout the continent, and whose taste and fashions set the standards of quality everywhere. During the American revolution France had been a valuable ally and was now seen by many as introducing at home the principles she had helped the Americans implement abroad. On this basis there were calls on the United States government to join the French in their revolutionary war against England, and, more threatening still, even favouring the adoption of Jacobin practices in America itself. Now the ties established between the two countries suddenly appeared too close for comfort. Adams himself was shaken as never before or after. His radicalism of the 1770s independence struggle was replaced by a conservatism that directed itself to holding down the threat from below. In 1790 he declared that 'In this country the pendulum has vibrated too far to the popular side, driven by men without experience or judgement, and horrid ravages have been made upon property by arbitrary multitudes or majorities of multitudes. France has severe trials to endure from the same cause.'[11] As President, John Adams declared 25 April 1799 a fast day, that God 'would withhold us from unreasonable discontent, faction, sedition, and insurrection'.[12] The key writings of this later phase are the *Defense of the Constitution of the United States* (1787–8), written to challenge Turgot's advocacy of unicameral parliaments, the *Discourses on Davila* of 1790, and the 1814 'Letters to John Taylor', a reply to a work in which Adams had been criticised from the standpoint of the Jeffersonian democrats. As our main concern is with the response to the democratic upsurge it is on writings such as these that we shall concentrate our attention.

To the radical optimists American independence had signalled a new start not just for the former colonists but for mankind itself. Away from the legacy of feudalism government could be established on the basis of Enlightenment rationalism. New government indeed could be introduced, and so it was, but a society is more than its governmental system. What of the populace? If the evils of the old world were to be confined to the eastern hemisphere there had to be a different type of person in the west. The New World could scarcely claim to be peopled by a dissimilar species from the old, so how could they establish a different and better nature? On the basis of Locke's theory of the mind as a *tabula rasa*, they believed that human nature was a blank page which filled up according to the events and impressions it encountered. In America rural living and the relative equality of conditions meant that the omens were particularly favourable. Tom Paine, whose *Common Sense* was influential in hastening the call for independence, believed, in a revealing phrase, that America was 'the Adam of a new world'.[13] From that perspective the world was not merely turned upside down, but was actually begun anew. The Adams of the new world had for a time shared this optimism. In hints of what others later developed into the notion of 'manifest destiny' Adams believed that America was blessed with opportunities denied to less favoured peoples.[14] By 1790, however, he was clearly engaged in a thorough reconsideration of his earlier views. Here again the contrast with Paine is instructive. Where Paine declares 'My country is the world and my religion is to do good'[15] Adams insists on the narrow limits of human affections. 'Almost all, confine their benevolence to their families, relations, personal friends, parish, village, city, county, province, and that very few indeed, extend it impartially to the whole community.'[16] Whereas Paine regarded people as not naturally antagonistic, as only placed in opposition one to another through the overlay of an unnatural system of government, Adams increasingly came round to the more Hobbesian view of natural and hence thoroughly ingrained human competitiveness and antagonism. 'Self-interest, private avidity, ambition, and avarice, will exist in every state of society, and under every form of government.'[17] The radical pursuit of equality Adams saw as a chimera. Whatever unnatural political attempts were made to oppose it, individual striving by a populace with unequal attributes would once again create a social hierarchy. Man's underlying, 'real' nature was not in fact different and better than the miserable human record of war, intrigue, deception and crime depicted in the sobering annals of history. In Adams's lifetime the sense of history as a long process of ascertainable improvement was developed. He well knew the writings of the Frenchman Condorcet, who was prominent among those who delineated mankind's passage from barbarism to civilisation and onward to the presumed imminent state of perfection. On such accounts the 'savages', such as the indigenous peoples that Adams had encountered in his New England childhood, were only tenuously part of the same species. Fascinating though they were to the Enlightenment intelligentsia, their interest derived from their being at the distant, opposite end of mankind's long developmental line. Adams, however, in the gloom that overclouded his earlier hopes, compressed this account, and was fearful that the veneer of civilisation might prove too thin to safeguard social order and the undoubted human achievements. 'Amidst all the refinements of humanity, and all the improvements of civil life, the same nature remains' as it did when 'savage, brutal man ranged the forests'.[18] In some circumstances human behaviour is also akin to that of the animals. 'When blood is once drawn, men, like other animals, become outrageous',[19] and 'without government, there is not a more savage beast in the forest'.[20] From this perspective America had no special privileges. She had presumed to start again, but was, for better or worse, part of world history. On this basis Adams felt free to draw upon accounts of ancient Rome and Greece, of medieval principalities and modern nations, in determining how America should order its affairs, for ancient and modern, barbarian and civilised, Europe and America, were all as one in terms of the human constituents from which they were respectively derived. Was there an element of deliberate ambiguity when, in June 1785, Adams informed the Queen of England, that 'Another Europe, madam, is rising in America'?[21]

'We the People of the United States', began the Preamble to the Constitution framed by fifty-five men who met in Philadelphia in 1787. In view of the extent of political rights at the time of its inception, we might well wonder who the first-person plural category was held to contain. In Europe the term 'the people' was often used to connote all categories below the aristocracy, with a demeaning adjective added when specifying its lower sections as 'the common people'. Adams held to a less sociological variant of this typology. In Europe the aristocracy were a distinct social stratum with legal privileges deriving from the feudal era. Those who are uppermost in power habitually inculcate the notion that they are simultaneously superior in quality. Adams concentrated on the latter sense and saw every society as necessarily creating an aristocracy who were set above the rest not so much by birth as by obvious personal qualities and the ability to inspire respect. Such was the aristocracy of an open society, and below them lay 'the people'.

However, the American Revolution was made against a King and his aristocratic government. The American colonists, paraded as one and united for ideological purposes, saw themselves as a lower echelon wrongly denied citizens' rights. In this context popular demonology looked upward for the threat to liberty. Oppression came from the few who monopolised power. This too was the view of Adams during the independence struggle, but for him it was only one part of a larger picture. Liberty was clearly endangered from above, but also could be undermined from below. Writing to his wife on the eve of the Declaration of Independence, he confided that 'the new governments we are assuming in every part will require a purification from our vices, and an augmentation of our virtues, or they will be no blessings. The people will have unbounded power, and the people are extremely addicted to corruption and venality, as well as the great.'[22] The radical cult of the people as the natural repositories of virtue and liberty Adams saw as hopelessly naive. Liberty was maintained by cultivated individuals operating in a context of constraining political institutions. 'The populace, the rabble, the *canaille*, move as naturally in the circle of domination, whenever they dare, as the nobles or a king.'[23] Even before the revolution in France appeared to confirm his prognosis Adams warned that once given the chance the people could be relied upon to introduce a frenzy of levelling that lasts until the revolutionary cycle closes with an exhausted, despoiled society prostrate before a new despot. Commenting later on Mary Wollstonecraft's study of *The French Revolution* Adams noted that 'those who were called the people were for butchering king, court, nobility, clergy and all the rich: even the National Assembly itself'.[24] Class war appeared ineluctable, as a natural consequence of inequality, for Adams saw 'the envy and rancor of the multitude against the rich . . . [as] universal and restrained only by fear or necessity'. The failure is evidently intellectual, for 'a beggar can never comprehend the reason why another should ride in a coach while he has no bread'.[25] Such people were not merely a threat to others; they were equally incapable of maintaining liberty even for themselves.

This brings us directly to the question of democracy. Our first duty at this point is to abide by Adams's own stipulation, and pay due regard to the question of definitions. At various times Adams sought both to enlighten his readers and to reduce the scope for disputes that were essentially terminological, by pronouncing on such key concepts as 'republic', 'monarchy' and 'democracy'. The value of this laudable endeavour is somewhat reduced by the lack of consistency in his various formulations. Adams mostly tended to define democracy in terms of what is now called 'direct democracy': a political system in which all the people assemble together in one body and thus avoid recourse to representatives. Adams implied a politics that lacked formal differentiating structures. He sometimes extended this to embrace a society similarly lacking in form. Democracy was thus an undifferentiated mass; it was anarchy, and thus had scarcely, if ever, existed, and was, in any case, next to impossible. Leaving it at that would dispose neatly of the democratic threat, but Adams did not leave it at that. Democracy was additionally the term applied to a unicameral parliament, presumably because in such circumstances the numerical preponderance of the people gives them unalloyed control. Apart from his conceptual forays, Adams used 'democratic' and 'democratical' as adjectives connoting the politics of the people. Thus a democratical element to the political system was regarded as both legitimate and necessary, so long as it was held in check by the executive and aristocratical branches. Democracy in this sense becomes dangerous only when it usurps the proper powers of the other elements of government, and, from being a part of the political system, attempts to form the whole.

In pursuit of examples of democracy, Adams starts where democracy itself was said to begin, in ancient Greece. The early signs were not auspicious. In Athens 'from the first to the last moment of her democratical constitution, levity, gayety, inconstancy, dissipation, intemperance, debauchery, and a dissolution of manners, were the prevailing character of the whole nation'.[26] For contemporary examples, in the middle 1780s, Adams looked to 'some of those states which have the name of democracies, or at least in such as have preserved some share in the government to the people'.[27] Those that merited consideration were San Marino, Biscay, seven Swiss cantons, and the United Provinces of the Low Countries. Unfortunately for the development of political science, under the bright light of close scrutiny these small states did not seem to merit the democratic label. San Marino and the Swiss cantons turned out to be mixtures of the three main forms, of monarchy, aristocracy, and democracy, while Biscay was described as 'a contracted aristocracy, under the appearance of a liberal democracy'.[28] Anyway, his pursuit concluded and in vain, Adams decided that the political practices of small communities of isolated, mountain people could have offered little guidance for the large, populous states of the American eastern seaboard. Had he stuck to that line all historical and empirical research would have been irrelevant. If the size factor was the crucial one, then America's own experiment was unique, and no prognosis concerning it could be derived from politics elsewhere. To this notion Adams did not adhere, for the classical sources on this question were not merely overwhelmingly prestigious; they also precisely verified his own insecurities. 'How does despotism arise?' asked Plato in *The Republic*. 'That it comes out of democracy is fairly clear'.[29] Democracy, then, according to unimpeachable sources, was both unstable in itself and liable to slide into despotism. Adams thus echoed a long-honoured suspicion when he noted that nowhere 'does human nature show itself so completely depraved, so nearly approaching an equal mixture of brutality and devilism, as in the last stages of such a democracy, and in the beginnings of that despotism that always succeeds it'.[30] The democratic pursuit was thus unavailing. It 'never lasts long. It soon wastes, exhausts, and murders itself. There never was a democracy yet that did not commit suicide'.[31]

Further evidence on this score was not long in appearing. Less than three months after George Washington was inaugurated as the first President of the United States, and John Adams as the first Vice-President, a rather more dramatic and violent course of events began in Paris. Adams was now more engaged in the minutiae of administration, but on the occasions when he turned again to the broader questions of democracy, he no longer had to enquire of bands of peasants in remote Swiss valleys, nor of dusty tomes on ancient republics. His prior expectations were now more than verified by the French performing roles he might almost have scripted for them. If, as we have noted, the French Revolution could claim a connection with the American, then the French brought to the surface all the evils Adams feared beneath his own country. It was, to change metaphors, the American dream turned nightmare.

Political expectations in France had been raised in inverse ratio to the possibility of satisfying them. From the depths of feudalism, superstition and illiteracy Adams thought it impossible that a sudden leap into rational, egalitarian bliss could be achieved. The gap was too wide; the preparations too inadequate. On the flimsiest of foundations people were preparing the most grandiose of structures. Reason, liberty, equality and fraternity were all invoked as key manifestations of the new age. Adams saw in it much of the opposite – stupidity, bloodshed, despotism and hatred. He was 'sure it would, not only arrest the progress of Improvement, but give it a retrograde course, for at least a Century, if not many Centuries.'[32] In some ways Adams's British counterpart was Edmund Burke, who had likewise vehemently opposed the French Revolution after having defended the American one. Burke, however, saw the French discarding all the elements of their old constitution; as having in fact made the complete break that they claimed. That was precisely the main source of his disquiet. Adams, in contrast, saw a continuity in French history. What they had produced was a variant of their *ancien régime*. The traditional powers were those of the nobility, the clergy, and the army. What the rise of Napoleon indicated was not the total obliteration of these elements, but the victory of the latter over the former two. The relative pluralism that existed when the state incorporated a diversity of forces was utterly destroyed once power was usurped by just one of them, the army.

The basic organisational principle of the army is rigid hierarchy. That their ascent should be the product of a movement nominally devoted to equality was an irony lost on most of their supporters, but not on Adams, who saw the whole lamentable course of events as an object-lesson on the foolishness of the proclaimed objectives.

As with Burke, egalitarianism was the aspect of Jacobin ideology that Adams took most seriously. Did the failure to match ideology with practice undermine the sincerity of the aim? Adams concluded that the motivation was real but partial. Under the label of equality was contained the passion people felt against those above them. It was one-half of a levelling spirit; the desire to bring superiors down to one's own station. As for the other aspect, there was precious little sign of people wishing either to descend the social hierarchy to attain the poverty of those below them, nor to bring the less fortunate up to their own level. The egalitarian thrust, then, in actual performance, was a misnamed reflection of ambition. The agitation created disguised the desire to see none higher than oneself, while complacently ignoring those below. Even so, the trauma of dislocation was immense, and at the cost of the wealth of society as a whole. In practice redistribution was bound to reduce the size of the economic cake as the uncertainties involved undermined productivity. This inconvenient fact tended to be ignored in the general scramble as those below the summit of the social hierarchy sought to gain from the general reordering, although, of necessity, only a few could ultimately be successful in this endeavour.

The French might purport to create equality by abolishing feudal privileges, but Adams thought the sources of differentiation were far wider than that. Had they abolished all previous surnames? If not, the prestige attaching to such as the Lafayettes and Mirabeaus would continue to produce their effects. What of the differences of wealth, property, intelligence and beauty? While these survived so too would their differential influence. Distinctions crushed in one sphere would find compensating effects in another, while the physical inequalities derived from nature necessarily remained beyond limitation.

As was common amongst his contemporaries, Adams sought to have nature on his side. Just as the various species have their proper and differentiated place within the whole natural order, so too did people within the social order. Nature herself has thus 'decreed that a perfect equality shall never long exist between any two mortals'.[33] Egalitarianism is thus declared unnatural and nature is made into a supreme, benevolent legislator. Her distinctions are intended 'for the order of society, and the benefit of mankind'.[34] This works nicely as an argument so long as nature is taken as the final court of appeal. When it suited his purposes Adams was happy to adopt this approach, although it sits oddly with his broader attitudes. Politics for him seems to have been the proper preserve of the cultivated and refined, of precisely those who had got furthest from the state of nature. Does not law and order seek something better than the law of the jungle? Adams knew that the beast lurked beneath the man, and anarchy behind government, but his opposition to the French revolutionaries was based precisely on his conviction that something better than their system had been achieved elsewhere and was in principle generally sustainable. In this sense society had provided guidelines that were more than a submissive capitulation to the forces of nature. Adams knew some of the French *philosophes* personally, and was well-acquainted with the works of others. When Adams mentions physical inequalities as if they were an argument against political egalitarianism, one can reply, with Rousseau, that it is precisely because the force of circumstances tends towards inequality that the forces of politics should be made to counteract them.[35]

More complicated than the appeal to nature is that to God, but at the point of claiming supernatural support, Adams drew back from the obvious inference. 'Physical inequalities are proclaimed aloud by God Almighty through all His works', we are told, yet Adams did not wish to deny equality of rights nor the role for politics to 'modify, organize, and arrange the powers of human society, that is to say, the physical strength and force of men, in the best manner to protect, secure, and cherish the moral, which are all the natural rights of mankind'.[36] This vague formulation, more characteristic of his opponents, in effect concedes the Rousseauist case that politics legitimately attempts more than mere submission to natural forces. The real question is where one draws the line. For Adams prudence dictates that one try to channel rather than obliterate natural passions. The revolutionaries, though they displayed passion and emotion to excess, thought that they were doing exactly the opposite. They thought that, with the cold precision of the social engineer, they were implementing the Age of Reason.

Among the many extraordinary features of the French upheaval, perhaps the most astonishing, to Adams, was the fact that it was not immediately seen for what it was by people of learning and presumed intelligence everywhere. Rather the contrary had happened. It was the intelligentsia who seemed to be its most fervent supporters, and who, in France itself, provided either its ideological or its actual political leadership. The salon *literati*, granted both a platform and the attendant prestige by the aristocracy it was busy undermining, had led the nation into atheism and ruin. One of their main English supporters was a friend of Adams, the scientist and Unitarian minister, Dr Joseph Priestley. Would not such a man immediately recognise the desecration of France for what it was? In a letter to Thomas Jefferson, in August 1823, Adams recalled a breakfast he had shared with Priestley shortly after Louis XVI had been guillotined. 'Do you really believe', Adams asked him, '"the French will establish a free, democratic government in France?" He answered, "I do firmly believe it."' Adams then got him to concede that there was no precedent for such a possibility in all of human history. '"Well, then, Sir, what is the ground of your opinion?" The answer was, "My opinion is founded altogether upon revelation and the prophecies."'[37] Priestley must thereby have merited inclusion with the distinguished category of 'encyclopedists and economists . . . Voltaire, D'Alembert, Buffon, Diderot, Rousseau, La Lande, Frederic and Catherine' all of whom could be declared 'totally destitute' of common sense. How they had then established their preeminence among men and women of letters would thus be hard to discern. Less problematic were their motivations, for their philosophy was evidently 'Atheism – pure, unadulterated atheism'.[38]

Knowledge, nevertheless, was at the forefront of the revolutionary ideology. The old regimes were stigmatised for their ignorance and stupidity; the new age, as Condorcet had made clear, rested on the diffusion of knowledge made easier since the invention of printing. Social optimism derived much of its support from the notion that knowledge of society could be gained, spread and consequently implemented in ways beneficial to society as a whole. As against this radical orthodoxy, Adams read the evidence of his times as demonstrating that education held out no moral advantages. It could be acquired by good and bad characters alike, and put to noble or evil ends. Ambition was central to human personality, and in the pursuit of advancement knowledge would be used as unscrupulously as any other resource. Rather than generating human equality, knowledge thus became another source of hierarchy, merely one more weapon in the social war of all against all. Rather than leading to the growth of rationality 'the more knowledge is diffused, the more the passions are extended, and the more furious they grow'.[39] Reading from Mary Wollstonecraft that 'The cruelties of the half-civilized Romans prove that the progress of sciences alone can make men wiser and happier' Adams wrote into the margin: 'Witness Marat, Robespierre, Collot, etc.'[40]

Different evaluations of the French Revolution had been a prime cause of the estrangement between Adams and Thomas Jefferson around the end of the eighteenth century. After both had retired from active politics they were brought back into contact by their mutual friend Benjamin Rush. Writing to Jefferson in 1813 Adams could not refrain from an element of gloating. Had not the course of events proved him right? What had happened to the heady expectations that formed the radical creed of twenty years earlier? 'Let me now ask you, very seriously my Friend, Where are now in 1813, the Perfection and perfectability of human Nature? Where is now, the progress of human Mind? Where is the Amelioration of Society? Where the Augmentations of human Comforts? Where the diminutions of human Pains and Miseries?'[41]

Whereas the radical optimists were full of self-congratulation for the age in which they lived, Adams did not see that much achieved. The 'perfectability of man' seemed an unwarranted doctrine; the science of government to have made no improvement for three or four thousand years. When liberty, as he saw it, existed only in the British Isles and North America, it was hard to feel certain it would be maintained even there, let alone advance with irreversible tread over the whole globe. Amelioration of conditions was possible, but Adams would go no further than that. In July 1814 Adams concluded that

> Our hopes however of sudden tranquillity ought not to be too sanguine. . . . Monarchy will still study to rival nobility in popularity; Aristocracy will continue to envy all above it, and despize and oppress all below it; Democracy will envy all, contend with all, endeavour to pull down all; and when by chance it happens to get the Upper hand for a short time, it will be revengefull bloody and cruel. These and other Elements of Fanatacism and Anarchy will yet for a long time continue a Fermentation, which will excite alarms and require Vigilance![42]

We have come once again to the notion of political fragility. Liberty involves the right to a voice, but misuse of rights threatens to

undermine them. Elections in the late eighteenth century were bois-
terous affairs. There was much banter, ribaldry, drunkenness and
corruption, with the complex electoral laws making for difficulties of
interpretation. Electoral officers were known sometimes to have used
this to their advantage, and permitted voters according to their
estimates of the likely partisan effect.[43] All this left Adams distinctly
uneasy concerning elections, and the more important the elections
the greater his unease. If they had to be held, as it seemed they did,
then the less frequently the better. It might be worthwhile electing
the President and Senators for life, and if that were not enough to
curb the electoral delirium, such offices might have to be made
hereditary. Just one month after independence Adams wrote: 'I fear
there is an infinity of corruption in our elections already crept in.'[44]
Unless it were overcome, thinking people, even in America, would
long for monarchy again. Such remarks are scattered through
Adams's writings and render surprising his astonishment that he
should be accused of monarchist leanings.

Adams's fullest consideration of the extent of the franchise is in a
long letter he wrote to James Sullivan in May 1776. The claim to
rights of representation had figured prominently in the independence
struggle, and Adams was aware that the rhetoric of government by
consent, although conveniently vague, led, in principle, further than
conventional opinion was prepared to go. Did consent require absolutely everyone in the community to voice their political opinions?
This he dismissed as impossible. He then moved on to some rather
basic and difficult problems. What gives a majority the right to
'govern the minority against their will? Whence arises the right of the
men to govern the women, without their consent? Whence the right
of the old to bind the young, without theirs?'[45] On these questions
Adams constructed an imaginary dialogue with Sullivan. The latter
was assumed to exclude women because ' their delicacy renders them
unfit for practice and experience in the great business of life'. War is a
'hardy' enterprise, and the cares of state 'arduous'. Furthermore it is
nature herself which has made women 'fittest for domestic cares' and
the 'necessary nurture of their children'.

Mention of children brought Adams to a brief consideration of
their political disqualifications. Firstly, they had not sufficiently developed suitable powers of judgement; secondly, they did not have 'a
will of their own'. This meant that they were not sufficiently independent to exercise a vote free from the economic or emotional control
of others, in this case presumably their parents. At this point Adams

realised that the reasons for excluding children from voting would also disqualify numerous adult males. Many of them remained somewhat undeveloped in political reasoning abilities, and were also without personal property and thus likely to be directed by a property-holder. Sullivan noted that the laws of the land and their attendant punishments applied to the unenfranchised as much as to the voters. Why those without political rights are obliged to obey the law is an awkward issue in liberal democratic theory, unresolved to this day. Adams concluded that some line must be drawn, and on the margins it is bound to seem arbitrary. A man can vote on his twenty-first birthday; another one day younger cannot. The line is fixed by convention, and the issue, thought Adams, is best left to convenient neglect. We might note that the age factor works reasonably if maturity is taken as the sole prerequisite for participation, but does nothing to justify the exclusion of women. The hard-world-of-politics argument works better to exclude women from the Presidency than from the right to go to their local church halls and cast an occasional vote. Adams effectively conceded that the whole philosophy of voting qualifications was in a state of confusion. The current limitations, which he supported, could not rationally be defended. It was political prudence which dictated that the issue be left dormant. Were it not, the whole social structure would be endangered.

> Depend upon it, Sir, it is dangerous to open so fruitful a source of controversy and altercation as would be opened by attempting to alter the qualifications of voters; there will be no end of it. New claims will arise; women will demand the vote; lads from twelve to twenty-one will think their rights not enough attended to; and every man who has not a farthing, will demand an equal voice with any other, in all acts of state. It tends to confound and destroy all distinctions and prostrate all ranks to one common level.[46]

Here at the end of the letter to Sullivan we come to the nub of his concern – that social distinctions will be upset. One part of the case against women, children, and propertyless men, that they have no will of their own, should not have been seen as a threat to the social order. If the unpropertied were liable to vote in a manner that demonstrated their dependence on the propertied, then property itself would be secure. On the one hand the unpropertied are disqualified for their lack of independent will; on the other, unpropertied men are feared precisely because they might exercise their will in a way that undermined property. In terms of the latter danger Adams recommended so subdividing the land that nearly all men might become, even in a small way, property-owners. In North America, a vast land with a small population, this was relatively easy, and land availability was later a major factor in the democratisation process. James Sullivan had suggested proportioning the male vote according to the amount of property held. A franchise somewhat to this effect was introduced in Prussia in the middle of the nineteenth century. Adams, however, declared the plan impractical as property-ownership was always shifting.

In 1817 news came to Adams that half-a-million people had petitioned the British parliament to grant annual parliaments and universal suffrage, two of the demands that were later to be incorporated into the Chartist 'Six Points'. Once again Adams conceded the theory/practice dislocation. In theory the right could not be denied; in practice 'an immediate revolution would ensue'.[47]

We thus find that the rights of property have precedence over the rights of mankind. If political decisions were determined by a majority of the whole society, those destitute of property would be preponderant. Adams, even in 1778, had the imagination to predict the ghastly outcome. Debts would be abolished, the rich taxed out of their wealth, and complete equality demanded. The idle would thus acquire wealth they in no way deserved, and thus fortified would commence, or continue, a life of debauchery. Once through with their ill-gotten gains the egalitarian demand would reappear so that the whole deranged cycle might recommence. 'Property is surely a right of mankind as really as liberty'[48] Adams tells us, but the logic of his argument requires that it become more so. Adams supposed the propertied in society to be 10 or 20 per cent; this then is the proportion of people who are to be protected by 'inviolable precepts'.

> The moment the idea is admitted into society, that property is not as sacred as the laws of God, and that there is not a force of law and public justice to protect it, anarchy and tyranny commence. If 'THOU SHALT NOT COVET', and 'THOU SHALT NOT STEAL', were not commandments of Heaven, they must be made inviolable precepts in every society, before it can be civilised or made free.[49]

We are told that 'property must be secured, or liberty cannot exist',[50] but also that 'in every society where property exists, there will ever be a struggle between rich and poor'.[51] Adams's frankness here is commendable. Liberty requires property; the propertied are few. The many will necessarily be resentful. Thus class struggle is an inevitable, permanent product of a society based on private property, and 'the great art of lawgiving consists in balancing the poor against the rich in the legislature'.[52] If the poor are so *balanced* when the rich are few, the obvious implication is that, per person, the poor count for less and the rich for more. Thus economic inequalities are transformed into political ones. Marx and Engels might even have agreed with this analysis, limited though it is, of the preponderance of property in the liberal constitutional state.[53] As for Adams, it is both rare and refreshing to find a defender of private property who is so devoid of humbug, and who is prepared to defend the rights of the few without indulging in insincere or implausible appeals to the general interest.

Adams, in fact, did not adhere to a concept of general interest, except perhaps in a very weak form. Society was composed of a diversity of interests, and the political trick was to allow all a certain sphere of influence, without anyone attaining preponderance. Adams's theory of mixed government derives from his view of human nature. No one person or group is to be trusted. All power corrupts and there are no impartial interests. Monarchy, aristocracy and democracy are all sectional interests that should be so placed that each part counteracts the other. At a time when Rochefoucauld, Condorcet and Mably had all favoured unicameralism, when revolutionary France had demonstrated its failings, Adams, who was stung to find himself wrongly associated with such proposals, made himself, by dint of repetition, the foremost advocate of multi-cameralism and checks and balances. In a single assembly there is no filter; the people would dominate and their majority would prove as despotic as that of any monarch. It was no coincidence that what Adams recommended bore not a little resemblance to the system of Great Britain – a representative assembly in which the voice of the people was heard, a Senate which represented property and the aristocracy, and an executive headed by the president or monarch.

The radical optimists of the late eighteenth century combined faith in the powers of reason with an emphasis on government by consent. The latter postulate led easily to optimism concerning the people and human nature. Thus their opposition to hierarchies both old and new. Adams belonged to a different tradition. He was hardly a defender of the *ancien régime*; how could a proponent of American independence be that? The principle of the old regimes was control through exclusion. The people were the objects of government, subject to sovereignty. Birth, power, property and education – all the preserves of the few – were the legitimate credentials for participation. The subtle, modern variant of this is control through subservient inclusion. The people are, usually of necessity, granted a share in the legislative process, but their influence is carefully filtered. This was Adams's position.

Almost since he entered public life Adams was burdened by a sense of unpopularity. His 1770 defence of British soldiers tried for murder hardly set him off on a popular footing. More significant than that, however, was his hostility to the French Revolution. He confided to Jefferson in 1813 that their opposed stands on this issue led to Jefferson's 'Unbounded Popularity' and his own 'immense Unpopularity, which fell like the Tower of Siloam upon me'.[54] He did not always even enjoy the compensation of having been proved right. 'Have I not been employed in mischief all my days?', he asked Benjamin Rush in 1811. 'Did not the American revolution produce the French Revolution? And did not the French Revolution produce all the calamities and desolations to the human race, and the whole globe ever since?'[55] In a society in which optimism is axiomatic, Adams, in the words of Gordon S. Wood, 'gave Americans as grim and as dark a picture of themselves as they have ever been offered'.[56]

In his views on controlled incorporation of the masses and his doubts concerning progress, Adams sounds a pessimistic and, hence, modern note. That knowledge can threaten as well as liberate may have sounded unduly negative to the Priestleys and Condorcets of his time, yet finds confirmation in the build-up of an awesome weaponry of mass destruction in our own. The optimism of Paine and Jefferson may have rendered them subjects of greater popular acclaim and even of academic attention, yet this very factor has trapped them within the history of their own more optimistic age.

Adams, however, speaks more directly and relevantly to a modern audience. His theory of checks and balances has become an orthodoxy of American thinking; his pluralism, his emphasis on freedom through diversity, connects him with the mainstream of all later liberal thought. Simultaneously, however, he foreshadowed the whole debate on mass society and the 'tyranny of the majority' through which Tocqueville, Mill, Nietzsche, Gustave Le Bon, and Ortega y Gasset were to voice their fears concerning the diffusion of power in the new commercial and industrial age.

Uncelebrated in his own time, Adams clearly deserves better of posterity. Unlike most of his contemporaries he had no illusions to lose. He who expected little from the modern age is in many respects at one with those who look back on two centuries of modernisation and find ample reasons to feel profoundly troubled.

4 G.W.F. Hegel

Hegel was six years old when the United States of America declared their independence of the British crown. While John Adams took part in the birth of a modern independent state, Hegel, the son of a civil servant in the government of Württemberg, later became concerned with the anachronistic survival of Germany's numerous outmoded governments. America he later described as 'the land of the future, where in the ages that lie before us, the burden of the world's history shall reveal itself'.[1] America had moved towards the greater cohesion of a 'more perfect union', but in contrast the German states had been content to slumber immobile within parochial particularisms that time had rendered ridiculous. Shlomo Avineri has described Hegel as 'the first major political philosopher of modern society' in that he 'introduced the dimension of change and historicity which has since become central to modern political thought'.[2] One key political feature of modern society is the emergence of the nation-state. In the aftermath of Napoleon's conquests of Germanic territory on the left bank of the Rhine, Hegel commenced his investigation of *The German Constitution* (1799–1802) with the cryptic statement that 'Germany is a state no longer'.[3] France, England and Spain had succeeded in pacifying and uniting their territories under a central administration. In this development Germany, ever since the Thirty Years' War, had been left behind. Germany, without either a common military or financial system, remained hardly more than a cultural concept, suffering, like Italy, a fragmentation that had long left her open to foreign invasion and spoliation. This fragmentation, which cut one small principality off from another and made a common course of action well-nigh impossible, also generated an attitude that separated individuals from sentimental attachment to their own principality. Germany was modern solely in terms of its detrimental separation of the state from civil society. Hegel noted that 'through the growth of the Imperial cities, the *bourgeois* sense, which cares only for an individual and not self-subsistent end and has no regard for the whole, began to become a power'.[4] Atomisation thus occurred both at the individual and the political levels as each individual gave priority to personal selfishness, whilst each state jealously guarded its autonomy. What was lost, and what had to be recovered, was a sense of the coherent whole.

Such was the lamentable German reality that generated a profound yearning for ancient Greece in Hegel and his educated contemporaries. There, they believed, the soul of man had not been fragmented by the division of labour. At the political level man and the citizen remained one, while between the individual and the state there was perfect harmony. This no doubt idealised version of ancient Greece functioned as the yardstick by which contemporary Germany was found wanting. Modern fragmentation was seen as the culmination of a protracted decline originating in ancient Rome, then deepened by Christianity, the Reformation, the French Revolution and the increasing division of labour generated by modern capitalism. Ancient religion had been essentially civic and hence had helped to unify the polis, whereas Christianity, with its focus upon the individual soul, concentrated the individual mind predominantly upon itself.

Ancient Greece, however, could not furnish a blueprint for modern times. Part of Hegel's critique of the Romantics stemmed from their desire to turn back to the political forms of medieval Europe. If that was impossible, how much less likely was it that the recreation of an even more distant and infinitely preferable situation might be attained. Raymond Plant has suggested 'that the whole of Hegel's philosophy may best be seen in terms of the pursuit of coherence'.[5] This the Greeks had attained on terms that were appropriate to their historical times and circumstances. The contemporary challenge was to move towards coherence in a manner appropriate to the modern condition.

For Germans of Hegel's generation the most striking intrusion of the modern into their provincial repose was the French Revolution, in both its theory and its rather different practice. It embodied the sweeping away of medieval cobwebs and the introduction of the notion of human rights and the consequent tendencies towards democratisation. Pre-modern assumptions had regarded freedom as a privilege, and thus confined to the deserving few. Now, though, rights were no longer to be unequally distributed on the basis of one's social position or exceptional desert, but were, in principle, granted to all alike in recognition of their common humanity. In place of the graded hierarchy of Estates there came into prominence the egalitarian concept of 'Man'. As Hegel noted in *The Philosophy of Right*: 'A man counts as a man in virtue of his manhood alone, not because he is a Jew, Catholic, Protestant, German, Italian, &c.'[6] In mocking this modern phantom the French reactionary Joseph de Maistre hoped to undermine the whole edifice of liberation that had been built upon it:

The 1795 (French) constitution, like its predecessors was made for *man*. But there is no such thing as *man* in the world. During my life, I have seen Frenchmen, Italians, Russians, and so on; thanks to Montesquieu, I even know that one may be a *Persian*; but I must say, as for *man*, I have never come across him anywhere; if he exists, he is completely unknown to me.[7]

For the Germans, the French Revolution constituted what Burke called 'an armed doctrine'. It imposed itself upon them not by the conviction generated by superior rationality but by the force of military conquest. What from one angle was a liberation from feudal obligations was, from another, the imposition of foreign rule and alien ideas. So whereas Adams was a prominent participant in the basic changes that his own country introduced, Hegel's situation placed him in the position of an observer of reforms imposed on Germany from outside.

A thinker's attitude to the French Revolution provides the most obvious criterion for estimating his whole approach to the broad modernisation process, of which democratisation is a major part. Of the four key thinkers in this study, the three Europeans, Hegel, Tocqueville and Carlyle, all saw that revolution as the prime symbol of the new age. Its significance thus extended far beyond its own particular time and country. To grasp the whole modern age one had to understand the revolution that was its most striking expression.

The unprecedented nature of the French Revolution was such that it made an immediate and dramatic impact on thinking people throughout Europe, particularly so in those countries in near proximity to France. The fall of the Bastille was at first widely welcomed as a heroic manifestation of will in action, a long-awaited synthesis of theory and practice, as a breath of fresh air and an intoxicating springtime of mankind. The metaphors regarded as most appropriate were of the casting-off of chains and the removal of shackles. The foremost poets of the time lauded its achievements, but with the onset of the Terror, their enthusiasm waned. The dream of emancipation turned into the nightmare of an oppression tragically modern in the severity of its imposed conformism. Hegel was affected by both aspects of this process, but not to the extent of ever becoming the Revolution's opponent. At first he had 'adopted the same kind of view of the French Revolution as many of his contemporaries, seeing in it an attempt to recapture something analogous to *polis* experience'.[8] Unsurprisingly, disappointment followed as an increasingly individualistic and atomised society destroyed all hopes of achieving a real community. Yet even towards the end of his life, some four decades after the storming of the Bastille, Hegel, sometimes wrongly viewed as an ideologue of Restoration, could still justify the necessity for revolution and simultaneously evoke the exhilaration that accompanied its outbreak:

> Before the French Revolution . . . the entire political system appeared one mass of injustice. The change was necessarily violent, because the work of transformation was not undertaken by the government. And the reason why the government did not undertake it was that the Court, the Clergy, the Nobility, the Parliaments themselves, were unwilling to surrender the privileges they possessed, either for the sake of expediency or that of abstract Right. . . . The conception, the idea of Right asserted its authority *all at once*, and the old framework of injustice could offer no resistance to its onslaught. A constitution, therefore, was established in harmony with the conception of Right, and on this foundation all future legislation was to be based. Never since the sun had stood in the firmament and the planets revolved around him had it been perceived that man's existence centres in his head, i.e. in Thought, inspired by which he builds up the world of reality. Anaxagoras had been the first to say that *nous* governs the world; but not until now had man advanced to the recognition of the principle that Thought ought to govern spiritual reality. This was accordingly a glorious mental dawn. All thinking beings shared in the jubilation of this epoch. Emotions of a lofty character stirred men's minds at that time; a spiritual enthusiasm thrilled through the world, as if the reconciliation between the Divine and the Secular was now first accomplished.[9]

For Hegel 'the history of the world is none other than the progress of the consciousness of freedom', and each of the stages of consciousness developed its appropriate political form. The Oriental knew that 'One is free' and thus produced political despotism; the Greeks knew that '*some* are free' and established the *polis* on the basis of a franchise that varied but was never universal; western Christendom knows 'that man as man, is free'.[10] As to the political form appropriate to this third stage, Avineri has noted that 'while no concrete historical state ever served Hegel as a model for the full realization of freedom, the modern constitutional monarchy as it evolved out of the

French Revolution and the Restoration seemed to him to move clearly in that direction'.[11]

To what extent, then, did Hegel share with the friends of the Revolution their view that freedom was now at hand? The answer is not entirely straightforward. Certainly, as many commentators have noted, freedom is a central concept of Hegel's philosophy. One aspect of it seems to consist of control over nature and in this sense freedom would be posited at the technological level. But technological mastery does not of itself produce freedom; it is merely a presupposition. When controlling nature, freedom is possible, for a major obstacle to it has been overcome. At a deeper level freedom consists of the self-determination of one's actions in conformity to reason, and here one sees how Hegel must be distinguished from the radical individualists of the revolutionary era who *granted* freedom as a trans-historical human right. For Hegel, *contra* Rousseau among others, man is not born free. As with J.S. Mill, so with Hegel, it was assumed that not all are fit for freedom. Rather than being an imperfectly recognised and wrongly withheld universally applicable human right, freedom, though the inherent destiny of man, is a hard-won and only gradually-attained human achievement. Thus for Hegel the French revolutionary breakthrough consisted of the *consciousness* of freedom not the practice of it. For Hegel, as Richard Schacht has pointed out, 'true freedom becomes possible only with the emergence of the properly organised state as an existing reality'.[12]

A characteristic of both proponents and opponents of the French Revolution was the view that it signified, for better or worse, a major breach, a wrenching free, from all previous history. Burke bemoaned the rejection of accumulated wisdom and experience, while Paine rejoiced in the removal of ancient superstitions and privileges. Hegel, in contrast to both, saw the events in France, however momentous, as still part of the *continuity* of world history. In this dawning of a new age 'the Germans contented themselves with theoretical abstraction', whilst the more audacious French 'immediately passed over from the theoretical to the practical'.[13] Thus for Hegel the French Revolution signified the rise to a position of preeminence of the idea that all are free. Whatever particular disfigurements occurred, world history had moved irreversibly forward under the sway of this new principle. This Hegel never sought to reject or deny and thus he opposed the anti-French, nationalist counter-movements which emerged in Germany between the defeat at Jena in 1806 and the victory at Waterloo nine years later. There could be no turning back. The new principles were the basis from which all politics should henceforth proceed. The practice of the Terror had disfigured and dishonoured ideas of freedom that remained valid notwithstanding. What Hegel wished to attain, then, was the rational implementation of ideas that the French had introduced, not for themselves alone, but for all mankind.

The intellectual background of both Hegel's thought and that of the French Revolution was that of the eighteenth-century Enlightenment. This tendency had both rationalistic and egalitarian elements. The effect of the former was to elevate intellect and education as the basis for political decision-taking. The general effect of the latter was the movement towards increasingly effective political representation of the middle and then the lower classes. A basic dilemma for modern politics is how these two principles are to be amalgamated. These are the questions we must consider in terms of Hegel's political recommendations. What level of priority was rationality to be granted? How was representation to be related to it? Was it rational to represent all? Of those who did qualify for representation, was it rational that they should be equally represented? How was representation to be organised, and how could an objective will be elevated above the various particularities and gradations into which modern society was divided?

In his Introduction to *The Philosophy of History*, Hegel noted that 'In a Constitution the main feature of interest is the self-development of the *rational*, that is, the *political* condition of a people; the setting free of the successive elements of the Idea'.[14] Here we have encapsulated the basis of his whole approach to politics. For him the central problem of human society was to facilitate the gradual realisation of rationality and, thereby, freedom. The 'political' was both an agent of this process and a symptom of the extent to which the wider social and cultural milieu had developed its full potential. This prior teleological concern conditions the secondary question of the relationship of the populace to the state structure, for this is determined by the state's purpose. By declaring this to be the achievement of impartial rationality Hegel thereby opened up the question of how the society/ state relationship should best be ordered and what category of person should be granted political influence. He thought that access to formal politics should be available only to those capable of furthering its revealed purpose. Rationality, in short, could be advanced only by those possessed of it. To those acquainted with the common identification of Hegel with conservative reaction, this might appear as the prelude to a rationale for keeping the rabble beyond the political horizon. It may function this way, but there is much else besides, for Hegel's thought does not facilitate simple one-sided categorisation. In his own distinct way, he was clearly within the Enlightenment tradition and, in a manner reminiscent of Bentham, the call for rationality is simultaneously a criticism of outmoded institutions that have lost all purpose except the narrow defence of sectional privilege and all laws that are mere historical lumber and quite devoid of overall coherence.

In his surprisingly materialistic analysis of the 1831 British Reform Bill, Hegel noted the important sense in which England had not yet entered the modern world. Since the Stein-Hardenberg reforms of 1807 Prussia had removed numerous ancient and outmoded laws that England now, alone among the major European powers, still operated. The wooden spoon for backwardness could thus be awarded to England on the basis of that country's entrenched system of aristocratic power and its associated sinecures, absurd game laws, ecclesiastical tithes and rotten boroughs. Habit and class privilege had induced a political torpor that left England 'remarkably far behind the other civilised states of Europe'.[15] Unconquered, and hence uninfluenced by Napoleon's Civil Code, England had not yet moved from the old legal accretions of positive law to the rational constitution. For the conservative clique led by the redoubtable Duke of Wellington the Reform Bill went dangerously far in opening the floodgates to democratic anarchy. For Hegel, on the other hand, its reforms did not go far enough. It failed to break with the traditionalist assumption that inherited property was the sole appropriate qualification for political power. 'Nowhere more than in England is the prejudice so fixed and so naive that if birth and wealth give a man office they also give him brains.'[16] Wealth was no guarantee of reason, ability or responsibility. For Hegel, England's social problems stemmed not merely from the widening gulf between the rich and the poor, but also from the irresponsible attitudes of the former to the latter. In his view the need for integration should be met not by political measures alone but by social reforms which would have the consequence of making an extension of political enfranchisement both plausible and safe. Thus it was not that Hegel wished to undermine wealth, but rather to insist that it be allied with other appropriate and necessary qualities.

To understand how the right balance should be struck requires consideration of the qualifications Hegel stipulated for entry into the state bureaucracy and into the legislature. In *The Philosophy of Right*, Hegel discounted birth as a qualification for entry into the Civil Service. Long before such practices were at all general he called for the '*objective*' factors of 'knowledge and proof of ability' as means towards the Napoleonic 'career open to talent'. This would guarantee that the state acquires the abilities it needs and also, since birth, wealth and other background factors appear discounted, gives 'every citizen the chance of joining the class of civil servants'. What seems to be a general democratisation of opportunity was in fact explicitly regarded as an appeal on behalf of the middle class. Hegel hardly spared a thought for the exclusion of the poor and the rabble from the political process. Like his contemporaries, the English Utilitarians, he wanted first to emancipate the middle class, for this was the class 'in which the consciousness of right and the developed intelligence of the mass of the people is found'. It thus forms 'the pillar of the state so far as honesty and intelligence are concerned. A state without a middle class must therefore remain on a low level', as the situation in Russia was held to indicate.[17]

The mode of entry to the Civil Service is thus by proof of knowledge and ability. We can assume some form of examination to be the means of attaining this position. The practice of competitive entry into the Civil Service was agreed to by Frederick William III of Prussia in October 1807, although it was introduced in Britain only in 1870.

That the task of administration necessitates certain qualifications is now virtually unquestioned. Hegel, however, also applied this concern to the legislature. It too had its own technical task; that of sharing in the law-making process, which should only be entrusted to those capable of dealing with its complexities. But there is also a representative function. This second task Hegel subordinated to the first. Representation could, then, only be widened to the extent compatible with efficient, knowledgeable and rational fulfilment of law-making. In our time, entry into the administrative and legislative structures of the state are by quite different means. We understand the interconnection between these areas but, as professions, treat them as requiring different qualifications. The concern that Members of Parliament or Congress possess sufficient education and ability for their task is never expressed in more than vague terms and without any formally granted certificate of qualification.

Hegel's recommended manner of entry to the lower house is mainly by elections, although the question of proper qualifications is equally important. 'People's representatives must not be picked at random, but rather one should choose the wisest from among the people, since not everyone knows, as it is his duty to know, what one's true and real will is, i.e. what is good for one.'[18] The approach here is similar to that of Marx, for whom the proletariat had a 'real will' which might well be at variance with their subjective preference. This approach leads to the quicksand of the 'false-consciousness' problem, where rescue is achieved through those who know better. Hegel's deputies are charged not so much with representing the people's wishes as with doing what is right. 'Hence their relation to their electors is not that of agents with a commission or specific instructions.'[19] Rationality and experience count above the representative function. Just as rationality was explicitly declared to have a particular social location, so we may suspect a corresponding limitation in terms of the importance Hegel attached to governmental and administrative experience. 'The essential thing is to place *suffrage* in the hands of a corps of enlightened and honest men, independent of the court.' The required consciousness of the general and a fitting opposition to the particular are acquired by 'habitual preoccupation with public affairs'.[20] The premium placed on experience would tend to restrict opportunities for advancement in these areas to those who are already in post. Those without such experience are ineligible to acquire it because they do not already possess it!

In his *Proceedings of the Estates Assembly in the Kingdom of Wurtemberg* (1817) Hegel expressed his distaste for the idea of salaried deputies. Without pay, one avoided the suspicion that office was sought for pecuniary reward. The consequence was to give 'preponderance in elections to property'.[21] Thus far entry to public office, whether to the bureaucracy or the lower house, has exhibited a dual character. The concern with proper qualifications broadens opportunity beyond what can be attained by inheritance, nepotism, or purchase, but simultaneously acknowledges the restricted social location of those with the requisite rationality and experience. On Hegel's criteria the class basis of power might well remain unaltered from before, although the allocation of positions within that class would be far more discriminating. In his system, hereditary power was not, as with Tom Paine, decried as such. All Hegel opposed was its irrational extended influence. In those spheres to which we now turn, the monarchy and the upper house of the legislative assembly, the hereditary principle found what Hegel thought to be its proper, rational application.

If we refer to the notes taken from Hegel's lectures and added by Eduard Gans to the *Philosophy of Right*, we get the impression that the institution of monarchy and its associated functions are more important than the particular incumbent. Hegel denied 'that everything depends on the monarch's *particular* character. In a completely organized state, it is only a question of the culminating point of formal decision and a natural bulwark against passion.' The monarch 'has only to say "yes" and dot the "i"'.[22] The monarch is thought to be able to attain universality through his own person because he is secure in his position which is raised above all classes and groups. This assumption overlooks the monarch's historical link with the landed aristocracy, whose legitimacy also stems from the inheritance principle. They thus have similar vested interests and rise but, as the French Revolution demonstrated, may fall together.

So long as the traditional rules of the political game are accepted, hereditary monarchy takes the succession question off the political agenda and thereby removes the chance that cliques and factions will disturb the unity of the state at its most precarious moment. This benefit Hegel presented as a consequence rather than a justification of hereditary monarchy. We appear to have something akin to 'figurehead' monarchy, but should note that the main text of *Philosophy of Right* presents a considerably more powerful monarch whose character must therefore be much more significant. Above the level of the Estates, Hegel recommended a supreme council or cabinet, whose members the monarch may both appoint and dismiss. Monarchy was held to be the essential character of the modern state, yet it is hard to resolve the uncertainties in Hegel's presentation of it. The greater the monarchical role the greater the significance of the monarch's character and level of ability. Hegel wished to avoid the element of chance that would result from elective or contractual monarchy, but failed to recognise the extent to which hereditary succession leaves monarchy the victim of genetic chance. For most of Hegel's lifetime the English throne was occupied by King George III, who, among other such incidents, once emerged from his coach in Windsor Great Park and addressed an oak tree as his cousin, Frederick the Great of Prussia.

The other area of hereditary power was that of the landed nobility, who constitute the upper house of the legislature and are charged with mediating between the monarch and the Estates. Their particular qualities derive from a guaranteed social position beyond all temptations of corruption and ambitious self-advancement. Their lands cannot be alienated; neither can they exhibit capricious preference in the distribution of their property at death, for primogeniture applies to them alone. Thus they are frozen into a feudalistic social form. In the important matter of wealth distribution they are without free will. They are beyond the tempestuous fluctuations of modern life, 'independent alike of the state's capital, the uncertainty of business, the quest for profit, and any sort of fluctuation in possessions'.[23] Thus Hegel accepted the norm that representation is best achieved in a bicameral parliament, and that an upper house composed primarily of the landed interest provides the most secure guarantee of political stability.

Where Hegel posited the need for political change, he did so in order that constitutions might be made more rational according to the criteria of the time. Here one is appealing not to the populace as a source of legitimacy but to rational insight, although how in practice one might decide between competing versions of what might claim to be rational and hence appropriate is nowhere made clear. Even so, this ademocratic criterion bypasses the whole question of consent and obligation as treated by thinkers such as Hobbes, Locke and Rousseau. For the latter, all representation necessarily produced misrepresentation, for no one part of the people could legitimately substitute for the whole. In Hegel's time 'democracy' connoted what we would now call 'direct democracy', that is that the whole citizen body be granted admission to the legislative assembly. This Hegel unequivocally rejected.

Having seen why representation mattered to Hegel, we should now ask how it was to be organised and to what degree participation might be extended. Representation was accepted as one of the basic characteristics of the modern state. 'The so-called Representative Constitution is that form of government with which we connect the idea of a free constitution; and this notion has become a rooted prejudice.'[24] Representation has the function of drawing the social orders in their various Estates into the state and, simultaneously, providing a check for the bureaucracy on the effectiveness of its activities. The awareness of a forum that functions both as watchdog and public critic furthers the incentive of officials and the Crown to devote themselves diligently and exclusively to the public good.

Although some degree of representation is essential, its precise extent is less important than its being properly organised. Hegel favoured a lower chamber based on the traditional notion of representation by Estates or legally established and recognised occupational groupings. The relevant unit was social function rather than geographical area. The landed gentry were to form the upper house of the legislature and business interests the lower. The relationship between the state and the people should only be mediated through an occupational interest group. 'The concrete state is the whole, articulated into its particular groups. . . . Hence the single person attains his actual living destiny for universality only when he becomes a member of a Corporation, a society.'[25] As for the powers of the Lower Chamber, Leonard Krieger has suggested that for Hegel the Estates form 'a representative body which had not the right of legislative co-determination but only the right of limiting the sovereign will of the monarch by granting or withholding monies'.[26] His source for this is Hegel's early work on *The German Constitution*. Whether the same point can be applied to the *Philosophy of Right* is unclear, although there Hegel emphasises the Estates' function of maintaining a level of public discussion and criticism that helps keep officials up to the mark.[27] Plamenatz asserts that in Hegel's opinion 'the Estates do not ordinarily put forward proposals of law'. Plamenatz finds this belief 'borne out by the experience of all modern states' and thus more realistic than 'the liberals and radicals of the early nineteenth century who assumed that it is for popular assemblies to make laws and for governments merely to carry them out'.[28]

The French Revolution provided Hegel's modern warning example of a state organising its parliament in opposition to the idea of corporate mediation. In consequence, power was acquired by 'fanatical priests [and] riotous, revelling despots and their minions, who seek to indemnify themselves for their own degradation by degrading and oppressing in their turn – a distortion practiced to the nameless misery of deluded mankind'.[29] Such atomisation Hegel regarded as quite contrary to a rational, organic order. A representative system based on the isolated individual and seen as a counter of the power of privilege and the executive fails to provide both a proper correspondence with the individual's real existence in a particular social context and the necessity for social unity. In contrast the corporations provide a source of cooperation and experience in public affairs which lifts its members above the level of personal selfishness and enables them to cultivate a broader outlook. An oddity of this system is that it structures society in terms of its separate social components and yet is still intended as a device to overcome particularity. Hoping to transcend individual selfishness, Hegel provided instead a structure that looks bound to replace it with sectional rather than general interests. Particularity has not been overcome but merely elevated. This has the advantage of providing the individual with a mechanism of integration, but what one is integrated into is primarily one's occupational grouping and only secondarily, if at all, the state itself. To an extent Hegel wanted rational bourgeois constitutionalism combined with a more traditional, even feudalistic, representation based on the Estates. This is a strange amalgam. Hegel wanted constitutions that were not the fossilised imprint of a bygone age, but rather, were in accord with their times. This notion of appropriateness, which is so central to his social and political analysis, now has a somewhat Marxist ring in its assumption of a coherent societal whole based on a socio-economic-political-legal fit. It lands one in the difficulty of deciding how accord or coherence are to be determined and arbitrated. If accord is decided by norms and conventions then one is not giving priority to a rationalistically coherent connection. Hegel wanted monarchy and Estates representation in a modern state and he rejected the idea of the atomised, individualistic voter as the basis of representation. In this respect his own ideas of what politically accords with, or is appropriate for a modern state, are highly idiosyncratic. As Marx put it in his *Critique of Hegel's 'Philosophy of Right'*, 'Hegel wants the medieval-estates system, but in the modern sense of the legislature; and he wants the modern legislature, but in the body of the medieval-estates system! This is the worst kind of syncretism.'[30]

If this is an anomaly, would it not be overcome by accepting modern trends and replacing the Estates by political parties? Pelczynski seems surprised that Hegel 'omits . . . all mention of party organization'.[31] We can see that parties could provide the important function of supplying a necessary intermediate structure between the people and the state and thereby also elevating the individual above formless atomisation. However, Hegel did not have available to him the modern experience of political parties and even if he had, one might suspect that they would not meet his requirements. Hegel probably agreed with Rousseau about the danger of factions. Indeed, stock eighteenth-century terminology aligned party with faction as something destructive of the general good and often near to treason. In any case, voluntary adherence to a party would appear to be shifting and unreliable, based on whim and caprice; not on the permanence of one's real social being but on what, at any particular moment, one happened to believe. What one is, the actuality of one's existence, was thought by Hegel to provide a better criterion for representation than what one happens to think.

Hegel thought that 'Electoral assemblies as unordered inorganic aggregates' have 'more in common with the democratic, even anarchical principle of separatism than with that of an organic order'.[32] Thus the French had misguidedly adopted a practice corresponding to that of ancient Greece during its democratic moments. Modern France and the city-states of ancient Greece, though, differ not only in size but also in mentality. Democratic constitutions akin to those of ancient Greece 'are possible only in small states'. There continual personal contact and proximity to each other as well as to the political stage 'render a common culture and a *living* democratic polity possible' in ways that cannot be reproduced in larger states. In the simple springtime of mankind, unmediated individual participation was possible and acceptable because 'the citizens are still unconscious of particular interests, and therefore of a corrupting element: the Objective Will is in their case not disintegrated'. Such a condition did not last. The rise of subjectivity 'plunged the Greek world into ruin, for the polity which that world embodied was not calculated for this side of humanity'. Corresponding difficulties had beset the attempt of revolutionary France to replace the Estates General with an assembly based on geographical constituencies. The campaign to introduce representative democracy into a large modern state was doomed from the start. 'In the French Revolution, therefore, the republican constitution never actually became a democracy. Tyranny, Despotism, raised its voice under the mask of Freedom and Equality.'[33] Democracy in its pure form was thus seen as appropriate to a particular historical phase long since departed.

> To hold that every single person should share in deliberating and deciding on political matters of general concern on the ground that all individuals are members of the state, that its concerns are their concerns, and that it is their right that what is done should be done with their knowledge and volition, is tantamount to a proposal to put the democratic element without any rational form into the organism of the state, although it is only in virtue of the possession of such a form that the state is an organism at all.[34]

Hegel explicitly accepted conventional classifications which designated Greek democracy as a political form compatible with slavery. It was the form in which only 'some are free' and slavery in fact was its necessary basis. That the citizens could be released for democratic participation presupposed a lower order occupied with necessary labour. A corresponding situation still prevailed. Greek democracy was as outmoded and irretrievable as Greek slavery, but Hegel still recognised the inevitability of society containing an underclass precluded from political activity, although how community could be achieved across such a divide is far from clear. Modern society seemed propelled towards inequalities that subject the lower orders to poverty and ignorance. 'Their poverty leaves them more or less deprived of all the advantages of society, of the opportunity of acquiring skill or education of any kind, as well as of the administration of justice.' 'The rabble' were obviously precluded from any hope of qualifying for the bureaucracy or of gaining representation through the Estates. Hegel quoted Ariosto to the effect that 'the ignorant vulgar reproves everyone and talks most of what it understands least'. Clearly the lower orders were not seen as even having the right to form an Estate. Not being possessed of rationality they were destined to be mere objects of administration, however benevolent, rather than full participants in the public life of their own community. Basic to Hegel's approach was his classification of the people as 'precisely that section which does *not* know what it wills. To know what one wills, and still more to know what the absolute will, Reason wills, is the fruit of profound apprehension and insight, precisely the things which are *not* popular.'[35] According to Pelczynski, Hegel 'never entertains the idea that . . . domestic servants, industrial proletariat, tenants-at-will, agricultural labourers, and so on, have any claims to be represented separately'.[36] They were ruled out of contention just as obviously as women and children. K-H. Ilting has referred to Hegel's 'odd rejection of universal and equal suffrage'.[37] The manner of rejection may conceivably have been odd, but the rejection itself was perfectly normal at the time Hegel was writing. In the section of *Philosophy of Right* on 'The State', Hegel mentioned the function of the Estates in stimulating a consciousness of public affairs. His explanatory notes take it as obvious that the political public 'prima facie excludes at least children, women, &c.'. Clarification of Hegel's ideas on the sexual division of labour is provided in the section on 'The Family'. Here we learn that man's nature is fitting for the political sphere and woman's is not. 'Man has his actual substantive life in the state, in learning, and so forth, as well as in labour and struggle with the external world.'

'Woman, on the other hand, has her substantive destiny in the family, and to be imbued with family piety is her ethical frame of mind.'[38] Differences of nature produce different mental capacities.

> Women are capable of education, but they are not made for activities which demand a universal faculty such as the more advanced sciences, philosophy and certain forms of artistic production. . . .When women hold the helm of government, the state is at once in jeopardy, because women regulate their actions not by the demands of universality but by arbitrary inclinations and opinions.[39]

More extended justification of the political exclusion of women and lower-class men was not required. Ruling assumptions concerning political access had not yet reached that crucial meridian which changed the magnetic pull from one pole to the other, when the onus of explanation rested on those who wished to restrict the franchise rather than on those wishing to extend it. Hegel obviously preferred the period when the wishes of 'people in general' had less force, and when the threat from the uneducated and unorganised was less apparent. Sound judgement was endangered by the falsity of public opinion. 'Whole peoples may often be prey to excitement or be carried away by passion to a greater extent than their leaders.'[40]

The conventional security against mass radical influence was, as we have noted, a wealth qualification for voting rights. Hegel made some interesting and unusual comments on this in his *Proceedings of the Estates Assembly in the Kingdom of Wurtemberg*. In 1815 the monarch of the recently-enlarged kingdom had summoned the Estates and presented them with a Constitutional Charter, the content of which gave rise to considerable conflict. The franchise, entirely normal for its time, was granted to men over the age of 25 with an income of 200 guilders from real estate. These qualifications Hegel declared irrelevant to a properly ordered state. 'Age and property are qualities affecting only the individual himself, not characteristics constituting his worth in the civil order.'[41] Property as a commodity preeminently ties its owner to his selfish, individual interests, to the detriment of universal concerns. Inherited property in entailed landed estates apparently does not fall under this disqualification, for it is a source of stability and thus the appropriate qualification for aristocratic composition of the upper house. The *fluctuating* fortunes of marketable property, in contrast, provide no guarantee of its owner's political reliability. Worth to the community, which is the qualification that really matters, derives from the nature of a man's office, social position, skill and ability. Age and wealth may be included as qualifications, but they should not be the only ones and they certainly should not be dominant. In any case, Hegel noted that in more extended electorates the citizen soon becomes relatively indifferent to his political rights. This is easily comprehensible, for franchise extension can be seen as a self-defeating attempt to devolve political power. Throughout his writings we find Hegel reiterating the view that as the number of voters increases so the real value of each particular vote is correspondingly lowered. Thus in the end popular suffrage would merely increase political apathy and leave power in the hands of a narrow caucus, exactly the opposite of what its proponents intended. Even for the enfranchised, voting is regarded as a poor system of appointment. Its dependence upon 'an accidental attitude and a momentary preference'[42] is so much less satisfactory than elevation on the basis of objective qualifications. This disadvantage is, in any case, unlikely to be crucial for, according to Pelczynski, Hegel insisted 'that the proper function of the Assembly of Estates is deliberative, that it may influence but must not control the government'.[43] Its task would appear to be little more than advisory. Rational bureaucracy is the prime characteristic of the modern state, and the Crown provides the effective centre through which this influence operates and thus the representative assemblies do not facilitate a preeminently parliamentary system.

We have noted that for a professed exponent of systematic rationality, Hegel's constitutional preferences seem beset with contradictions. Monarchy is attained by birth, but one joins the bureaucracy on merit. Only the corporations embody a representative aspect. Representation, then, has its place, but it is only one element of the system. And even within the representative sector, other qualities also have to exist. 'The external guarantee, a property qualification, is, if taken by itself, evidently just as one-sided in its externality as, at the other extreme, are purely subjective confidence and the opinion of the electorate.'[44] The popular will has to be countered and filtered. This concern for the politics of balance underlies Hegel's refusal to take a simple choice between monarchy, aristocracy and democracy. In spite of the primacy of monarchy, all three elements have their part to play. Hegel saw constitutional monarchy as the rational unity of the three forms. Democracy has its restricted sphere, but monarchy itself is also not without limitation, for legislative power is shared with the representative bodies. 'Without such a representative body, freedom is no longer thinkable.'[45] In accord with contemporary radical proposals, the French Revolution had produced a unicameral assembly. Conservatives, in contrast, desired a check on the more popularly elected lower house and thus insisted on bicameralism. Hegel also wanted the Estates divided into two assemblies, so as to overcome 'the accidental character' of 'a snap-division',[46] although given the powerlessness of the assemblies, part of the rationale for this division would appear to be lost.

If Hegel's system seems a strange amalgam of ancient and modern, hereditary and representative, this in no way detracts from its plausibility, for similar criticisms could be made of the British parliamentary system with its elected lower house, its nominated and inherited membership of the upper house, and its hereditary monarchy. J-F. Suter has noted that 'in some respects Hegel's system of representation bore the mark of English institutions'.[47] A major point of difference might be that Hegel regarded his system as an emanation of rationality, but does one not still find the British parliamentary system bestowed with a comparable aura of excellence – that History, God, or a benevolent fate have contributed to the gradual emergence of a political pattern that rational constitutionalism would have been unable to equal? The consequence of this view was that it left untouched systems that had become anachronistic. Political developments have their proper rhythm, in which harmony is maintained with the prevailing cultural and historical context. Retarded development is criticised on the same methodological grounds as attempted leaps into what is taken to be the future. Just as he thought it ludicrous to attempt any return to the constitutions of Antiquity so Hegel also decried the utopian notion that 'the form of a constitution were a matter of free choice, determined by nothing but reflecting'.[48] This mentality, characteristic of emergent liberal thought, assumes that the individual could be presumed to exist as a bearer of rights even before the creation of society and the state. For Hegel, on the other hand, it was only the existence of the state that made actual rights possible. Here we have the antithesis of the individualistic social-contract mentality that believes constitutions can be framed out of the thin air of a state of nature, and derive their legitimacy from the consent of those who will be bound by them. Legitimacy for Hegel was not based on the modern notion of popular consent nor the ancient ones of prescription or divine right. He belonged to that strand of the Enlightenment tradition associated with reformist, bureaucratic autocracy. Improvement was possible only within the constraints imposed by existing conditions and the guidance of those with real understanding. Thus Hegel's basic attitude to both the individual and the state serves to differentiate him sharply from liberal individualism. It seemed to Hegel that liberalism, though it performed the necessary task of destroying outmoded institutions, was inadequate in replacing them with an atomised society possessed of a too-weak sense of community. 'The bad', he noted, 'is that which is wholly private and personal in its content; the rational, on the other hand, is the absolutely universal.'[49] For Hegel, the universal is represented by the state and here too, the gulf between him and classical liberalism is wide. For the latter, the state was an object of suspicion, certainly necessary for liberals are not anarchists, but equally certainly in need of curbs and limitations. It was from the state that the danger to freedom was thought to emanate. For Hegel, in stark contrast, the state was the source of rights and freedom. It was an object deserving of veneration, 'the actuality of concrete freedom' and 'the march of God in the world'.[50] Whereas liberals wanted to limit the state's economic role, Hegel thought it had a responsibility to regulate commercial relationships for the benefit of all.

In terms of Hegel's view of the democratic movement we can see that his concern for representation was motivated by a strong desire to integrate all sections of society into a coherent whole. However, representation should be to a largely advisory chamber, and thus integration was intended to produce affirmation rather than general legislative powers. Political decisions should remain the preserve of the specially qualified. Hegel belongs to a line of thought that stretches from eighteenth-century enlightened despotism through Saint-Simon and Comte to the English Fabians and the Russian communists. This political tradition believes that bureaucratic power is not merely efficient but, more controversially, simultaneously able to perceive and implement a general interest. The basic problem here, then, is the notion of bureaucratic objectivity. In terms of Hegel we do not need to bring evidence, starting with that of Marx and continuing with Michels and later elite theory, which was not available to him. Hegel was well versed in, and an admirer of, Rousseau. For Rousseau the general will must come from all and apply to all. Will could not be represented. If it was it would thereby become particular. This, we might suggest, is the inherent fate of even the Hegelian bureaucracy. Bureaucracy, then, becomes an interest alongside others. Hegel recognised that modern society produced a poverty-stricken rabble who were beyond political integration, yet he still thought that some kind of general interest in principle existed. In this sense his ideas lend themselves less successfully to liberal democracy than do those of John Adams, for whom the interplay of conflicting and inherently contradictory forces was an unavoidable part of modern politics.

5 Alexis de Tocqueville

In 1857, just two years before his death, Alexis de Tocqueville wrote to his nephew Hubert of his investigation of family documents in the 'charter room' and how he had 'encountered the line of our fathers through nearly four hundred years, always finding them again in Tocqueville, and their history mingled with that of the whole population that surrounds me'.[1] This letter is more than just the response of an older man forced out of the political arena and ruminating on his place in the wider order of things, for the weight, and indeed the presence, of history, both personal and national, were central to Tocqueville's sense of self-identity and purpose. The name of his Norman baronial ancestor, Clérel de Tocqueville, can be found in a document from the Court of William the Conqueror. Half a dozen of his immediate relatives were guillotined in the French Revolutionary Terror. His father was in prison and rescued from a similar fate by the fall of Robespierre. Tocqueville's whole identity was conditioned by being a member of a family that had a long history and a profound sense of belonging to an aristocratic class with appropriate obligations and outlook. His contemporary, Karl Marx, once remarked that the lord does not so much inherit the land as that the land inherits him.[2] Thus Tocqueville had a circumscribed place in society bequeathed to him by historical circumstances. Though born a *Comte*, Tocqueville rejected the title, as he also rejected the legitimist politics of the rural notables with whom he intermingled, sitting to the left of centre in the French parliamentary assembly. Yet to the end he still bore the traits, manners, tastes and obligations of the aristocracy into which he had been born.

'A seigneur', as Esmond Wright has noted, 'had a role to play'[3] and thus Tocqueville found himself on the political stage. His first campaign for election to the Chamber of Deputies, in 1837, failed amid cries of 'No noblemen!'[4] In 1839 he gained election from the nearby district of Valognes with 317 votes against 241, and was re-elected for the duration of the July monarchy, which fell in 1848. In 1842 Tocqueville had become a member of the General Council in the *département* of La Manche, a position he greatly enjoyed and in which he could both demonstrate and confirm his strong appreciation of local government as a bulwark against over-centralisation. As a member of the national Chamber of Deputies Tocqueville recom-

111

mended a gradual extension of the franchise, free education for the poor, prison reform and the ending of slavery in the French colonies.

As had happened to his father, Tocqueville found himself a witness to the revolutionary outbreaks which France was now experiencing almost in each generation. Tocqueville's report of it, his posthumously published *Recollections*, is, in terms of quality and immediacy, virtually unparalleled as an eye-witness account of a major revolutionary outbreak. Following the February 1848 Revolution and the abdication of King Louis Philippe, Tocqueville was elected to the new Constituent Assembly and chosen for the legislative committee which was to write the constitution. In May of the following year he was elected to the new Legislative Assembly and was then chosen by Louis Napoleon as Minister of Foreign Affairs. Tocqueville remained in this position for a mere five months, until Louis Napoleon formed a new cabinet at the end of October 1849. Immediately after Louis Napoleon's coup of 2 December 1851 Tocqueville, in the company of 230 other representatives of the Assembly, was arrested and imprisoned for a few days. He refused to take an oath of loyalty to the new Empire and consequently his political career came to an end.

Politics' loss of Tocqueville was a gain for social science, for having risen to fame on the basis of his writings on America, Tocqueville's departure from the public stage gave him the opportunity to analyse social change in his own country. His first volume of a planned series on the French Revolution, *The Old Regime and the French Revolution*, appeared in 1856. Of the second volume only notes are extant, for Tocqueville died of tuberculosis at Cannes in 1859. He was only 54.

Writing about Tocqueville's switch from the public life of the Assembly to the solitude of the study, Michael Hereth suggested that Tocqueville's 'main goal was political activity, not literary fame',[5] yet Tocqueville himself recognised that his preeminence lay more in the field of thought than of action. To his distant cousin Louis de Kergolay, with whom he shared a voluminous correspondence, he wrote in 1850 that 'my true worth is above all in works of the mind, that I am worth more in thought than in action'.[6]

So, like John Adams, Tocqueville both practised and contemplated politics. He did not reach the same political heights as Adams, but then Adams never achieved the analytical and stylistic excellence of Tocqueville's writings. Adams saw in France an awful warning of how America might decline, while Tocqueville saw in America what France might achieve: a free democratic order from which all hereditary political power had been effaced. Like Adams, Tocqueville accepted the great revolution of his country and sought to turn it to the best advantage. Again, like Adams, his subject was 'the Atlantic revolution' (to borrow a later term), for both acknowledged that reciprocal ideological influences linked their countries in spiritual affinity. More like Hegel, however, Tocqueville had an overriding sense of history as an ascertainable logical sequence with no turning back and no guarantee of its destination. Instead of Hegel's 'world spirit' we have, in the concept of 'providence', what may be another term for a similar phenomenon. For Tocqueville it was through the gradual extension of democracy that providence had its most evident manifestation.

Tocqueville had been in the United States for less than a year, from May 1831 to February 1832. The ostensible purpose of the journey, made with his friend Gustave de Beaumont, was the study of American penal institutions. Their report appeared in 1833 as *Du système pénitentiaire aux Etats-Unis et son application en France.* However, this was only one of the fruits of a short visit put to distinctly good effect. Tocqueville's basic intention in visiting America was broader still, and in terms of 'application to France' he had in mind the character of modern society as a whole. His two volumes on *Democracy in America* were published in 1835 and 1840 respectively. Tocqueville became an instant celebrity and, ever since, the works have been accorded classic status.

For Tocqueville the peculiarity of America was the purity and extent to which it had developed the modern form of democratic society. In Europe, with its dense historical encumbrances, the forms of modernity remained somewhat opaque. In contrast 'The emigrants who colonised the shores of America in the beginning of the seventeenth century somehow separated the democratic principle from all the principles which it had to contend with in the old communities of Europe, and transplanted it alone to the New World.' There it developed with such particular rapidity that it 'seems to have nearly reached its natural limit'.[7]

Tocqueville's broad outline of this democratic process, and indeed much that is basic to his general outlook, can be found in his powerful and much-quoted Introduction to the first volume. In it he is most lyrical not about the country he had recently visited and on which he was reporting, but on the homeland to which he returned. This serves as a reminder of what can easily be overlooked, that a work whose impact on educated Americans has been immense, was in fact not written for them. It was a French traveller's report back to his countrymen of the future he had witnessed and which they were destined eventually to experience. Tocqueville confessed that 'in America I saw more than America,' for 'it appears to me that, sooner or later, we shall arrive, like the Americans, at an almost complete equality of condition'. In this view 'the democracy which governs the American communities appears to be rapidly rising into power in Europe'. To understand where this trend might lead, one must witness its most developed form. Accordingly Tocqueville crossed the Atlantic in pursuit of what he termed 'Democracy in America'. The United States represented the most advanced stage of democratic development because it had been born free, without an indigenous aristocracy to overthrow. Circumstances had rendered it democratic from the start. Its general equality of conditions, egalitarian spirit, and politically-engaged citizenry signified, for Tocqueville, the essence of democratic life.

Contemplation of seven hundred years of French history appeared to confirm that similar processes were at work on both sides of the Atlantic. France, with its longer recorded history, provided better evidence of the duration of the democratic trend. As new modes of power emerged 'the value attached to high birth declined'.[8] At one time nobility could only be inherited; by the thirteenth century it could be purchased or conferred. In the conflicts of attrition between the crown and the nobility either side might grant the common people influence in order to tip the scales of power in a desired direction. As a result, 'In France, the kings have always been the most constant of levellers.' In time the invention of 'printing and the spread of learning opened the same resources to the minds of all classes'.[9] For Tocqueville, from the Crusades through to the introduction of municipal corporations, firearms, protestantism, commerce, manufacture and the discovery of America, the social consequences of the egalitarian trend had been consistent in their tendency.

Among the striking features of Tocqueville's presentation of this democratisation process is his insistence upon its utterly inexorable nature. To the reactionaries of his time he frames rhetorical questions in a form which renders possible only negative answers. 'Would it, then, be wise to imagine that a social movement, the causes of which lie so far back, can be checked by the efforts of one generation? Can it be believed that the democracy which has overthrown the feudal system, and vanquished kings, will retreat before tradesmen and capitalists? Will it stop now that it has grown so strong, and its adversaries so weak?'[10]

Summing up the cumulative social changes in France since the eleventh century, Tocqueville concluded that 'the noble has gone down on the social ladder, and the commoner has gone up: the one descends as the other rises. Every half-century brings them nearer to each other, and they will soon meet.' France follows next behind the United States in this process, for in no other 'country in Europe has the great social revolution . . . made such rapid progress'.[11] England, with its distinctive history, was also moving in the same way. What better proof could there be of the extent of the process than that so many Christian countries, in spite of their differing starting points and 'following such different roads', were still heading in the same direction.[12] 'Whithersoever we turn our eyes we perceive the same revolution going on throughout the Christian world.'[13]

Here it becomes apparent that Alexis de Tocqueville, the cultivated aristocrat and defender of French imperial rule in Algeria, held assumptions common among the upper classes of his time, that the world was divided into civilised and barbarian, or Christian and pagan. Which conceptual scheme had predominance was of little consequence, for the one merged into the other. The favoured portion of the globe was progressive and apparently predestined to dominate the stationary and, hence, backward regions. But what factors placed some countries on one side of this great divide and the rest on the other side? What moved some countries forward and held others back? Nineteenth-century social science emerged as, in large part, an attempt to answer this great question. For Marx social change derived from contradictions in the mode of production; for Mill from the free development of ideas; for Durkheim from an increasing division of labour. For Tocqueville, who here had more in common with the clerical reactionaries, the guiding hand of God lay behind the visible social processes.

In his introduction to *Democracy in America* Tocqueville emphasised that the whole book had

been written under the impression of a kind of religious terror produced in the author's mind by the view of that irresistible revolution which has advanced for centuries in spite of every obstacle, and which is still advancing in the midst of the ruins it has caused. It is not necessary that God himself should speak in order that we may discover the unquestionable signs of his will. . . .

The gradual development of the principle of equality is, therefore, a Providential fact.[14]

This insistence on a divine and providential underlay to human history characterises both Tocqueville's early and later writings, both in his private letters and his published books. Of the beginnings of the 1789 French Revolution he wrote that 'one of the laws of Divine Providence . . . was shaping human destiny in that momentous phase of our history'.[15] In the unfinished second volume on the 1789 revolution Tocqueville pondered on how 'some of the most trivial scenes in history' had in aggregate produced 'immense events . . . Hairbrained or narrow-minded ministers, dissolute priests, futile women, rash or mercenary courtiers, a king with peculiarly useless virtues' had all been instruments of a plan beyond their comprehension. 'I marvel at the almighty power of God, who, with instruments as weak as these, can set the whole mass of human society in motion.'[16] Tocqueville wrote to Arthur de Gobineau that 'to me it is Christianity that seems to have accomplished the revolution' in modern moral philosophy. Christianity, Tocqueville reminded his friend, 'put in grand evidence the equality, the unity, the fraternity of all men'.[17] Christianity was therefore incompatible with the ideas of racial inequality for which Gobineau was to become notorious. Christian equality was for Tocqueville the basis of the social equality, the democratic levelling process, which he observed. In Tocqueville's mind God's providential plan is to history what continental drift is to geography, or gravity was to physics; it is the basic law of movement to which all other changes are subordinate.

The God who set this process in motion, who watches over it and guides it, for reasons that Tocqueville pondered but did not claim to understand, is the God of Christianity. In a study of Tocqueville's religious views Doris Goldstein pointed out that he regarded both Islam and Hinduism as 'socially pernicious' and the latter 'a religion worth less than unbelief'.[18] God had chosen to advance only the Christian nations. Tocqueville, who found the idea of inequality distinctly distasteful when based upon racial differences, nevertheless accepted it when grounded in theology, and seems to have been unaware of this important disparity. The Christian God had favoured the Christian nations with social progress denied to the heathen. Tocqueville pointed out to Gobineau that

A few million men who, a few centuries ago, lived nearly shelterless in the forests and in the marshes of Europe will, within a hundred years, have transformed the globe and dominated the other races. Seldom has Providence shown us an aspect of the future so clearly. The European races are often the greatest rogues, but at least they are rogues to whom God gave will and power and whom he seems to have destined for some time to be at the head of mankind. Nothing on the entire globe will resist their influence. I have no doubt about this.[19]

At the most overt level Tocqueville outlined a process of democratic levelling. Equality was growing within the countries with which he was concerned; that is, the major Christian nations. This process within Christendom is one that simultaneously advances the democratising countries and increasingly differentiates them from the rest of the world. Furthermore growing equality *within* Christendom continually accentuates the distinctiveness of it as compared with the rest of the world.

Tocqueville here, in the broad panorama of his thought, clearly belongs within the recognisable tradition of western post-Enlightenment thought. We have seen that for Hegel, as with Marx, the course of history had an ascertainable broad outline. For both Hegel and Tocqueville it had a theological basis. For them both, as for Marx, European superiority was presumed. Where Tocqueville noted the preeminence of Christendom, Hegel had elevated the Germanic world, broadly defined, whilst Marx assumed the superiority of European capitalism which was destined to create a world in its own image. Just as Tocqueville favoured French colonial rule in Algeria so did Marx that of the British in India. We can, then, agree with Robert Nisbet that 'it is impossible for the student of nineteenth-century thought to miss the affinity between Tocqueville and such system-builders of the age as Comte, Hegel, and Marx'. Nisbet notes 'the same kind of cosmic principles of change or development, of patterns of uniformity, and of inexorabilities and immanent ends that we are accustomed to seeing in the century's major philosophers of history'.[20]

Yet, for a number of reasons, Tocqueville's concept of Providence remains rather unsatisfactory. If we draw on some of the more obvious points of comparison, we can see that for Marx the basic causes of social change were not beyond empirical investigation. The same is true of Durkheim's theory of the progressive development of the division of labour in society. Abraham Eisenstadt has noted that Tocqueville 'hardly attempted to prove his basic premise: that the regime of democracy, long in the making, was irresistible'.[21] The reason for Tocqueville's omission is that theologically-based explanations are not dependent upon empirical verification. The process itself could be observed in history, as Tocqueville sought to demonstrate, but the cause of the process could not. Quite simply, Tocqueville's belief in the divine origin of the process of democratisation rested on faith.

The oddity of Tocqueville providing the democratic process with a divine basis is that he did not seem to have been markedly religious. He lost his faith at the age of 16 and never came to terms with this loss. One critic has noticed how Tocqueville 'consciously or unconsciously pushes the philosophical-theoretical questions aside, to make room for the realm of political activity interesting him'.[22] Writing to Louis de Kergolay on religion reduced Tocqueville to exasperation: 'Enough of this matter: if I plunged into it often, it would drive me crazy.'[23]

Tocqueville at his desk was as much a politician as Tocqueville in the National Assembly; and we can see how his doctrine of Providence might help reconcile those of his own class to the modern social order. The Roman Catholic church had been the largest landowner of the *ancien régime* and the monarchy had claimed to rule by divine right: in respect of both its property and its ideology the Catholic church in France was identified with the old order. Jacobinism, the agent of the new order, was seen as derivative from the impiety and heresy of Voltaire and Rousseau. The Enlightenment had upranked reason and downgraded faith. The revolution confiscated church lands, discarded the Christian calendar, closed the churches and substituted the cult of the Supreme Being for the worship of Jesus Christ. Edmund Burke, in an account that Tocqueville knew well, saw the revolution as an attack not just on French Catholicism but on Christianity as such. All along the line a simple equation seemed to hold good. On the one side, the old regime, monarchy, aristocracy and the Roman Catholic church; on the other, the *philosophes*, the Terror, democracy and secularism. Tocqueville's achievement was to break through these standard distinctions and to assert that God had not abandoned mankind; that all the attributes and changes of modern society were still part of His design. The consequence was inescapable. Christians should not oppose but rather come to terms with the modern world.

In this vein we should also understand Tocqueville's constant reiteration of democracy as not just providential but also inexorable. In the Preface to the second volume of *Democracy in America*, Tocqueville declared himself 'firmly convinced that the democratic revolution occurring before our eyes is an irresistible fact and . . . it would be neither desirable nor wise to try to combat it'.[24] Combining the inevitability thesis with the providential one implies that 'to attempt to check democracy would be in that case to resist the will of God'. This enabled Tocqueville to move towards his desired conclusion that 'the nations would then be constrained to make the best of the social lot awarded to them by Providence'.[25]

We arrive, in consequence, at a view that democracy is inevitable, the attempt to combat it both futile and heretical and that the question of its acceptance should be taken off the political agenda. According to Marvin Zetterbaum, Tocqueville 'by assigning the defence of democracy to history or Providence . . . removed himself from the partisan fray' whilst still being able to promote the democratic cause.[26] This intimation that Providence was a rhetorical device would carry more conviction if Tocqueville had otherwise been characterised by a desire to avoid 'the partisan fray'. Our argument, to the contrary, has been that Tocqueville felt a social obligation to engage in current debate. We shall see that he regarded the encouragement of active citizenship as one of the merits of democracy. If this is so, how are we to align the determinism of Providence with the democratic ideal of active citizenship? Robert Nisbet mentions Tocqueville having 'a concept of predestination translated into the field of social evolution'.[27] If so, would not the logical response be one of fatalistic acceptance of the consequences? What scope does such a theory allow for politics as an activity in the democratic age?

The interplay between democracy and freedom was one of Tocqueville's main concerns. The providential dynamic of democracy involved a broad determinism at the level of the general social process, but democracy was not of just one type. It had its variations and it was within these external bounds that free political activity was not merely possible but in fact essential. It is far from clear to what extent Tocqueville was actually a friend of democracy. Other contemporary philosophers of history often conflated a prediction with an ethic and were prone to present as inevitable what for them was simultaneously desirable. In Tocqueville's case this is not so. Democracy was not so much desirable as inevitable. It was fraught with intrinsic dangers against which constant vigilance was required; but vigilance, to have its effect, had to be allowed some scope. The resolve of mankind had to be allowed the power of implementation and, therefore, Tocqueville rejected the full application of a deterministic theory. Such an approach was declared false and overdrawn and likely to produce distressing moral consequences. A reduced emphasis on human capacity and freedom 'can never produce aught but feeble men and pusillanimous nations'.[28] *Democracy in America* concludes with a notion of freedom within constraints that invokes comparison with Marx's efforts to come to grips with the same problem. Whereas Marx wrote that 'Men make their own history but they do not make it just as they please'[29] and that society could not 'leap over the natural phases of its development nor remove them by decree. But it can shorten and lessen the birth-pangs.'[30] Tocqueville produced a formulation as follows:

> Providence has not created mankind entirely independent or entirely free. It is true, that around every man a fatal circle is traced, beyond which he cannot pass; but within the wide verge of that circle he is powerful and free: as it is with man, so with communities. The nations of our time cannot prevent the conditions of men from becoming equal; but it depends upon themselves whether the principle of equality is to lead them to servitude or freedom, to knowledge or barbarism, to prosperity or wretchedness.[31]

In his preface to the twelfth edition of *Democracy in America*, written in 1848, Tocqueville concluded, in like vein, that: 'According as we establish either democratic liberty or democratic tyranny, the fate of the world will be different. Indeed, one may say that it depends on us whether in the end republics will be established everywhere, or everywhere abolished.'[32]

Democracy, then, could range from liberty to tyranny. This makes it sound as if Tocqueville used the term so loosely that it could apply to almost any form of government. Of America, Tocqueville wrote that he was 'far from supposing that they have chosen the only form of government which a democracy may adopt'.[33] Modern usage of the term 'democracy' involves a narrower conception than that adopted by Tocqueville: the term is now a description not of a type of society but of a particular type of government. Specifically, present western usage equates democracy with freely-chosen government. From such a perspective Tocqueville's concept of 'democratic liberty' is virtually a tautology. Conversely 'democratic tyranny' would appear a contradiction to those for whom the two terms are mutually exclusive.

Tocqueville used 'democracy' to refer to a basic egalitarian tendency in society: it therefore encompassed far more than the formal political structure. In addition to the political manifestations of democracy he also included the social, ideological and legal changes that were undermining the time-honoured formation of graded ranks and hereditary advantages enjoyed by his forebears. Democracy, accordingly, denoted not so much a precise constitutional arrangement, as the general movement attacking the traditional system of inherited privileges. It can best be understood in terms of its antithesis, for its primary definition derives from what it is not. Democracy had removed the fixed barriers to social mobility imposed by aristocratic societies. It is not that all immediately become equal but, rather, that all have a chance to alter their social condition. From Tocqueville's perspective, democratic society seemed virtually classless, for in comparison with the Estates system of earlier times the social groupings of modern society were 'composed of such mobile elements that they can never exercise a real control over their members'.[34]

Aristocracy and democracy are what Nisbet refers to as Tocqueville's 'two great ideal-types' held 'in a kind of dynamic tension, a dialectical opposition'.[35] Democracy, defined as the anti-aristocratic movement, was certainly Tocqueville's basic understanding of the term. However, we must concede that his usage was not always consistent. Within Tocqueville's writings, democracy was sometimes specified as a social *condition*, sometimes as a social *tendency*, and sometimes as a type of *government*. The latter usage might appear to be the same as that commonly applied today, but that would be misleading. Even where Tocqueville referred to a democratic state or government we are still not justified in regarding the nature of government as the only criterion. Democracy in government would be one part of democracy in society. This aspect is apparent in the following passage as is also Tocqueville's characteristic binding of origins and destinations:

> Gradually the distinctions of rank are done away; the barriers which once severed mankind are falling down; property is divided, power is shared by many, the light of intelligence spreads, and the capacities of all classes are equally cultivated. The State becomes democratic, and the empire of democracy is slowly and peaceably introduced into the institutions and manners of the nation.[36]

As Tocqueville's conception of democracy is defined in terms of its social manifestations, his comments on voting rights and the formal political structure have been relatively neglected. If we examine his attitude on these questions we find that the wider the franchise the more concerned Tocqueville was to filter its radical impulses. In

broad terms, Tocqueville would probably have accepted the notion
of a correlation between social and political change, but varying rates
as well as means of change make it possible for politics to curb the
speed of social change, although not its overall direction. Formal
political structures are suited to function as brakes on the social
movement, because constitutional arrangements are produced deliberately and self-consciously, whereas the broad process of social
change operates through a dynamic beyond human control. This will
become more apparent if we examine Tocqueville's comments on the
franchise and the societal character not only of the United States but
also of some of the European nations in which he took an interest.

Tocqueville's assertion that 'all the states of the Union have
adopted universal suffrage'[37] can seriously mislead the modern
reader. His own notes on the electoral qualifications in force mention
residential qualifications varying between three months and two
years, and property qualifications of varying severity in the states of
Massachusetts, Rhode Island, Connecticut, New Jersey, South
Carolina and Tennessee. 'In the United States', we are also told,
'except slaves, servants, and paupers supported by the township,
there is no class of persons who do not exercise the elective franchise,
and who do not indirectly contribute to make the laws'.[38] Here
Tocqueville omitted any mention of women, although in other contexts he had much to say about them. Either we must assume that
Tocqueville held to a notion of 'virtual representation' in which
women, like children, were taken to be adequately represented by
the head of the household to which they belonged; or else that the
omission of women from the area of political power was so natural as
not properly to count as an exclusion. Nevertheless, in remarking on
the vibrant political culture of America, Tocqueville noted that 'even
the women frequently attend public meetings and listen to political
harangues as a recreation from their household labors'. This is in a
context where political debating clubs are said to be 'a substitute for
theatrical entertainments'.[39]

When Tocqueville wrote that 'every American citizen can vote or
be voted for'[40] we must assume that he meant it tautologically, i.e.
that not all the inhabitants of the United States were citizens and
citizenship was thus defined as the right to 'vote or be voted for'.
Tocqueville never forgot the considerable numerical presence of
black and native American sub-citizens, and his portrayal of their
plight shows a humanity and understanding that has stood the test of
time and compares very favourably with the writings of his European

contemporaries about the various indigenous peoples with whom they came into contact.

What then of 'Democracy in America' when Tocqueville was all too aware of its limitations as well as of its extent? We may say that democracy was the characteristic of the white male community. 'In' America might be understood in the sense of 'within'. In the multiracial American society it was the white, mainly Protestant community which possessed the advanced social and political forms he wished to observe and understand. Tocqueville wrote of the Indian tribes being treated as foreign nations: they were within the same broad geographical domain but not the political community. A rudimentary notion of 'internal colonialism' is implicit here. The same might more obviously be said for the slave plantations of the south. In this respect a thunder cloud hovered permanently on the horizon. Not even the abolition of slavery could remove it, for what was at stake was the willingness of the white races to intermingle and live in peace and equality with their black compatriots. Tocqueville feared that as legal equality increased so would social prejudice become more bitter. He saw no way to escape what he regarded as the inevitable fate of those who disregard nature's laws. 'The more or less distant but inevitable danger of a confrontation between the blacks and whites of the South of the Union is a nightmare constantly haunting the American imagination.'[41]

Clearly the democracy that Tocqueville found in the United States was not a benefit spread evenly over the country. It was, rather, the dominant tendency which was gradually overcoming obstacles in its path. He acknowledged that the prevailing social equality had not penetrated so fully into the political world. The triumph of political equality was thought to be merely a matter of time. As new states west of the Appalachians were added to the Union, their suffrage requirements were, from the start, broader than those of the older states to the east. The latter would, in time, have to change in accord with the prevailing tendency.

When a nation begins to modify the elective qualification, it may easily be foreseen that, sooner or later, that qualification will be entirely abolished. There is no more invariable rule in the history of society; the further electoral rights are extended, the greater is the need of extending them; for after each concession the strength of the democracy increases, and its demands increase with its strength, the ambition of those who are below the appointed rate is irritated in exact proportion to the great number of those who are above it. The exception at last becomes the rule, concession follows concession, and no stop can be made short of universal suffrage.[42]

In volume two of *Democracy in America*, Tocqueville referred to the French as 'a democratic people'.[43] Such a designation may well have fitted the general social mores but would seem less applicable to the political constitution introduced by Louis Philippe, which (as we noted in Chapter 1) still left over 97 per cent of adult males without the vote. A considerable further extension took place after the 1848 February revolution when a universal male franchise was introduced. This created a total electorate of about nine million people. Tocqueville was able to describe France as democratic even before that revolution, not just because of the 'democratic constitution of our civic society',[44] but because he believed that the battle against aristocracy had been completed by 1830 and that a civil society on another class basis had replaced it. The French Revolution for Tocqueville could not simply be confined within the years 1789–94. That brief timespan did not even delimit its primary phase – that of removing aristocratic power. As he noted in his *Recollections*:

> Seen as a whole from a distance, our history from 1789 to 1830 appears to be forty-one years of deadly struggle between the *Ancien Régime* with its traditions, memories, hopes and men (i.e. the aristocrats), and the new France led by the middle class. 1830 would seem to have ended the first period of our revolution. . . . All that remained of the *Ancien Régime* was destroyed forever. In 1830 the triumph of the middle class was decisive and so complete that the narrow limits of the bourgeoisie encompassed all political powers, franchises, prerogatives, indeed the whole government, to the exclusion, in law, of all beneath it and, in fact, of all that had once been above it. Thus the bourgeoisie became not only the sole director of society, but also, one might say, its cultivator.[45]

Tocqueville regarded England, in spite of its more extended franchise, as less democratic than France. In 1840 France had double the population of England and Wales but only about a third of the number of electors. However, the basic tendency of its state and society was bourgeois while that of England was still thoroughly aristocratic. 'The aristocracy makes the laws, applies them, and judges breaches of them. The whole thing is consistent, and England can properly be called an aristocratic state.'[46] In 1849 Tocqueville described England as the only country 'in which an aristocracy still rules'.[47]

In early 1848 Tocqueville addressed the Academy of Moral and Political Sciences about a book entitled *On Democracy in Switzerland*, written by M. Cherbuliez, the Professor of Public Law at the Academy of Geneva. Tocqueville noted that 'all the constitutions of the cantons are now democratic, but democracy does not show the same aspect in all'. Some were representative democracies in which power was granted to elected assemblies. Others were what M. Cherbuliez referred to as pure democracies, now better known to the political science profession as 'direct democracies'. These Tocqueville took to be 'the last venerable ruins of a vanished world'.[48] It should not surprise us that, as in America, so in France and Switzerland, Tocqueville could describe as democratic a political system that excluded women from the suffrage.

In this sense, as in others we have noted, Tocqueville was a man of his times. His own self-understanding was rather different from this, for he thought circumstances had raised him above the partiality of contending factions. 'Aristocracy was already dead when I started life and democracy did not yet exist, so my instinct could lead me blindly neither toward one nor toward the other'.[49] We can share with G.A. Kelly a suspicion that Tocqueville was more partisan than he admitted: 'the models of the two societies are laid side by side and exposed in endless dialogue: not exactly *yin* and *yang*, for we quickly perceive that aristocracy prevails on the moral plane, while democracy has the last, best answer – the right of history'. Thus 'Tocqueville takes up his station as the *eiron*: the enlightened aristocrat, preaching to stupid, nostalgic and rancorous peers; the reluctant democrat, chiding the fondest appetites of the mob'.[50]

Tocqueville was not merely caught between aristocracy and democracy; he was, in his attitude toward democracy itself, caught between his hopes and his fears. Was it possible that democratic societies would play politics with such consummate skill that the advantages would be maximised and the disadvantages reduced? Tocqueville's first impressions of American democracy were favourable. In the townships of New England he found a commendable level of participation, local government, civility, political morality and freedom. For Tocqueville freedom implied the notion of the possibility of politics, and politics was understood as more than just administration; it implied discussion, argument, compromise, adjustment, exchange and it had to be extensive; not just a debate within the circle of the executive few, but an activity of involved citizenship by the dispersed many, what in his foreword to *The Old Regime* he described as 'a community of free citizens'.[51]

Politics was not just a matter of reaching wise decisions but also of their being the decisions of the whole community. In the words of Doris Goldstein, Tocqueville 'shared the Greek view that political life was inherently dignifying, and that participation in it elevates men from the material preoccupations of daily life'.[52] Here we reach the nub of Tocqueville's ambivalent attitude to democracy. Political life is a primary good. He advocates politics as an activity of the people but is not sure that they can be trusted. He pursued a balance between an elitism motivated by self-interest and mass activity uninformed by wisdom. The shoals through which the democratic current must pass require of it the most careful navigation. Democracy could be passive or active. Tyranny might be imposed on the passive many by the powerful few, or by an active majority imposing itself on all who think differently. Ideally leadership should be used to guide the majority towards its own good. 'The first of the duties which are at this time imposed upon those who direct our affairs, is to educate the democracy; to renovate, if possible, its religious belief; to purify its morals, to regulate its movements; to substitute by degrees a knowledge of business for its inexperience, and an acquaintance with its true interests for its blind instincts.'[53]

Tocqueville feared the power of the egalitarian process and was anxious lest it submerge other important values. Democratic societies yearn for both equality and freedom but the passion for the former is so predominant that the latter is endangered. 'They call for equality in freedom; and if they cannot attain that, they still call for equality in slavery. They will endure poverty, servitude, barbarism; but they will not endure aristocracy.'[54]

Under aristocracy the people had, of course, not ruled at all. They were constrained by their rulers, and their rulers were subject to convention and divine command. The process of modernity, though, was associated with the removal of constraints. In the 1789 French Revolution, classes without political experience had come to power and had abandoned both God and history. Their only measure was their own happiness and they had pursued this through an indiscriminate and violent process of levelling. Tocqueville's first priority was to secure liberty within democratic societies. In this endeavour religion had a vital role to play. It alone could impose limits on the passion for gratification that a democratic society legitimated. Religion alone could provide a sense of boundaries and rules to which people might confine themselves and without which civilisation was unthinkable. Therefore Tocqueville, who had doubts about the truth of Christianity, was quite convinced of its social utility. In a democratic society it was even more necessary than before, for since the external constraints of hierarchy were less severe, the internal ones had to be more effective. In America, though the state and church were divided, religion was still 'the first of their political institutions, for though it did not give them the taste for liberty, it singularly facilitates their use thereof'.[55] In a manner partly reminiscent of Rousseau, Tocqueville desired a civic religion which would bind people together to an extent which the laws themselves could not guarantee.

In medieval Europe the concept of 'citizen' hardly existed. Irrespective of their will, individuals were bound up with, and into, their particular Estates. This gave them a sense of belonging which modern society could not equal. 'No one could regard himself as an isolated unit.'[56] Now each individual was on his own, privatised and cut off from wider supports, and devoted merely to personal selfishness and material wellbeing. Such a condition threatened the survival of genuine citizenship. Unless intermediate institutions could be generated or strengthened, an increasingly passive mass might find itself at the mercy of a centralised despotism. This is what seemed to be happening, for in Europe most of the 'secondary powers . . . have already disappeared; all are speedily tending to disappear, or to fall into the most complete dependence. From one end of Europe to the other the privileges of the nobility, the liberties of cities, and the powers of provincial bodies, are either destroyed or upon the verge of destruction.'[57] Such centralisation negates democratic citizenship. It 'perpetuates a drowsy regularity in the conduct of affairs'.[58] Citizens become subjects under the sway either of a centralised class of public officials, or else of a new rising class of manufacturers. Class rule, of course, was the characteristic of the *ancien régime*. Its reappearance under democracy would, one might argue, leave society no worse off than before in this respect. Tocqueville acknowledged that an 'aristocracy of manufacturers' has at least the advantage of being more open to ability than its predecessor, but what it lacks is a deeply-inculcated sense of broad social responsibility. Any new aristocracy, of state power or of private wealth, would be a negation of much that was worthwhile in the democratic ethos.[59]

In Tocqueville's view, democracy walks a tightrope above the abyss of despotism. If the people are passive they facilitate the emergence of irresponsible new elites; if they are active, too little subservient to cultured leadership, they produce the so-called 'tyranny of the majority'. After his first electoral defeat in 1837, Tocqueville complained to de Beaumont, of 'the blindly democratic passions of the lower class'.[60] The danger of an unchecked majority is that it provides no guarantee for the liberty of the minority. This is the in-built limitation of democratic government. 'No obstacles exist which can impede or even retard its progress, so as to make it heed the complaints of those whom it crushes upon its path. This state of things is harmful to itself, and dangerous for the future.'[61] The constitutional means of alleviating this danger lay through the greatest distance between the people and the executive consistent with the appearance of popular power. Consequently, Tocqueville preferred indirect and infrequent elections and the establishment of a bicameral legislature. He disliked the use of the referendum because this gave too direct an influence to the people. 'The most rational government', he had written in 1831, 'is not that in which all interested parties play a role, but that which is directed by the most enlightened and moral classes of society.'[62] Democracy, which, at its best, produces the finest examples of participatory citizenship, would thus, at its worst, produce the opposite, a passive mass where diversity of opinion had become as flattened out of existence as diversity of rank. Democracy was, therefore, simultaneously a dream and a nightmare. In America Tocqueville had found the material for a dream. In the case of his own country, he feared a nightmare.

For Tocqueville democracy had always contained positive and negative tendencies. He managed to describe the process in relatively neutral tones until 1848, when it became too threatening and increasingly adopted a socialist terminology that he was wont to dismiss as monstrous and grotesque. Class struggle was one aspect of the unacceptable face of democracy. In late 1847 Tocqueville, on behalf of his parliamentary friends, had drafted a programme for the next legislative session. In it he noted that

> the French Revolution, which abolished all privileges and destroyed all exclusive rights, did leave one, that of property. . . . But now that the right of property is the last remnant of a destroyed aristocratic world, and it alone still stands, an isolated privilege in a levelled society; when it no longer has the cover of

other more doubtful and more hated rights; it alone now has to face the direct and incessant impact of democratic opinion. . . . Soon the political struggle will be between the Haves and the Have-nots; property will be the great battlefield.[63]

The battle, in fact, took place sooner than anyone had foreseen, and in it Tocqueville unequivocally and wholeheartedly aligned himself against the revolutionary elements. In his *Recollections* of those days, he noted that 'Socialism will always remain the most essential feature of the February Revolution, and the one that left the most frightening memory.'[64] Panic and emotional distaste coloured Tocqueville's account of French socialism to an extent that badly affected his judgement. He failed, for example, to acknowledge the federalist and decentralist aspects that were so marked in the French socialist tradition. His description of Louis August Blanqui betrays an unusual lack of detachment. The revolutionary leader, said Tocqueville, had a 'dirty look like a pallid, mouldy corpse . . . he looked as if he had lived in a sewer and only just come out'.[65]

Tocqueville viewed socialism as the worst aspect of democracy. It set one class against another, glamourised violence, exalted materialism and confirmed centralisation. On all these counts it was singularly incompatible with the preservation of freedom. These features of socialism gave it particular appeal in France; not that Tocqueville is explicit on this point, but it lurks as a subtext beneath the surface of his analysis. Like Burke writing on France, but thinking of England – 'solicitous chiefly for the peace of my own country'[66] – even Tocqueville's writings on America had France in mind. France was the European country in which democracy had made most progress, but it increasingly seemed to be democracy at its worst. Tocqueville attempted, as a member of the so-called 'Party of Order', to banish the socialistic elements of the 1848–9 Revolution, but rather than achieving democratic liberty the counter-revolution swung to the other extreme and produced the long, dull torpor of Bonapartism.

During the last years of his life, Tocqueville, in 'internal exile' from practical politics, sought to come to terms with the political traditions of his own country. In the Foreword to *The Old Regime and The French Revolution*, he acknowledged that 'I have never quite lost sight of present-day France'.[67] The work 'was partly an attack on Bonapartism', as one modern commentator has reminded us.[68] In the same Foreword, Tocqueville described freedom as being 'out of fashion'. Later we are told that during the *ancien régime*, 'France had not yet become the land of dumb conformity it is now'.[69] In the planned second volume Tocqueville made a few notes on 'The Peculiar Physiognomy of the Revolution'. One states 'The upper classes distrustful of liberty, the lower classes inclined to violence: that is France.'[70] The use of the present tense is significant, as for Tocqueville the French Revolution had not yet run its course. France continued to display the tendencies of sixty years earlier, and the great revolution itself was not the clean break with the earlier times that writers such as Burke had imagined. Centralisation was not a product of the Revolution but of the pre-revolutionary system. France had moved with the general democratic trend, but the implication and fear behind Tocqueville's comparative account is that his own country was a flawed democracy. Unsurprisingly he sometimes confessed to moments of gloom. In April 1848 he wrote to de Beaumont: 'I expect little in the future. I hardly see anything there but disastrous events for us and for France.'[71] Even from the time of his most optimistic work, the first volume of *Democracy in America*, there were intimations, which became more pronounced later, that the Anglo-Saxons were adjusting more effectively to democracy than the French.

This raises the question of whether the American and French experiences could be compared in the way that Tocqueville originally assumed. Beneath the general aspect of the broad democratic tendency, each country re-emerged with its own distinctive traditions. First, the Americans began with very localised powers. The townships were there before the states, and the states before the federation. At the time of their revolution local autonomy was deeply entrenched. For the French, in contrast, decentralisation had, as we have seen, already been undermined by the *ancien régime*.

Secondly, in terms of the social place of religion, the Americans had again done better. 'An American sees in religion the surest guarantee of the stability of the State and the safety of individuals . . . Much the same may be said of the British.'[72] On the contrary, in France the triumph of unbelief among the upper classes and the intellectuals had helped undermine the moral fabric of the civic order. The people that Tocqueville studied in America he termed 'Anglo-Americans'. He gave due prominence to their Christianity, but perhaps failed to give proper significance to their Protestantism. The Christian designation allowed Tocqueville to align France with the Anglo-Saxon nations. Roman Catholic and Protestant categories would, of course, have set them apart. Tocqueville's work, with its strong emphasis on the social function of religion, cries out for a fuller sociology of religion. Tocqueville might, for example, have turned his analytical powers to the question of whether Roman Catholicism and Protestantism had different propensities to produce a culture of citizenship and freedom.

Thirdly, class also was a factor which placed the French at a disadvantage. 'The French nobility had stubbornly held aloof from the other classes.' The nobles spurned the bourgeoisie, who in their turn despised the peasantry. Class conflict was the inevitable result. For the English aristocrats, in contrast, 'no sacrifice was too great if it ensured their power. . . . in England during the eighteenth century it was the poor who enjoyed exemption from taxation; in France it was the rich'.[73] Tocqueville sometimes seemed resentful of his aristocratic ancestors, who acted so that revolution became the only means whereby barriers to democracy could be overcome. They had maintained a haughty distance from trade and the commercial classes, whereas the English had been happy to embrace new wealth. 'What distinguishes [the English aristocracy] from all others is the ease with which it has opened its ranks. . . . As everybody had the hope of being among the privileged, the privileges made the aristocracy, not more hated, but more valued.'[74] The British 'had succeeded in gradually modifying the spirit of their ancient institutions, without destroying them'. The French, armed with the purity of abstract doctrine, had done the opposite. In Britain, theory and practice intermingled; the one was in harmony with the other. 'In France, however, precept and practice were kept quite distinct and remained in the hands of two quite independent groups.'[75] Britain, of course, remained less democratic than France. Its tradition of compromise and gradualism meant that it had not travelled so far along the democratic road. To Tocqueville this might well have been one of its attractions.

Fourthly, America had achieved democracy peacefully, whereas France had moved towards it by way of revolution. Part of Tocqueville's task in studying America comparatively was to distinguish what was democratic from what was revolutionary. Though France appeared in a poor light when compared with Britain and the United States of America, it was certainly not Tocqueville's view that the latter societies had escaped from the maladies to which democracy was prone. Seymour Drescher has noted that Tocqueville 'like many French observers . . . looked on the rapid industrialisation of England as a gigantic and dangerous gamble. The English people had simply been carried away by the passion for wealth.'[76] The second volume of *Democracy in America* already showed less optimism than the first. It was from his American experience that Tocqueville drew the conclusion that 'despotism, therefore appears to me peculiarly to be dreaded in democratic times'.[77] The democratic movement drew sustenance from the opposition to servitude, yet threatened to reproduce it in a new form, for equality provided no necessary defence against the tyranny of the majority and the centralisation of the state. As a force, democracy seemed virtually unstoppable and freedom sometimes almost unsustainable. If he had to choose, it was certainly the latter that he was most concerned to defend. It was freedom, also, which was the most precarious. In his later years Tocqueville regarded himself as in opposition, not merely to Napoleon III, but to the whole course of events in his own country and beyond.

How, finally, are we to understand Tocqueville? He is famous for a theory of history that is simple in broad outline, yet it was one that his own investigations did not fully verify. Democratic equality was presented as a remorseless continuing process, yet in America it had evidently acquired 'all the practical development which the imagination can conceive'.[78] This was a society in which women were still excluded from political rights but for Tocqueville, attempts to grant the sexes equal rights would be preposterous, resulting in 'weak men and disorderly women'.[79] The abolition of slavery, were it to be achieved, would, Tocqueville thought, produce not racial equality and harmony, but still greater racial inequality.

Tocqueville was an aristocrat who accepted democracy; a politician without charisma, without oratorical ability and without a party with which he could easily identify. Alfred Cobban once described him as a 'progressive Conservative' and Raymond Aron as 'a liberal conservative, resigned to democratic modernity'. Roger Boesche concludes his book on *The Strange Liberalism of Alexis de Tocqueville* with the remark that 'his political thought frustrates all attempts to categorize it'.[80]

Tocqueville was an activist whose finest achievements were intellectual; and a non-believer uneasy about the void before him. Too rational to feel at ease with religion he was too traditionalist to be comfortable without it, 'a political plight which', according to a recent commentator, 'makes him sympathetic to modern minds'.[81] Robert Nisbet has written of Tocqueville's 'analysis of modern totalitarianism'.[82] This view, widely held, is obviously anachronistic. It is truer to say that Tocqueville's analysis provides the basis for much of the later discussion on the social structure of freedom. The best American commentators know that his knowledge of their country was not always deep; also that some of his judgements were inaccurate.[83] Nevertheless they, rightly, cannot leave him alone and find in his writings a source of continual insight and inspiration.

6 Thomas Carlyle

From the French aristocrat full of doubts and uncertainties we turn to the clear convictions of the Scottish stonemason's son. Thomas Carlyle was born in 1795 in Ecclefechan, a small village in Dumfriesshire. His parents were strict Calvinists and wanted him, the oldest of their nine children, to enter the ministry. This opportunity he declined and soon came to believe that religious principles were easier found outside of churches than within. Yet in a broader than pulpit sense, preaching became his vocation, and though he wore no clerical garb, the hard theology of his parents provided the moral framework for his verbal assault on the modern world.

One aspect of their creed was the Protestant work ethic. Time is money and the talents with which one is endowed should be put to beneficial effect. That we have St Paul's Cathedral, explains Carlyle, presupposes an art that originated long before, with the humblest, clumsiest efforts of construction. That we have English literature presupposes the earliest, most inarticulate semi-grunting attempts at communication. Culture, in all its forms, is thus a product of work by many hands over distant times. The names of those to whom we are indebted may have largely disappeared but the example is one that civilisation ignores at its peril. 'Produce! Produce!', says Teufelsdröckh, an incarnation whose German name (of sorts) indicates where Carlyle was looking for inspiration, but whose intermittent use of capital letters for nouns perhaps shows that the acculturation was only partial. 'Were it', Teufelsdröckh continues, 'but the pitifullest infinitesimal fraction of a Product, produce it in God's name! 'Tis the utmost thou hast in thee; out with it then. Up, up! Whatsoever thy hand findeth to do, do it with thy whole might. Work while it is called To-day, for the Night cometh wherein no man can work.'[1]

Out beyond his obscure village Carlyle found not only that there were those who did not work, but more offensive still, that just such people monopolised wealth and prestige. The aristocracy, the ruling class inherited from feudalism, had turned decadent and cultivated show and appearance rather than devote itself to its proper purpose of rule with responsibility. Privilege without obligation seemed to Carlyle the most reprehensible usurpation of position. In France such people had got their just deserts. That a similar fate awaited their

English kindred could not be discounted.

Yet the old regime had at least maintained the outer forms of community, neglected though the inner reality had become. What a contrast modern society presented! Cold, impersonal and as mechanical as the new industrial world, it was full of interconnections yet devoid of real community. From Goethe, Fichte and Novalis, the German writers that so profoundly influenced him, Carlyle learnt that society is properly organic and that only common spiritual bonds can transform a human aggregate into a worthwhile community. Teufelsdröckh, we learn, is

> one of those who consider Society, properly so called, to be as good as extinct . . . 'Call ye that a Society,' cries he again, 'where there is no longer any Social Idea extant; not so much as the Idea of a common Home, but only of a common, over-crowded Lodging-house? Where each, isolated, regardless of his neighbour, turned against his neighbour, clutches what he can get, and cries "Mine!" and calls it Peace, because, in the cut-purse and cut-throat Scramble, no steel knives, but only a far cunninger sort, can be employed?'[2]

As Carlyle saw it, the nineteenth century was reaping the sour fruits of the ideologies sown in the eighteenth. 'The monster UTILITARIA'[3] was breaking the social aggregate into individual fragments and then, having pitted one man in competition against the other, in effect declaring one man the enemy of another, goes on to pronounce that the object of life is the pursuit of the greatest happiness. The age suffered from a surfeit of panaceas, and liberal constitutionalism threw paper guarantees around like confetti: rights of man, greatest happiness principle, free trade, abolition of slavery and the enactment of rule of law. These Carlyle aggregated into the 'UNIVERSAL ABOLITION-OF-PAIN ASSOCIATION'.[4] Meanwhile out in the real world, 'the Working Millions' were granted 'a liberty to die by want of food'.[5] An unattainable ideal was placed within a competitive framework that directly contradicted it. The nation of shopkeepers had come to fear more for their stomachs than their souls and their vision of hell consisted of the terror of not making money. For Carlyle society would find greater contentment if it focused its ethics on the values of work, duty and reverence. Unfortunately the work ethic had long been directed, or rather misdirected, towards the narrow pursuit of profit within a *laissez-faire* context. This was the dominant 'dismal science' that averted its gaze while its human victims were buffetted by the regular rise and fall of the economic tide. Its individualist postulates left its selfish practitioners and dominant advocates without any obligations of leadership or real sense of community. Public squalor and environmental neglect were the inevitable results. 'Is Industry free to tumble out whatever horror of refuse it may have into the nearest crystal brook? Regardless of gods and men and little fishes. Is Free Industry free to convert all our rivers into Acherontic sewers?'[6]

Carlyle's attack on the dominant trends of English society left him no more favourable to those of France. 'Liberty, Equality and Fraternity' was the appealing battle-cry of the French Revolution. Liberty, for Carlyle, was what it produced in over-abundance, with licence, bloodshed and anarchy the result. There was too much chatter about the Rights of Man and not enough consideration of their duties. As for equality, such reduction of the established hierarchy to an undifferentiated rubble negated all opportunity for the proper leadership that modern societies so urgently required. Equality was also, as it had been for Burke, an idea at war with nature. 'The Universe itself is a Monarchy and Hierarchy'[7] and so the species of 'two-legged animals without feathers'[8] was well advised to harmonise with the divine order. Fraternity was a fine objective but could not be pursued alongside the individualist postulates that encumbered it. The ideologies of Enlightenment and revolution in France and of economic individualism in England had, in spite of their variations, led in a similar direction – to moral, social and political anarchy.

'The time is sick and out of joint.'[9] Thus wrote Carlyle in *Signs of the Times* in 1829, an essay title that indicates the prime concern of nearly all his extensive literary output. Even the historical studies were underscored with topical intent for, following the abdication of real social responsibility by the Church, history became the only reliable storehouse of human instruction. Both the glories and the follies of the past were laden with guidance for the present. That past mistakes be recognised and not repeated was as vital as deriving wise counsel from the actions of history's great men. In a period of turmoil no question seemed more important than that of knowing which way to turn. Signposting, however, could be entrusted only to those capable of true guidance. Herein lay the basis of the prevailing crisis. Leadership was the vital attribute for social health, yet those entrusted with the task were no longer capable of its proper exercise. Though necessarily structured into its separate parts society remains essentially one. When those with power and responsibility cut themselves adrift from the lower orders, and put pleasures and profits above general welfare, it is a clear indication that the ills of society are bordering on the terminal. In England *noblesse oblige* was a thing of the past. The titular aristocracy was given over to frippery, idle luxury, and bloodsports. 'What shall we say of the Idle Aristocracy, the Owners of the Soil of England; whose recognised function is that of handsomely consuming the rents of England, shooting the partridges of England, and as an agreeable amusement (if the purchase-money and other conveniences serve), dilettante-ing in Parliament and Quarter-Sessions for England?' Carlyle regarded the new commercial plutocracy as cold and calculating, dominated by the heartless Mammonism of Utilitarian ethics and laissez-faire economics. Its need was to 'understand that money alone is *not* the representative either of man's success in the world, or of man's duties to man'.[10]

For Carlyle the truth of power is that it carries the obligation of proper leadership. If one part of society is out of order, the inevitable consequence is a corresponding though dissimilar derangement in the other, in this case an untended people expiring in wretchedness and poverty. *Laissez-faire*, proclaimed as a policy of freedom, was functioning as one of neglect. With cash payment as the 'sole nexus of man to man',[11] those for whom work was simply not available were treated worse than animals. Carlyle noted the irony that the 'no work/no pay' equation was applied only to the manual worker and not to those for whom affluent leisure was regarded as a fitting way of life. 'How to deal with the Actual Labouring Millions of England? this is the imperatively pressing Problem of the Present, pressing with a truly fearful intensity and imminence in these very years and days. No Government can longer neglect it.'[12] Thus Carlyle in *Past and Present* (1843), a work which elicited the following praise from Friedrich Engels in a review published in the *Deutsch-Französiche Jahrbücher* (1844): 'Of all the fat books and thin pamphlets which have appeared in England in the past year for the entertainment or edification of "educated society", the above work is the only one which is worth reading . . . the only one which strikes a human chord, presents human relations and shows traces of a human point of view.'[13]

Carlyle's message was that the people's real needs have to be attended to as a matter of urgency. Guidance from a wise and caring shepherd is what is required. If those responsible for order and justice fail to provide it an abandoned flock will look to its own meagre resources. Obedience may be 'the primary duty of man',[14] but this is conditional upon obligations being met. There is here a rather Lockean note; that if obligations are not fulfilled revolt will ensue. But whereas for Locke conditional rebellion was a natural right, for Carlyle, who did not care much for the notion of rights, it was a natural consequence. Its occurrence was thus all the more inevitable. Neglect produced not merely the possibility of revolt contingent upon human choice but the certainty. This was the message that Carlyle thundered out to the perpetrators of the old aristocratic neglect and the new plutocratic disdain. Like an Old Testament prophet or a modern John Knox he warned that retribution was at hand and that it would wreak vengeance in the most destructive and arbitrary manner. His philosophy was that error cannot endure. 'All lies have a sentence of death written down against them, in Heaven's Chancery itself.'[15] Power without the exercise of responsibility was false and shortsighted. One way or another the truth would emerge.

Thus we come to what Carlyle saw as democracy. It was the phenomenon of mass politics taking the place of exhausted aristocratic rule. This Carlyle reiterated as the dominant tendency of his time. 'Democracy is everywhere the inexorable demand of these ages, swiftly fulfilling itself', he wrote in 1843. 'You cannot walk the streets without beholding Democracy announce itself.'[16] The message was repeated constantly after the revolutions of 1848–9 and again at the time of Britain's Second Reform Bill.[17] For Carlyle it was more than a mere constitutional or parliamentary arrangement, for it included the rebellious citizen spirit prevailing against constituted state power. Carlyle exhibited a certain negative sympathy for it as such; sympathy with the grievance rather than with the proposed solution. One disorder produces another. Unnatural neglect produces an unnatural and, hence, unstable response. There is an ambivalence in Carlyle's attitude to the disorders of his time. Though utterly contemptuous and also fearful of the rabble mass, for a time he could not conceal a certain glee at the prospect of the rich getting their just deserts. The spectre of violence is held out as an awful possibility with Carlyle hovering on the borderline that separates the issue of a warning to be heeded from the designation of a fate richly deserved.

Without the great French Revolution 'one would not know what to make of an age like this at all.'[18] Here lay the supreme indication that the old injustice could not endure; that the Day of Judgement awaits those who depart from God's law. Where Hegel noted the movement of the world spirit, and Tocqueville the inexorable march of providence in a democratic direction, from Carlyle we have the inevitable elemental force of natural justice. For the new commercial England of the cash nexus and Individual Mammonism, there could be no warning so apposite. 'Our England, our world cannot live as it is. It will connect itself with a God again, or go down with nameless throes and fire-consummation to the Devils.'[19] England might be on the move, a veritable hive of bustle and activity, but it was moving along the wrong path. Democracy itself, in the collective voice of 27 million, might command the direction, but if the path led over Land's End, as Carlyle believed, then England would soon find its firm foundations replaced by 'ocean-deeps and roaring abysses.'[20] Carlyle's epic on *The French Revolution* appeared in 1837 and thundered out the warning familiar also from the writings of Disraeli, Heine and Marx. Society could not remain as it was. The proximity of luxury and poverty were taken to be incompatible with social harmony. In certain situations an earthquake becomes the only means of complaint. Where Marx and Heine saw it producing communism, Carlyle held before the English aristocracy the fate of their French counterparts half a century before.

His record of these events has less historical accuracy than some that could be recommended, but no one could better convey an atmosphere of social cataclysm. The first part of Carlyle's account had to be rewritten after John Stuart Mill's maid mistakenly used it as kindling. Intended to stop a fire, it had instead been used to start one. Carlyle got back to work and produced what became one of the literary successes of the time. He was now a public figure with enough financial security to enter into some hard bargaining with his publishers. His interpretation received a second lease of life when Charles Dickens used it as the basis for *A Tale of Two Cities*. The French Revolution also dominated the outlook of Marx and Engels and, appropriately or otherwise, served as their basic model of how one social order is transformed into another. Thus, whether in history, literature or social theory, revolution's fearful image could not be ignored. Carlyle warned that high civilisation, the highest Europe had known, could plunge into ferocious barbarism with scarcely a warning and hardly a pause for breath.

Since Burke, a dominant strand of British thinking had viewed the French Revolution as a frenzied outburst of unjustified lunacy. A rationalist clique had somehow enticed a nation away from the traditional verities. Carlyle rendered this interpretation shallow not so much by denying it as by outlining the social and moral condition that made it possible. He believed that the aristocracy had succumbed to the temptations that privilege provides. They had 'nearly ceased either to guide or misguide' and had become 'little more than ornamental figures'. Of them and the clergy Carlyle asked 'What are you doing in God's fair Earth and Task-Garden; where whosoever is not working is begging or stealing? Wo, wo to themselves and to all if they can only answer: Collecting tithes, preserving game!' What of the monarch himself? 'Their King has become a King Popinjay',[21] weak, vacillating and obviously no hero, notes Carlyle. Dressed as the leader he was by descent born to be, he nevertheless proved himself quite unfitted for real leadership. Increasingly isolated from the people, he was unresponsive to their needs and ignorant of the real processes undermining a system he took to be eternal, and hence, as it turned out, woefully incapable of meeting the crisis once it came. With their material needs unmet, the people were also denied spiritual leadership, for a sham aristocracy found their natural companions in a sham clergy. The clergy's actions had become those of a propertied class collecting tithes and filling their larders. With the abnegation of true priesthood, a void was opened up to be filled by the Gospel according to Jean-Jacques. Thus Carlyle did not, like Burke, blame the *philosophes* for undermining religion in France, for the church had made itself contemptible. Once the faith had disappeared, no powerful barrier blocked the emergence of scepticism and 'French Philosophism'. With the king, aristocracy and clergy diverted from their proper responsibilities, Carlyle inquired of the condition of their dependent lower orders. 'Such are the shepherds of the people: and now how fares it with the flock? With the flock, as is inevitable, it fares ill, and even worse. They are not tended, they are only regularly shorn. They are sent for, to do statute-labour, to pay statute-taxes. . . . Untaught, uncomforted, unfed; to pine stagnantly in thick obscuration, in squalid destitution and obstruction: this is the lot of the millions.'[22]

The explosion of the French Revolution was thus almost a self-inflicted wound. Contributory negligence was a primary cause of the rape of France, for questions not listened to on earth are answered in heaven with dreadful ferocity. Sin leads to destruction and what Sodom and Gomorrah were to ancient Israel the French Revolution seemed to be to modern times. The democratic harvest may have been rapidly gathered in but it had been maturing for centuries past and the irony of biblical prophecy did not escape Carlyle's attention. 'Here, however, though by strange ways, shall the precept be fulfilled, and they that are greatest (much to their astonishment) become least.'[23]

'The French Revolution means here the open violent Rebellion and Victory, of disimprisoned Anarchy against corrupt worn-out Authority.'[24] Such was democracy in its violent and demonic prelude. As a destructive force it had some merit. On the constructive side it had serious defects. Carlyle's use of terms was not always exact but we may take the designation of 'anarchy' as applicable more to the various intermittent outbursts of popular fury and violence, and 'democracy' as referring to such constitutional arrangements as the calling of the Estates General, the baptism day of Democracy',[25] the creation of the National Assembly and the voting of the Constitutions of 1791 and 1793. In this situation anarchy and democracy advanced some way together in mutual reinforcement, but anarchy by its nature was even less durable. Democracy could establish a more settled order, although one based on premises at variance with human nature. Carlyle was pleased to observe that the principle of universal suffrage was confined within the aery realm of political humour, for not even French radicalism could achieve its actualisation. The division between *citoyen actif* and *passif* had confined electoral privilege to those paying a 'yearly tax equal to three days' labour'. Thus practice mocked principle, a mockery from which Carlyle himself could likewise not refrain. 'Nay, might there not be a Female Parliament too, with "screams from the Opposition benches", and "the honourable Member borne out in hysterics"?' This is as obviously ridiculous, and therefore presented in the same context, as a 'Children's Parliament'.[26] These gibes are clichéd and tasteless, but nevertheless interesting for their combination of radical reasoning and reactionary assumptions. On the former aspect it seems that Carlyle understood the logic of the radical cause better than did many of its proponents. He at least saw that the language of universal political rights contained no intrinsic justification for the exclusion of women. Mention of a children's parliament, even in jest, is also interesting as perhaps, even if only subconsciously, realising the dilemma of their relationship to parliamentary democracy. Yet Carlyle lurched from left to right, for he imagined not the inclusion of women and children in one parliament with men, but their having separate parliaments – in effect a recreation with new content of the medieval system of Estates.

What democracy the French achieved in practice proved unavailing on a number of scores. Economic problems remained and bread shortages had outlasted the demise of the old aristocracy. A revolution that proclaimed fraternity had instituted the Reign of Terror, and so a movement fuelled by opposition to one tyranny had replaced it with another. The more moderate revolutionaries, the Girondins, were treated with contempt by Carlyle. He associated them with the legalistic middle-class respectability that he so opposed in Britain. No solution to the social problem could be expected from them. The extremist Jacobins were viewed with greater favour. At least they understood the needs of the people. Their leader, the 'seagreen' Robespierre, had been the meanest member of the Estates General, but the final result of their mercurial rise and fall was merely the replacement of one sham aristocracy by another. Democracy by violence had instituted a levelling process, but equality it could not achieve. The impossible, by definition, was beyond attainment. Violent egalitarianism merely brought France to the lamentable condition achieved in Britain by more gradual means. 'Aristocracy of Feudal Parchment has passed away with a mighty rushing; and now, by a natural course, we arrive at Aristocracy of the Moneybag. It is the course through which all European Societies are, at this hour, travelling. Apparently a still baser sort of Aristocracy? An infinitely baser; the basest yet known.'[27] A financial, capitalist aristocracy hardly even laid claim to the social responsibilities traditionally adopted by their landed predecessors. Power without responsibility was justified by proclaiming the ethic of individual aggrandisement as conducive to the general good. Thus was selfishness elevated to a form of altruism. This may sound like a presentiment of Marx, but, as we saw with Tocqueville, there was also a strand of conservative thought which decried the heartlessness of commercial wealth. Already at the time of the French Revolution Burke had noted that 'the age of chivalry is gone. That of sophisters, economists and calculators' had succeeded it.[28]

The democratic movement in Britain could be welcomed as a punishment for past errors, but was otherwise of little avail. Eleven years after the passage of the 1832 First Reform Act, Carlyle took stock of its consequences and declared himself unimpressed. For the 'Tenpound Franchiser' it seemed to matter little who misrepresented him in Parliament. MPs of each side continued primarily to serve their own small clique and ignored the real needs of the nation. The only slight benefit derived from the parliamentary fixation was that it helped keep politics off the streets. Violence was thus replaced by oratory. Carlyle's criticism was a rather different one from the disillusion that gave birth to Chartism, for he had a lower estimate of the supposed parliamentary panacea. The Chartists' demand for an even wider franchise was, at best, only an amplification of prevailing disorders; an extension of the very mentality it ought to overcome. It was still within the logic of representative government, a creed that could only produce more bribery, mammonism and place-seeking. The malpractices of the few are extended to the many. It was a multiple futility to assume that franchise extension guaranteed the solution of pressing national problems. Electoralism had firstly encouraged the myth that what could be was ascertained by the counting of heads. Secondly, it had ignored the point (familiar to us from Hegel) that, as the franchise is extended, the power of each individual voter is correspondingly reduced. Thirdly, it functioned as a diversion from the fundamentally important question of how that vote was used. Fourthly, it concentrated on the legislature, the talking section, whereas Carlyle was more concerned with the active, doing part, the executive.

In the mid-1840s Carlyle was still relatively unworried by the prospect of the ignorant getting the vote, for there was little worth defending in the way their 'betters' had used it. After the 1848 revolutions his attitude hardened. Failure was all around. Not merely failure in achievement, plenty of that though there was, but also, yet more serious, a failure to understand what had to be done. From the Baltic to the Mediterranean the monarchs, by their spineless capitulation to the mob, had acknowledged their redundancy. 'Not one of them turned round, and stood upon his Kingship, as upon a right he could afford to die for, or to risk his skin upon; by no manner of means.' So even monarchy itself seemed to lack the faith that the democratic tide could be turned. Kings had once provided far-sighted and courageous leadership. All that they were now good for was playacting. 'They had merely got-on the attributes and clothes of rulers, and were surreptitiously drawing the wages, while the work remained undone.'[29] Such was Carlyle's February 1850 retrospective on the turbulence of the previous few years. The oddity of his account is not so much that he distorts by over-generalisation but that it reads like a plausible statement of nearly two years earlier. Then the kings had fallen like ninepins, politics had become an affair conducted by masses on the streets, and fear and uncertainty abounded. Carlyle, however, was writing in the aftermath of revolution. By and large (and France was a large exception) the monarchs had reasserted themselves, albeit with certain constitutional compromises. Carlyle chose not to go into this. Perhaps for him a constitutional monarch was no monarch at all, for Carlyle's basic point is that kings were no longer what they had been.

The same, it seemed, could be said of parliaments.

> The old Parliaments were authentic entities; came upon indispensable work; and were in earnest to their very finger-ends about getting it done. . . . In modern Parliaments, again, indeed ever down from the Long Parliament, I note a sad gradual falling-off in this matter of 'veracity,' – which, alas, means a falling-off in all real use, or possible advantage, there can be to mankind in such Institutions.[30]

Parliament at best could be an advisory body; but 658 'miscellaneous persons' could not hope to accomplish any proper business, least of all with 27 millions, 'mostly fools' listening. Time and again Carlyle berated the idea of voting as a panacea. Throughout the world more and more people seemed to believe that if more and more people voted then all would be well. Such people would vote for this or that 'so this or that will thenceforth *be*.'[31] For Carlyle what could be was determined by the implacable nature of reality rather than by the transient inclinations of the many and, certainly, the fool's vote was of no value in deciding the issue of what it was wise to do. Given the bribery and drunkenness surrounding the electoral circus Carlyle concluded that 'the mass of men consulted at hustings, upon any high matter whatsoever, is as ugly an exhibition of human stupidity as this world sees'.[32]

By the time of the 1867 Reform Act Carlyle was referring to 'the unanimous vulgar' and their 'torrent of brutish hoofs and hobnails'.[33] 'Shooting Niagara' was his term for what others saw as Disraeli's 'leap in the dark'. Carlyle began by pondering democracy and the baleful influences of 'Penny Newspapers', 'so-called religions' and 'unlimited Free Trade', but his account, published in 1867, was a distinctly unusual contribution to the thriving national debate on the issue of reform, for it was pitched at a rather more fundamental level. Such questions of precise detail as to whether the town labourer should be granted privileges unavailable to his counterpart in the countryside or whether constituency boundaries be redrawn in accord with recent shifts of population were not on Carlyle's agenda. For him there was no intrinsic moral or practical merit in political participation. 'Manhood suffrage', treated as one of the 'stupidest absurdities', is ridiculed by juxtaposition with 'Horsehood, Doghood'. As for its concomitant '"the equality of men"', any man equal to any other; Quashee Nigger to Socrates or Shakespeare; Judas Iscariot to Jesus Christ; – and Bedlam and Gehanna equal to the New Jerusalem, shall we say?'[34] No such assumptions could set society aright. Whether achieved through violence on the streets or votes in parliament, democracy was seen as a false response to social needs.

What, in Carlyle's opinion, should have been occupying the attention of the British people was the question of proper leadership. Britain had the fortunate advantage of a 'Titular Aristocracy' who 'are not hated or disliked by any Class of the People, but on the contrary are looked up to . . . by all classes, lower and lowest class included'.[35] This deference, in terms of all Carlyle had written over the previous four decades, must have seemed rather more than the aristocracy deserved. Just a year before, when addressing Edinburgh University students in 1866, Carlyle declared that for about six hundred years, that is from 1066 until the time of Charles I, England had got aristocrats on the basis of their desert. From that time, however, it became the practice that a peerage could be purchased. As its price went up its true value went down. That, however, was no longer the main point. The urgent question in 1867 was whether 'a body of brave men, and of beautiful polite women, furnished *gratis* as they are' could 'be good for something, in a society mostly fallen vulgar and chaotic like ours!' Could they combine with their unrecognised humble superiors, 'the unclassed Aristocracy by nature . . . who derive their patent of nobility direct from Almighty God'? One aristocracy was already gradually coming into contact with another. This partnership offered the best prospect Britain had that 'Cosmos be achieved upon this our unspeakable Chaos'.[36]

As an alternative to the prevailing focus on representation Carlyle recommended a little more concern with sovereignty. The proper relationship between monarch and parliament had long been completely upset. How could the 'national palaver' conduct business with any prospect of efficiency or rectitude? The question of how democracy and sovereignty could co-exist was certainly 'the hugest question ever heretofore propounded to Mankind'.[37]

Democracy was shallow. It only facilitated the expression of surface opinion. At that level the people's views were clear, but Carlyle chose to regard them as a kind of code for their actual wishes. These, he conveniently concluded, consisted of a cry for real rather than bogus leadership. The message he chose to derive from Chartism was that the people actually wanted guidance more than votes. This coincided with his own inclination not to let the people rule, but to advocate that the best rule over and for them.

The emphasis here is similar to the one that led him to deride Utilitarianism as a Pig Philosophy. Democracy was concerned merely with quantity, whereas Carlyle regarded moral tone and the quality of leadership as the most essential. Democracy sought changes at the superficial level of the constitutional system rather than in the mentality of the people. It forgot that greatness had been found 'under strange outward circumstances: Saint Paul and his brother Apostles were politically slaves'.[38] Cortez and Pizarro came from the society that produced the Inquisition. Such was his hatred of European liberalism that Carlyle chose instead to laud the infamous dictator Rodriguez Francia who had sent Congress packing and ruled as dictator of Paraguay from 1814 until his death in 1840. A society based on authority and obedience was held preferable to the style, manner and content of emerging liberal democracy. In the latter spiritual concerns had given way to a mechanical age of systems and calculations, but 'we shall never, by all the machinery in Birmingham, discover the True and Worthy'.[39]

As against the system-mongers, Carlyle believed that if you got the right leader to the top, the system would take care of itself. 'Get *him* for governor, all is got; fail to get him, though you had Constitutions plentiful as blackberries, and a Parliament in every village, there is nothing yet got!'[40] In Carlyle's view real worth was extremely difficult to recognise. It never had and never would be attained through a universal vote. 'The worthiest, if he appealed to universal suffrage, would have but a poor chance. John Milton, inquiring of universal England what the worth of Paradise Lost was, received for answer, Five Pounds Sterling.' To decide who was up and who was down, who should rule and who should serve, was not the prerogative of man. Adapting Calvinist theology to politics Carlyle decided that it was God who had created born leaders and born slaves. To enfranchise the latter was the Devil's Gospel, an invitation to 'folly, knavery, falsity, gluttonous imbecility, lowmindedness and cowardice'.[41] To realise the need to replace general representation by the heroic free man was one thing. How to recognise the right person and how to elevate him was quite something else.

Book Two of *Past and Present* (1843) was based on the medieval Latin chronicle of Jocelyn of Brakelond. The hero Samson is a member of a twelfth-century monastic community. Through a process of discussion among the twelve monks he is chosen as Abbot. Without hustings or ballot-box, wisdom is recognised and elevated to the highest position. Samson was without previous experience in governing but, having learnt the art of obeying, he thereby had the first prerequisite for ruling. He succeeded old Abbot Hugo, who had allowed the monastery to fall into debt and decay. Abbot Samson, by contrast, had a developed sense of veracity and, impartial as to previous friendships and enmities, brought the fittest men to the top. Lazy monks and unjust bailiffs soon learnt that the days of disorder were gone. Overcoming many difficulties, Samson, who remained Abbot for thirty years, eventually brought order, vitality, solvency and spirituality to his community.

The moral for modern times was, first, that quality, from however humble a source, should be recognised and put in charge; and second, that the process is accomplished by more thoughtful and quieter means than the competitive babblings of the electoral process. The mode of emergence to leadership was very important for Carlyle. If the process were mystical it was likely to produce a better result than if it were mechanical and explicitly articulated. The truer feelings of men lie beneath the surface and emerge only as a result of a contemplative frame of mind and a proper mental orientation. There are intimations here of Rousseau's distinction between the General Will and particular individual wills, for the individual conscience has to be tapped at a deeper level than that of selfish reaction. 'Votes of men are worth collecting, if convenient. True, their opinions are generally of little wisdom, and can on occasion reach to all conceivable and inconceivable degrees of folly; but their instincts, where these can be deciphered, are wise and human; these, hidden under the noisy utterance of what they call their opinions, are the unspoken sense of man's heart, and well deserve attending to. Know well what the people inarticulately feel, for the Law of Heaven itself is dimly written there.'[42] In contrast a contested modern election produces selfishness, ambition and partisanship. As such it is unable to attain the optimal benefit for society as a whole.

What has appeared as a total opposition to the idea of democratic choice now needs some slight modification, for there was, at this stage, an element of consent in Carlyle's approach. He wanted the rulers to be both acceptable and accepted by the populace at large. What he opposed was the modern method of political mediation. His politics was not one of choice on the model of consumer purchasing, but of the more spiritual and reverential acceptance such as should, for example, exist in the relationship of a congregation to a Church dignitary. Furthermore Carlyle, notwithstanding his opposition to most of the Enlightenment and revolutionary ideology, accepted the axiom of the career open to talent. Abbot Samson was 'the son of poor parents'[43] and throughout his lengthy catalogue of heroes Carlyle delighted in emphasising their humble origins. Martin Luther was 'brought-up poor, one of the poorest of men'.[44] Robert Burns was a Scottish peasant. Neither the barber Richard Arkwright nor book-keeper Robert Clive were born to life's advantages. In tracing the emergence of James Watt, Carlyle depicts the contrast between the luxury and frivolity of the aristocracy and the striving under adverse conditions of society's natural leaders. 'Neither had Watt of the Steam engine a heroic origin, any kindred with the princes of this world. The princes of this world were shooting their partridges; noisily, in Parliament or elsewhere, solving the question, Head or Tail? while this man with blackened fingers, with grim brow, was searching out, in his workshop, the Fire-secret; or, having found it, was painfully wending to and fro in quest of a "moneyed man", as indispensable man-midwife of the same. Reader, thou shalt admire what is admirable, not what is dressed in admirable.'[45] There is here a kind of social rather than political democracy in that the ablest man might come from any part of society and should not have his path blocked by anachronistic and dysfunctional social attitudes.

This approach clearly delegitimises prevailing power structures. The nobility, by reneging on their obligations, were effectively forfeiting all claims to be regarded as a 'real' aristocracy. 'How many of our Titular Aristocracy will prove real gold when thrown into the crucible?' Carlyle hoped that some worth might still be found in them, but otherwise looked to 'the unclassed Aristocracy by nature, not inconsiderable in numbers, and supreme in faculty, in wisdom, human talent, nobleness and courage, "who derive their patent of nobility direct from Almighty God"'.[46] As for kings, Carlyle was all in favour of having them, but not necessarily of the hereditary variety. 'The King merely *dressed* in King-gear'[47] was worth less than the likes of Cromwell and Napoleon who, by dint of ability and personality, forced themselves into national leadership. Cromwell, indeed, had been implicated in the death of an hereditary monarch. He was rated above Napoleon who did not remain true to the forces that propelled his ascent but took on the imagery of his opponents. Carlyle's leader reaches the top by force or acclamation rather than inheritance. This is the politics of populist paternalism in that the elite, although strictly differentiated from the mass, both draw on and are accepted by the lower orders in whose service they operate.

Carlyle's longest and last major work, however, was a biography of a hereditary monarch, the *History of Frederick II of Prussia, called Frederick the Great*. Frederick was a friend of Voltaire. He flirted with the Enlightenment and was thus, unwittingly, in some ways implicated in the French Revolution. He was the best that the eighteenth century could produce, but for Carlyle that was no great praise, and clearly he was an unlikely hero for Carlyle to devote six volumes and thirteen years of writing to. Albert La Valley has suggested that Carlyle was probably attracted to Frederick 'not merely by chance but by the continuity of the Prussian state as the one centrally stable and masterful human organization around him'.[48] The Prussian monarchy had been alone in resisting the democratic contagions of 1848–9 and so obviously had some mettle that others lacked.

The mentality and apparatus of military might were advantages that Frederick II had inherited. In Carlyle's account it appears that the real hero of Prussia's ascent was Frederick's father, Friedrich Wilhelm. Neither contemporary nor modern scholarship concur in this flattery. Professor Trevor-Roper notes that 'this brutal, boorish tyrant ruled his country by stick and gallows, hanged innocent men without compunction, and forced his eighteen-year-old son to witness the summary execution of his closest friend.'[49] Carlyle did not deny these aspects; nor was he deterred by them. Friedrich Wilhelm's merit is that he was a man of action who, immediately he had the chance, set about doing the right thing. Carlyle insisted that all people should at least be doing something. His heroes are doing something positive and decisive, like Jesus driving out the money-lenders, and Cromwell the parliament. Friedrich Wilhelm set about creating a Prussian state that was trim and efficient. Looking neither right nor left in fear of those he might upset or offend, he ensured that work was rewarded and idleness sent packing. Unlike Napoleon, who set up his own court, Friedrich Wilhelm reduced his to the bone, discharging 'a whole regiment of superfluous official persons, court-flunkies, inferior, superior and supreme, in the most ruthless manner.' Here was a king who, more than any other, made what Carlyle now wanted, a revolution from above. He had inherited court fruppery, flunkies and lackies and left 'a Prussia made after his own image; the most thrifty, hardy, rigorous and Spartan country any modern King ever ruled over; and himself (if he thought of that) a King indeed'. Such a man, Carlyle thought, 'would not have risen in modern Political Circles; man unchoosable at hustings or in caucas'.[50] The son came to a throne in good order. The father had put it there and so clearly seems the greater hero. Yet both had inherited the monarchy. It was, thus, sheer chance that placed them both in the right position.

While Carlyle was writing his history Prussia was preparing for its greatest triumphs, the victories over Austria and then France, followed by the creation of the German Empire in 1871. What Carlyle admired in Prussia was its military spirit and no-nonsense manner. Here words gave way to deeds and the army that owned a nation ensured that order, discipline and regulated work prevailed. The Prussian victory at Sedan prompted the following entry in Carlyle's journal:

> No war so wonderful did I ever read of, and the results of it I reckon to be salutary, grand, and hopeful, beyond any which have occurred in my time. . . . Alone of nations, Prussia seems still to understand something of the art of governing, and of fighting enemies of said art. Germany, from of old, has been the peaceablest, most pious, and in the end most valiant and terrible of nations. Germany ought to be President of Europe, and will again, it seems, be tried with that office for another five centuries or so.[51]

From Abbot Samson to the Prussian kaisers is a long journey. In his earlier works Carlyle hoped for the elevation from below of recognised merit. By the time of his later writings the emphasis had gradually shifted. It now seemed that any stirrings from below were too dangerous. A false democratic spirit was afoot and so an established hierarchy should not be upset. If it was corrupt the best hope lay in self-renewal, as, according to Carlyle's account, had happened in Prussia. On this model retribution was to be averted by not incurring it in the first place. Thus the later Carlyle, who softened his earlier criticisms of aristocracy, hoping that some among them might prove worthy of the title, similarly came to await the arrival of monarchs possessed of the inner essence of rule and not merely the outer garments.

Carlyle's critique of industrialism and parliamentarism is both incisive and powerful; his depiction of alternative orders is fairly clear although somewhat sketchy and distinctly anachronistic, but we are given little indication as to how society is to get from here to there.

We know that old evils cannot endure. But do not new evils replace them? It seems a divine command that those best fitted to be shepherds of the flock should become so, yet, taking his earlier example, it is hard to see how the leadership process of a small medieval monastery can provide a model for industrial nation-states. Carlyle, who scorned elected leaders, would no doubt have been equally contemptuous of elevation through competitive examinations. Such processes were, in their separate ways, equally mechanical and equally distant from the search for authenticity and virtue. Furthermore, no one made it more clear than Carlyle himself that the social/economic basis for real unity and community no longer existed. Out of what other fabric, then, was it to be spun? Ideas are not enough. We know from Carlyle's account of the French Revolution that ideas only have their full effect when material conditions provide a basis for their acceptance. History, we gather, works with a purpose, yet that purpose seems to be retribution, justice in its negative rather than its positive aspects; a justice that is vengeful and destructive, but not one out of which a fair and settled order can easily emerge.

Having begun his literary career as an advocate of political responsibility, Carlyle closed it as one of obedience, intolerance and strict sovereign authority. His love affair with Germany led him from romantic literature to Prussian militarism. The Prussian political model may be more plausible and slightly less anachronistic than the medieval monastic one, in that it did survive into the twentieth century, but can hardly be deemed adequate for modern times. Its subordination of democracy and human rights to militarist authoritarianism would, for Carlyle, be seen as a virtue, but could hardly have advanced its continuing legitimacy in a twentieth-century context. For Carlyle true legitimacy comes not from the inheritance of a title but through manifestly deserving it. So here again, as with the elevation of Abbot Samson, the production of the right man for the right job is problematical. The chance of birth is as uncertain as any other method.

Though he looked backward Carlyle was not reactionary in the sense of wanting a return to the medieval past. He accepted and in some ways admired industrial society. It exhibited a vast display of energy with world-transforming consequences, but remained sadly lacking in coherent organisation. From the example of medieval society it might well derive a proper sense of purpose and order. The army was the modern institution which, more than any other, maintained a clear continuity with its earlier history. Ideally Carlyle would have liked the military model to be spread outward to envelop the politics and economy of modern societies. An organised economy would thus resemble the army in being explicitly structured, hierarchical, cohesive, purposive and authoritarian. One critic notes that 'Carlyle would like to be the drill sergeant of the future',[52] but in his last years there seemed little prospect of this as Carlyle came to feel increasingly isolated and unheeded. The times remained as sick and out of joint as ever and Carlyle scarcely knew which way to turn. Better then, he concluded, to stand still and hope that the established authorities could prove worthy of the trust reposed in them. In early career Carlyle comes near to baying for blood; he ends by keeping his fingers crossed.

Carlyle, so numerous modern commentators assure us, is now virtually unread. He is also said to be unreadable, yet hard-headed publishers have kept his major works in print. Carlyle's baroque, idiosyncratic style, a source of awe and astonishment to his contemporaries, is not easily penetrable to ours. Yet in his time Carlyle was a luminary of the London literary scene, and a friend of Browning, Dickens, Ruskin, Thackeray and Tennyson. Even before leaving his native Scotland he referred to 'us English',[53] yet as a rural Scot in the urban, English metropolis, with a spoken accent that singled him out almost as much as his literary style, he revelled in being both in and out of place. As an outsider on the inside he was, even more than Marx at the same time, ideally positioned to be suitably appalled by his surroundings. Yet, unlike Marx, who was hardly known outside German emigré circles, Carlyle used his alienation from the dominant ideologies to become a public figure.

Though without disciples Carlyle's voice provided the cardinal, contemporary moral critique of the new liberal, industrial order. His earlier writings, typified by *Signs of the Times* (1829) and *Chartism* (1840), railed against the miseries suffered by the labouring classes and the frivolities enjoyed by their rulers. This earlier Carlyle long enjoyed the widespread approval of the political left, appalled though they often were by the turn taken by his later writings. Engels' enthusiasm of 1844 turned to scorn a few years later. Reviewing *Latter-Day Pamphlets* (1850) Marx and Engels deplored 'the decline of literary genius' and its replacement by 'highly indignant bluster'. Engels later concluded that 'the February [1848] Revolution made [Carlyle] an out-and-out reactionary. His righteous wrath against the Philistines turned into sullen Philistine grumbling at the tide of history that cast him ashore'.[54] It is tempting to follow Engels in using the mid-century revolutions as convenient markers for a shift of attitude. The same can be done for Marx and Engels themselves who never again recovered their earlier optimism after the working classes of Europe failed to consolidate their revolutionary break-through. For Tocqueville the 1848–9 revolutions also marked a watershed, but of a different type, for his mistrust of democracy deepened perceptibly after witnessing the anarchy that accompanied the eruption from below. For Carlyle, however, no clear-cut dividing line is available. The *frisson* of revolution produced the satisfaction of divine justice meted out but also disgust at the stupidity and anarchy that accompanied it. Carlyle was less appalled by the rise of the masses than by the political demands made in their name. His concern for duty, order and discipline gained primacy before the February Revolution, as can be seen in *On Heroes and Hero-Worship* (1841), *Dr Francia* (1843) and *Cromwell* (1845), and continued through to his six volumes on Frederick the Great (1858–65). Idle-ness, the Calvinists' *bête noire*, had first flaunted itself at the summit of society. Carlyle's later research unearthed it at the base. As the attack on court flunkeydom and dandyism decreased, the focus of condemnation turned to the 'Demerara Nigger', the Irish potato-eaters and thirty thousand alleged seamstresses who could not knit a stitch. Now the extreme right found more to their liking. Bismarck wrote to Carlyle on his eightieth birthday and the Kaiser awarded him the Prussian Order of Merit. In our own century Goebbels and Hitler have been among his admirers and a wide body of opinion regards Carlyle as a precursor of fascism. In the final balance Carlyle's emphasis on opportunity, consent and responsibility weighs less heavily than his acclaim for any regime that crushed all intima-tions of liberal democratic pluralism. Was not this an implicit accep-tance of the impossibility of achieving the type of community that he had recommended in *Past and Present*? This left only the stark alternatives of democracy or autocracy, with Carlyle opting unequi-vocally for the latter.

PART III Democracy and Discrimination

7 'Beings of an Inferior Order': The Ideology of Black Subordination in the USA

The extension of citizenship in the west was only achieved through the gradual removal of formidable legal and ideological barriers. Political power was by convention the preserve of rich, propertied men. This position they rationalised as the rightful reward of wealth and intelligence. Changing social mores gradually facilitated the entry of the unpropertied and female upon the political stage. In Europe, race as a political factor did not figure as prominently as in the United States of America. The major European imperial powers ruled over vast numbers of black subjects, but they were far away in territories ruled under quite different principles from those declared at home. The situation of the United States was quite different. It, in effect, had internal colonialism. Its Third World of black subjugation was on territory contiguous with that of its free, more liberal north. As the United States was also the country with the most explicit attachment to modern freedoms, this relationship was eventually bound to be a source of conflict. Democracy, as we have been using the term, is, centrally, about the rights of citizenship. In all the European imperial countries racialist ideologies have placed particular ethnic groups below the level of democratic rights. The ideology of black subordination that we shall outline from American evidence, is, then, a particularly stark instance of a much broader part of western thinking.

Behind the liberatory phrases of the United States Declaration of Independence lay a profound irony. Thomas Jefferson, whose inspired words have provided linguistic ammunition for radicals ever since, was himself a slave-owner. Did his enslaved blacks not deserve inclusion among 'all men . . . endowed by their Creator with certain unalienable Rights'? Presumably so, for Jefferson's original draft of the Declaration included a passage, later struck out by Congress, in which he attacked George III's complicity in the slave trade: 'He has waged cruel war against human nature itself violating its most sacred rights of life and liberty in the persons of a distant people who never offended him, captivating and carrying them into slavery in another hemisphere, or to incur miserable death in their transportation thither.'[1] It was, of course, easier to attack the slave trade, especially when treating it as the king's transportation, than to disturb the social arrangements of his own country. Yet those rights of 'life and liberty' violated by being carried into slavery, presumably remained equally violated when held therein. Some certainly saw it this way for in the few decades after the revolution a number of slave-owners, influenced by Enlightenment ideas, freed their slaves. Between 1790 and 1810 the south's free black population grew from 32 357 to 108 265, whilst from Pennsylvania in 1780 through to New Jersey in 1804 every northern state freed its slaves. But Jefferson doubted the capacity of the free blacks to integrate successfully into the wider community, and in 1782 recommended to the state of Virginia that their slaves be set free and colonised elsewhere, a pattern of thinking that led to the founding of the American Colonization Society in 1817 and of Liberia three years later.

The universalistic language of primary legal documents provides a powerful argument for political incorporation. This the United States for long managed to resist and the exclusions imposed on blacks and women were not overcome until well into this century. When the Constitution was framed, certain presuppositions concerning exclusion from 'the people' were of basic influence and thus too self-evident to require explicit delineation. For later generations such assumptions can no longer be taken for granted and it is a service to us that the public discussion on ratification of the Constitution occasionally brought to the surface important aspects of the dominant view. In the second number of *The Federalist Papers*, for example, John Jay declared his satisfaction

> that Providence has been pleased to give this one connected country, to one united people; a people descended from the same ancestors, speaking the same language, professing the same religion, attached to the same principles of government, very similar in their manners and customs.[2]

Providence had acted with convenient and characteristic discrimination. Dislodged native Americans and displaced Africans were obviously excluded from this united community of white, Anglo-Saxon Protestants. Jefferson's clause against the slave trade had been omitted from the Declaration to accommodate the wishes of South

Carolina and Georgia. Tom Paine, by that time a falling star, had wanted an anti-slavery clause in the Constitution, but his hopes were dashed for similar reasons. A 'more perfect union' was difficult enough both to achieve and sustain as it was. A challenge to slavery would have ruined the possibility of securing the southern states for the new federation. Thus the Constitution, though not directly explicit, was clear enough on this issue. The Senate was to be composed of two members from each state. This equality of representation benefited the less populous states and countered the influence of numbers represented in the lower house. Here self-interest pulled in different directions. The larger the electorate the larger the state's representation, but also the greater the likelihood of the suffrage being exercised by elements deemed undesirable. Article 1, Section 2, of the Constitution declared that the numerical basis for representation 'shall be determined by adding to the whole Number of free Persons, including those bound to Service for a Term of years, and excluding Indians not taxed, three fifths of all other Persons'. Slaves thus came into the gaze of the Constitution's framers as 'other persons'. In strict logic three-fifths Congressional weighting should have given each slave three-fifths of a vote, but the precise franchise qualification was left for each individual state to determine, with predictable results.

The free blacks clearly occupied an economic category different from that of the slaves. What, then, were to be their political rights? Myrdal noted that 'at the time of the making of the Constitution, free Negroes had the right of suffrage in all the original states, except South Carolina and Georgia'.[3] Six states in fact never excluded blacks from the franchise, but as these were all in New England and New York, where few of them lived, the consequences were slight. Other states altered their constitutions so as explicitly to exclude black voters.[4] In time the vestiges of eighteenth-century radicalism declined in significance as America's black population was categorised as subject to rather than part of 'the people' of whom the political order consisted. The best-known and most influential evidence of this attitude is the testimony of Chief Justice Taney in the 1857 Dred Scott case. To determine whom the Constitution protected, the Chief Justice decided to probe the mental world from which it derived. At that time, he concluded, blacks

had for more than a century before been regarded as beings of an inferior order, and altogether unfit to associate with the white race, either in social or political relations, and so far inferior that they had no rights which the white man was bound to respect; and that the Negro might justly and lawfully be reduced to slavery for his benefit.[5]

Thus blacks were within the domain of the Constitution but outside its protection; subjects but not citizens. In the south, black voting would have been impossible whatever the law stated, for the country contained two sectors with different socioeconomic forms; slavery on the one side, free wage labour on the other. In terms of economics Barrington Moore has argued that the two systems could in fact coexist. 'Plantation slavery in the South . . . was not an economic fetter upon industrial capitalism. If anything the reverse may have been true; it helped to promote American industrial growth in the early stages.'[6] But, as he also realises, the political consequences were more destabilising. Congress, the executive and the Supreme Court took decisions binding on all the various states. Norms of citizenship were bound to be established whose range could not be too diverse. Thus the question of which side would dominate at the centre became a crucial one.

The nature of the federal balance of power could not be finally settled by the Constitution while the country was still expanding. From the original east-coast states, migration westward brought in new territories that in time attained their own separate statehood. How each new member would align on the slavery issue was a source of continual tension for both sides. The Missouri Compromise of 1820 balanced the admission of Missouri as a slave state with Maine as a free one, and prohibited slavery from territory north of 36°30'. (This was repealed in the Kansas–Nebraska Act of 1854.) In 1846 the Wilmot Proviso banned slavery from all territory taken from Mexico. The southern slave states were clearly on the defensive. The growth of population in the north was shifting the political balance in Congress their way. For the white south the anti-federalist and states' rights theories best suited their interests. The slave-holder Thomas Dew voiced his unease about the north outvoting the south. A situation had emerged, he complained, in which one set of people were legislating for another. Similar unease was the basis of John Calhoun's rather tortuous theory of 'concurrent majorities'.[7] Calhoun's plan would have given socioeconomic minorities, by which he meant the white south, a veto on the decisions of the majority. Thus government decisions would represent the whole community rather

than temporary and unstable majorities. The search for constitutional safeguards as well as the rise of an explicit pro-slavery
ideology, to which we shall now turn, were clear indicators that the
'peculiar institution' was entering its terminal phase.

Britain had banned the slave trade in 1808, but not until 1833 were
slaves in the British dominions purchased and set free. It was in the
second quarter of the nineteenth century that slavery was pushed
decisively on to the defensive. In 1831 Nat Turner's slave insurrection
brought to the surface the owners' suppressed insecurities. In the
same year, in the relative safety of Boston, Massachusetts, William
Lloyd Garrison founded his abolitionist journal *The Liberator*. A
year later he organised the New England Anti-Slavery Society. In
1833 the American Anti-Slavery Society was founded, followed in
1838 by the American and Foreign Anti-Slavery Society. The same
general drift was even clearer elsewhere in the western hemisphere.
During the 1820s slavery had been abolished in Guatemala, Mexico,
Argentina, Peru, Chile, Bolivia and Paraguay. In the early 1840s it
came to an end in Colombia, Venezuela and Ecuador (although not
in Brazil until 1888). Meanwhile, in the southern states of the USA,
the extent of slavery was increasing. There had been less than seven
hundred thousand slaves in 1790. By 1830 their numbers had grown
to over two million, reaching a peak of just under four million in
1860.

It has often been noted that whereas left theorising is provoked by
particular social conditions, conservative theorising emerges on the
defensive, as the justification of a *status quo* under attack. In the case
of the slave-owners it was the steady drift of opinion away from their
own standpoint that brought forth the articulation of a conservative
ideology in their defence.

If, as some believe, the south was another country, then the
slave-owners might have felt secure in their own practices and not
had to justify them in terms appropriate for outside opinion. In fact,
although the south had another social system and a different form of
economy, it spoke and addressed the north in a common language
from the standpoint of a shared cultural background. Throughout the
considerable bulk of slave-holding apologetics the constant frame of
reference is that of western civilisation and Christianity. This appeal
was thus to standards that had the highest status wherever European
culture was established. Ironically, part of their selection from within
that culture drew from aspects that their forebears had left Europe to
escape. In place of the New World–New England ideology of capi-

talism and individual freedom we find an appeal to the Old World medievalism of corporatism, estate, community, stability, fixed hierarchy, *noblesse oblige* and, the very essence of feudal mentality, the inheritance of class position. Thus, the ideology of the white south has its place, as Eugene Genovese noted in respect of George Fitzhugh, with the Romantic reaction that emerged in Europe in the late eighteenth century as the nostalgic cry of a sinking social order.[8]

If the slave-owners were nearer to the reactionary mentality of the Old World than the egalitarian one of the New, we must consider how they related to what has since become established as the American ideology – the ideas of the 'founding fathers' as embodied in the 1776 Declaration of Independence and the 1787 Constitution. It was on the basis of the inalienable rights asserted in the Declaration that, in 1831, William Lloyd Garrison decided to 'strenuously contend for the immediate enfranchisement of our slave population', and in our own time the 1968 National Advisory Commission on Civil Disorders noted that 'Negro protest, for the most part, has been firmly rooted in the basic values of American society, seeking not their destruction but their fulfilment.'[9]

White southerners, however, preferred to emphasise the Constitution, which ordered their affairs in relation to each other, rather than the Declaration delivered to the former colonial power. The Constitution had left slavery intact and had allowed each state to regulate its own electoral franchise. The equal provision of seats for each state in the Senate stemmed the domination that the more populous industrial northern states might have imposed over the more agricultural southern ones. In allowing each black a three-fifths weighting in estimating appropriate state influence in the House of Representatives, the mass of unenfranchised blacks unwittingly and irrespective of their will strengthened the federal power of southern whites.

In the south, the liberatory rhetoric of the Declaration was derided for what in truth it was – a legacy of the over-abstract, rationalist philosophy of the Enlightenment. White southerners could echo de Maistre in finding that mentality devoid of application to particular circumstances. In 1837 William Harper of South Carolina made nonsense of the claims that men are born free and equal possessors of certain inalienable rights. Rather he thought that 'no man was ever born free. . . . Man is born in a state of the most helpless dependence on others'. Similarly 'men', or as Calhoun pointed out, children, are born to great inequalities of condition. So-called natural rights pertain solely to an imagined state of nature, but people are born into pre-existing societies with their respective hierarchies and conventions. From these they derive the specific rights which are appropriate to their particular circumstances. Thus against the abstract universalism of the Rights of Man, the defenders of slavery recommended respect for historically established conventions and laws. As for Jefferson's utilitarian 'pursuit of Happiness' as an unalienable right, Harper asserted much the opposite; that the whole purpose of law was precisely to restrain people from what they might classify as their happiness. As against the radical Enlightenment optimism which tended to the belief that mankind would benefit from being set free, a mentality that often approached anarchism, the conservative reaction asserted instead that human nature is unruly and needs to be controlled. Harper belonged to a class and a period of history convinced of the causal link between radical liberal ideology and the French Revolutionary Terror. Behind the high-flown abstractions of Jefferson they feared the desecrations of Robespierre. 'And', asked William Harper, 'is it by this . . . well-sounding, but unmeaning verbiage of natural equality and inalienable rights, that our lives are to be put in jeopardy, our property destroyed, and our political institutions overturned or endangered?'[10] In *Slavers Ordained of God* (1857) the Reverend Frederick Ross identified Jefferson's Declaration with atheism. 'All this, every word of it, every jot and tittle, is the liberty and equality claimed by infidelity. God has cursed it seven times in France since 1793.'[11]

Conservatives defend what is and thus move the argument from the abstract to the concrete. At the abstract level no universal rights could be found; in concrete existence, meanwhile, slavery was declared well-nigh ubiquitous. According to Harper it had existed in all societies until quite recent times. It was in fact 'as much in the order of nature, that men should enslave each other, as that other animals should prey upon each other'.[12] White southerners claimed not to have imposed slavery on black Africans. All they did was to change their masters, for slavery had already been their condition under black masters, prior to westward transportation.

For John Calhoun, United States Vice-President from 1825 to 1833, it was the ubiquity of the class-divide that was most significant. The politics of equality flew in the face of all recorded history. Slavery could in fact be defended as the most stable and just means of perpetuating this pattern. It was a more effective means of domination than any plausible alternative. As for American ideals, James Hammond, the owner of 147 slaves, noted in 1845 that 'our Presidential chair has been occupied forty-four out of fifty-six years by slave-holders'.[13] In 1847 the ex-slave and anti-slavery campaigner Frederick Douglass mentioned the same general point, but on the basis of slightly different arithmetic and an entirely different political stance. 'The Government', he said, 'was on the slaveholder's side, as might be seen from the fact that for forty-two out of fifty years, the Presidential chair had been filled by a slaveholder . . . to be a slaveholder was a qualification almost indispensable to the election for any public office and a non-slaveholder had no chance of being chosen President.'[14]

Slave-holding had the most distinguished antecedents as the owners themselves were not slow to indicate. Had not Aristotle defended slavery, declaring that 'by nature some are free, others slaves, and that for these it is both right and expedient that they should serve as slaves'?[15] The master–slave relationship was regarded as akin to that between husband and wife and between father and children. In each instance 'the same wide discrepancy between two sets of human beings' justified the former dominating the latter. Thus for millennia one form of domination was used to justify others, in contrast to the modern situation where one form of liberation has pulled others behind it. However, in Antiquity slavery was the basis from which civilisation and freedom were held to derive, the labour of the many facilitating the cultivation of the few. Similarly, in the nineteenth century, James Hammond, declaring himself in possession of 'abundant leisure', devoted part of it to composing a 'Letter to an English Abolitionist'. Thus the labour of his slaves gave their master the facility to justify their subservience. To the connoisseur of alienation the irony is quite compelling. This, though, was just a minor instance of this pattern. 'Let it be remembered', wrote William Harper, 'that all the great and enduring monuments of human art and industry – the wonders of Egypt – the everlasting works of Rome – were created by the labor of slaves'.[16]

If knowledge of the classics was a sign of the cultivated mind, acquaintance with the Bible was the southern gentleman's moral credit card. How convenient it was to be able to parry the thrusts of purer-than-thou northern clerics and English Quaker philanthropists with the words of Holy Scripture. There was no theory/practice divide here. Biblical theology proved eminently practical as a weapon in the class struggle. Devotion to scriptural learning was simultaneously useful both as a means for pacifying slaves with Christianity and combatting abolitionist tracts with a powerful counter-polemic.

As an indication of the latter we may consider Thornton Stringfellow of Virginia. He had been ordained as a Baptist minister in 1814 and, as the son of a slave-holder, came in time to inherit both the human property and the near thousand acres of land that went with them. He regarded 'the guardianship and control of the black race by the white' as 'an indispensable Christian duty to which we must yet look, if we would secure the well-being of both races'. It is questionable whether he performed this duty adequately, for come the Civil War 'his seventy slaves ran away to the Yankees'.[17] Even so, we shall consider a Biblical investigation he conducted two decades earlier, his *A Brief Examination of Scripture Testimony on the Institution of Slavery* (1841). Stringfellow rested his case rather heavily on a problem of linguistic usage. How was one to understand the category of 'men-servants and maid-servants', which, among others, Abraham was found to own after famine had driven him to Egypt? Here Stringfellow, like others of his persuasion, was happy to follow Dr Johnson's assertion that over the years the meaning of the concept 'servant' had gradually softened. Originally it was synonymous with 'slave'. Thus reinterpreted, slavery could be found spread all over the pages of the Old Testament. Particularly explicit in its terminology was a passage from Leviticus in which Stringfellow found all the justification he required for the purchase of human beings as property and the continued possession of their offspring forever:

> Thy bond-men and thy bond-maids which thou shalt have, shall be of the heathen that are round about you: of them shall ye buy bond-men and bond-maids. Moreover, of the children of the strangers that do sojourn among you, of them shall ye buy, and of their families that are with you, which they begat in your land. And they shall be your possessions. And ye shall take them as an inheritance for your children after you, to inherit them for a possession, they shall be your bond-men forever.[18]

Thus had God given his laws to his chosen people. Stringfellow regarded the Old Testament as the record of 1500 years of Jewish history and divine advice. During this period a lot occurred that was creditable but also much behaviour fell well below the due standard. From on high God was kept busy delivering necessary encouragement, advice and reprimands. On the ground, excesses occurred that the less charitable would have found hard to tolerate. It was, consequently, according to Stringfellow, decisively significant that God's strictures on one-and-a-half millennia of sinful behaviour contain not one complaint concerning the institution of slavery as such. The conclusion could not be more clear-cut. The God of Abraham and Isaac clearly accepted and condoned the ownership of human property.

Turning to the New Testament, Stringfellow took it as beyond dispute that no record exists of Jesus ever challenging or rejecting the institution of slavery. Stringfellow proceeded to quote chapter and verse from the numerous admonitions to obey the powers that be. 'Servants be obedient to them that are your masters.' 'Submit yourselves to every ordinance of man for the Lord's sake.' Others before and since have used the scriptures for quite different purposes, but clearly those who did their homework could find ample support for the conservation of the white American south. So long as control was combined with proper guardianship, the slave-owners believed they need feel no moral qualms about the society they dominated.

From the above we can already infer one part of what this guardianship entailed. From the backwardness of heathen Africa the slaves had been rescued and brought to the benefits of Christianity. According to LeRoi Jones[19] the provision of true religion had not at first seemed necessary. The slaves were categorised as beasts and thus inappropriate recipients of the gospel message. Nevertheless, following the Nat Turner revolt, slaves without religion appeared particularly dangerous and so many slave-holders 'came to see Christianity primarily as a means of social control'.[20] The provision of Christianity also became a useful part of the slave-owners' self-defence. They were, they claimed, raising their slaves one step up the ladder of civilisation. Their slaves' place was, necessarily, still a lowly one, but in that place they were given proper care and guidance. In the ideology of the slave-owners, the plantation was one large family and the family itself the most basic and natural institution. From all time and in all circumstances it had cohered in a structure of mutually advantageous hierarchy. Alongside the relationship of husband to wife and father to children, that of master to slave fitted quite appropriately. In this extended family one found a community of mutual responsibility, concern and affection in which the weak obtained their most secure defence. In childhood and old age the slave was granted a level of care and security unavailable to workers in the north. In the words of George Fitzhugh of Virginia, who was perhaps too blunt for his side's own good, 'to protect the weak, we must first enslave them'.[21] Thus emerged the vision of slavery as a kind of conservative welfare state. In this organic community tasks were allotted according to suitability as slaves were freed from responsibilities they were deemed incapable of exercising. 'Slaves', said Fitzhugh, 'never die of hunger; seldom suffer want.'[22] From the cradle to the grave these 'perpetual children'[23] were held to enjoy a lifetime of minstrel sing-along as they laboured beneath the warming sun. The permanence of childhood was a constant theme. In 1923 Klansman William Joseph Simmons declared that 'the mind of the pure negro, compared to the white, on the average does not get beyond the age of twelve years'.[24] Childhood involved paternal authority and, of course, as with all children, punishment might sometimes be necessary. However, the occasional flogging, said James Hammond, 'is not degrading, and unless excessive, occasions little pain'.[25]

To the slave-owners any indications that their charges required a change of status were unquestionably the consequence of outside interference. It was the existence of subversive abolitionist tracts which supposedly made necessary the injunction against black education. Away from 'zealous and overheated philanthropists' the slaves remained 'the happiest of the human race'. These words of Thomas Dew were echoed by many others, among them James Hammond again, who declared southern slaves 'the happiest three millions of human beings on whom the sun shines'.[26]

If slavery was so beneficial and if it were the most stable and humane way of regulating the inevitable divide between owners and labourers, why then should its benefits be confined to blacks alone? George Fitzhugh, following the logic of classical and biblical slavery, where there had been no racial basis, recommended that it be also extended to white workers. This suggestion was hardly tactful and did not serve to enhance white working-class support for the 'peculiar institution'. More common was the view that the blacks had certain peculiarities which fitted them well for their role in the southern economy. In 1844 the ethnologist Josiah Nott delivered his 'Two Lectures on the Natural History of the Caucasian and Negro Races', part of a growing school of 'scientific' racism that, later in the century, developed into racial Darwinism. Here Nott outlined as scientific findings the view that nature herself had confined the black to limited and lowly tasks. Compared to the Caucasian 'the head of the negro is smaller by a full tenth . . . in consequence of which the anterior or intellectual portion of the brain is defective'. Also 'the teeth point obliquely forward and resemble in shape those of car-nivorous animals'.[27] The 'inferior' nature of the black physiognomy seemed clearly to indicate the appropriate level of occupation. 'If there are sordid, servile, and laborious offices to be performed', thought William Harper, 'is it not better that there should be sordid, servile, and laborious beings to perform them?'[28]

Harper was desirous of 'fulfilling the first great command to subdue and replenish the earth'. How else were the fertile soils of the southern states to bring forth fruit than as a product of slave labour? All history seemed to prove that no other social formation was sufficient to bring under cultivation the tropical type of climatic region. 'The black man was placed in Tropical Africa', thought Josiah Nott, 'because he was suited to this climate and no other.' Once moved northward 'a cold climate so freezes their brains as to make them insane or idiotical'.[29] Thus divine providence had, it seemed, effectively designed the black for both a hot, sultry climate and mundane, patient physical work within it. How ideal this evidently was for the species as a whole! How important it seemed that nothing ever disrupt the pattern that God and nature so clearly intended.

For all that, and this was the main impetus to pro-slavery writings, into the southern 'Eden is coming Satan in the guise of an abolitionist'. The natural order was under attack, as also was the basis of the United States economy. Under what other arrangements, asked William Harper, could the produce of 'our great southern staple' be assured?[30] Southern whites enjoyed reminding their northern opponents that the slave economy, though differently constituted from theirs, was vital to the country as a whole. The abolitionists, it seemed, hypocritically attacked a system of production from which they themselves benefited, and in which, therefore, they too were implicated. For all conservative thought there is a strong presumption in favour of existing arrangements. The morality of historical origins weighs less heavily than the hard facts of current existence, which are assumed to have emerged and been adapted in response to real, practical requirements. Such was also taken to be the situation in the American south.

The abolitionists, however, wished to convert the slave into a wage labourer. To the owners there were clear reasons why this would not work. The slaves were said to be quite unfitted for such a transformation. They were not yet ready for an introduction to free wage labour and, on some accounts, never would be. Slaves were thus better left in the condition for which both nature and nurture had prepared them. The experience of the free blacks was held to prove conclusively that they were morally unfit for freedom, and incapable of the self-discipline characteristic of the white worker. Rising crime and relapse into natural indolence were held to be the clear consequences of releasing blacks from their overseers' control.

William Harper's imagination on the perils of emancipation ran further than that of many others of his persuasion. Given political rights, blacks were, he thought, likely 'to act in concert' and thus accrue even more influence than their numbers warranted. Easily made the prey to demagogues, the deteriorating situation would produce a scale of white emigration likely to exacerbate the chaos left behind. 'Thus matters will go on, until universal anarchy, or kakistocracy, the government of the worst, is fully established.'[31]

Clearly, to many white southerners, slavery was more than just an economic arrangement. It was also the only plausible means of dealing with the racial divide. Two races so utterly different in nature and aptitude could not exist in mutual equality. One would necessarily dominate the other. Harper feared that emancipation would thus lead to 'a war of extermination'.[32] The superior nature of white civilisation would almost certainly result in their victory, and so slavery once abolished would later have to be reintroduced.

If black and white could not live together in freedom, might they not have to live apart? For some the proper corollary of emancipation appeared to be deportation. Having been brought from Africa by force the blacks would be returned there by the same means. To this prospect Thomas Dew addressed himself in his 1832 essay on the 'Abolition of Negro Slavery'. Slavery, he presumed, could not be abolished unless Congress was willing to repay the owners the value of their human property and cover the immense costs of transportation and recolonisation. As a means of purchasing the destruction of the southern economy he thought the whole enterprise would be a financial disaster. Economy and stability thus jointly required the undisturbed continuation of the southern *status quo*.

We have thus far presented slave-owners on the defensive. When, in 1845, James Hammond penned his 'Letter to an English Abolitionist' he produced a powerful counter-attack. From what basis did the English presume to disparage southern slavery? Were Britain's Chartist riots a recommendation for their own standards of civil peace? Did shipment to Australia for petty theft represent their sense of legal justice? In British government reports on factory conditions, Hammond found that her Majesty's own commissioners provided a damning indictment of the treatment of the English labouring poor. If a comparison were to be made he concluded that 'in Great Britain the poor and labouring classes . . . are more miserable and degraded, morally and physically, than our slaves; to be elevated to the actual condition of whom, would be to these, *your fellow citizens*, a most glorious act of *emancipation*'.[33] Clearly, as Hammond judged it, what irked the English was not so much the practice of slavery as the mere name. Call it something else and it seemed less reprehensible.

This line of thought was pursued with greater intellectual rigour by George Fitzhugh, whose 'Southern Thought' appeared in 1857. Fitzhugh undertook to attack the basic philosophy of modern capitalism. The *laissez-faire* ideas of Adam Smith seemed merely high-falutin' selfishness, a catechism chanted by the rich while they trod down the poor. Under this system the labourers were herded together in squalid urban degradation. Unlike American slaves they were cut off from the classes most capable of raising their morals and refining their manners. As a means of regulating the class divide capitalism appeared both immoral and irresponsible. The isolated 'free labourer' was in fact 'a slave, without the rights of a slave'; the employer 'a master, without the obligations of a master'.

What a poor contrast this seemed to the condition it replaced. Under feudalism, thought Fitzhugh, the

> baron and the priest vied with each other in their care of the vassal. This was feudal slavery; and what is modern liberty? Why, quietly, slowly, almost insensibly, the poor have been turned over from the parental and protective rule of kings, barons, and churchmen, to the unfeeling despotism of capitalists, employers, usurers, and extortioners; and this was called emancipation!

Such language will be familiar to students of western thought, though we may not expect it from this quarter. In the nature of its critique, as well as its virulent tone, it sounds, of course, like the language of socialism. Of this Fitzhugh was quite aware. 'From the writings of the socialists . . . we can derive both facts and arguments quite sufficient to upset the whole moral philosophy of the day.'[34] Had not Marx himself employed a similar equation, declaring the term 'free labourer' a euphemism for the 'wage-slave'? This, then, is just one instance of the strange but partial affinity between left- and right-wing thought. It was in fact European conservatives who first provided a comprehensive critique of capitalism. Socialists had drawn on these insights and attempted to turn them in an egalitarian direction. Both groups were thus united in what they were against and agreed in opposing a social order based upon capitalist market economics and liberal, individualist political theory. That was the negative side. In terms of positive recommendations the slave-owners looked, obviously, not forward to socialism, but back more to ancient slavery for the ideological justification of their position.

The steadily declining power of the south meant that their desires eventually had less effect than what the northern states decided for them. Self-determination was part of the American creed, as the Democrats pointed out, but military defeat kept the south within the union against the wishes of its political leaders. The work that the Constitution had left undone might in time be completed. On the first day of 1863, in the middle of the Civil War, President Lincoln issued his famous Emancipation Proclamation. This freed the slaves in all areas in rebellion against the federal government, that is, in precisely those states where the President's writ did not run. With the end of the war a more consequential liberation could be introduced. In 1865 the thirteenth amendment to the Constitution abolished slavery within the United States. Five years later the fifteenth amendment turned explicitly to voting rights, which were not to 'be denied or abridged by the United States or by any State on account of race, color, or previous condition of servitude'. The black had now won citizenship and full political rights, at least on paper. In crucial respects, though, the south remained a law unto itself. Laws can be changed faster than attitudes, and the southern white notion of black disqualification was largely unaffected by military defeat, and, according to some commentators 'among the far-reaching results of the process of emancipation was a significant increase in white racial animosity toward blacks'.[35] This was the period of the rise of the Ku Klux Klan and of 'black order' which forced blacks into oppressive labour contracts and extended the punishments for vagrancy and such conveniently vague offences as 'malicious mischief' and 'insulting gestures'. The slaves had been kept below the level of citizenship not just because they were slaves, but more basically because they were black. With liberation the slave as slave achieved nominal freedom, but as black remained exactly as before. Thus to enforce the federal will, the south had to be subjected to a form of occupation by the northern victors, as was again the case in the 1950s and 1960s.

The south, once again, had historical precedent on its side, for in imposing a black male suffrage the fifteenth amendment required federal jurisdiction of an area that the fifty-five of Philadelphia had, in framing the Constitution, deliberately left to the discretion of the individual states. Non-citizen blacks had previously counted as three-fifths of a person in terms of states' weighting in the House of

Representatives. With the end of slavery each black citizen was now to count as one. This obviously redressed the imbalance in Congressional power that had so troubled the white south in the previous decades. Yet their strengthened federal power should no longer have been white power, but rather a southern federal representation of black and white citizens alike. During the period of Reconstruction, moves in this direction commenced. Between 1868 and 1876 blacks in South Carolina formed a majority of the lower house, the only state where this happened. Two blacks were elected to the Senate, both from Mississippi, and fifteen to the House of Representatives.

However 'nothing angered former Rebels (some of whom were temporarily disfranchised) more than the "spectacle" of blacks voting'. This violated the whole theory of appropriate levels. In 1833 Richard Colfax had already asserted the black 'brute' physiognomy as a political disqualification. He held that the black man's 'want of capacity to receive a complicated education renders it improper and impolitic that he should be allowed the privileges of citizenship in an enlightened country'.[36] The woman who taught the slave Frederick Douglass to read was given a severe reprimand by her husband. 'A nigger should know nothing but to obey his master – to do as he is told to do. Learning would *spoil* the best nigger in the world. . . . It would forever unfit him to be a slave.'[37] According to the 'Proceedings of the Constitutional Convention of the state of Alabama' (1901), 'there is in the white man an inherited capacity for government which is wholly wanting in the negro'.[38]

Such attitudes lay behind the reassertion of white political supremacy in the decades after the Civil War. The means thereto were to impose on the blacks a harder form of the disqualifications that were accepted as normal in the north and, indeed, virtually everywhere else. In place of an explicit colour bar, other barriers were erected to achieve the same purpose. The black male was not merely black; he was, or more significantly, could be, designated as vagrant, criminal or illiterate, according to the convenience of those empowered to make the judgement. Having been excluded from education under slavery, newly-liberated blacks were necessarily the least-educated section of the population, and thus easy victims for exclusion on this count. In 1890 the Mississippi Constitutional Convention introduced a poll tax, residential requirements, and an 'understanding clause', which called for an accurate comprehension of the state constitution. Whites were rarely questioned under the latter, but many of those who might otherwise have failed to qualify were rescued by the so-called 'grandfather clause'. This gave the vote to all men who could prove direct descent from someone qualified to vote before 1867, that is, before the passing of the 1868 fourteenth amendment, which it appeared to infringe. This pattern was soon followed by other southern states, the purpose being, in the language of the 1898 Constitutional Convention of Louisiana, 'the purification of the electorate' and the elimination of 'the mass of corrupt and illiterate voters who have during the last quarter of a century degraded our politics'.[39]

Consequently in the actual politics of the post-liberation south we find the key positions, such as the judges, the electoral registration officers and the police chiefs, still held by whites deeply imbued with the ideology of their own racial supremacy. This they were still able to enforce, firstly, because 'the mere letter of the law may give no hint of the abuse that is possible under it';[40] secondly because segregation and discriminations not established by legally constituted powers were imposed by the white social dictates of lynch law; and, thirdly, because federalism provides a convenient facility for localised intransigence.

As late as 1918, at a time when full voting rights for all classes and both sexes was at the top of the western liberal agenda, Kirk H. Porter could declare that in the United States of America 'public attention has ceased to focus upon the negro cause; it is looked upon as lost, or not worth saving'.[41]

Until the Civil Rights movement of the 1950s and 1960s southern blacks were excluded from the normal liberal democratic rights of citizenship. Once again it took federal action to try and enforce racial justice in the American south. In the crucial area of education a 1954 Supreme Court decision (Brown *v.* Topeka) overturned an earlier ruling allowing 'separate but equal' schooling for black and white children. Both races, henceforth, had to go to school together. They did not, as yet, vote together. In *Why We Can't Wait*, Martin Luther King cited the case of Birmingham, Alabama, where in January 1963 blacks constituted 'two-fifths of the city's population' but only 'one-fifth of its voting strength'.[42] This situation was countered by the 1964 Voting Rights Act, which permitted federal registrars to operate in counties where less than half of the eligible voters were on the voting lists. In consequence, whereas only about three per cent of southern blacks were registered to vote in the mid-1940s, the figure was nearer 70 per cent a quarter of a century later.

Since 1776, the United States of America has seemed a beacon of liberty to many progressive Europeans. In that it was the first major power to dispense with any form of hereditary political office, it was regarded as the first modern democracy. But in terms of the racial disqualifications it imposed until three decades ago, it may be regarded not as the oldest surviving western democracy, but as one of the youngest.

8 'Exalted by their Inferiority': On the Subjection of Women

'In every society', wrote Gunnar Myrdal, 'there are at least two groups of people besides the Negroes, who are characterised by high social visibility expressed in physical appearance, dress, and patterns of behavior, and who have been "suppressed". We refer to women and children.'[1] Childhood, to which we shall refer in the conclusion, is, however, not a permanent condition. In respect of 'suppression', children escape from their political disqualifications soon after becoming aware of them. For us the more appropriate comparison is that between blacks and women, for both situations are unchangeable.

A hierarchy of permanent orders, with each Estate accepting its preordained place, had been a cardinal feature of medieval society. The emergence of liberal constitutional systems in the late eighteenth century was accompanied by an ideology of popular sovereignty, equal opportunity and the 'career open to talent'. That the fixity of genetic inheritance could be taken to correspond with the permanent and unchosen allocation to a particular social sphere appears incompatible with the declared beliefs of liberal democracy. An unstated and perhaps unconscious boundary to liberal ideology thus emerged in its application. Just as some were to be more sovereign than others, so too was opportunity to be more equal for some than others. In particular, the social barriers that had long accompanied the genetic distinctions of race and sex were allowed to remain much as before and in some cases even got worse. In France some privileged women had, for over five centuries, been allowed to vote at both local and national levels. It was not until after the proclamation of the Rights of Man that, in the constitutions of 1791 and 1793, the political rights of women were explicitly denied. It is hard to know how much to make of this, for political exceptions in medieval France should not distract from the overall situation concerning women's allotted role. Their exclusion or under-representation from all areas of power and influence is a characteristic common both to medieval and modern society. In 1869 John Stuart Mill observed that the power relationship between the sexes was the last relic of the old and anachronistic law of the strongest. In the areas of race and sex the great revolutions of the United States and France lit a slow fuse but had little immediate impact. Thus the divide between medieval and modern was less sharp than many supporters of liberal constitutionalism assumed. The traditional enclosures which kept women in their supposedly natural place were still buttressed with the old classical and theological orthodoxies which, in certain chosen areas, were left relatively unscathed. Furthermore, in the late nineteenth century they were granted the additional prestigious confirmation of scientific support. It was with some understatement that Mary Wollstonecraft, a pioneer campaigner for women's rights, noted that 'many ingenious arguments have been brought forward . . . to account for, and excuse the tyranny of man'.[2]

In March 1776, a few months before the signing of the Declaration of Independence, and at a crucial stage in the dispute between the British government and their American colonists, the future first Vice-President and second President of the United States of America received a strongly-worded letter from his wife. Abigail Adams wrote threatening rebellion against tyranny, but her theme was not the one which preoccupied her husband, that of colonists against the 'mother' country, but rather of women against men. 'If particular care and attention is not paid to the ladies', she wrote, 'we are determined to foment a rebellion, and will not hold ourselves bound by any laws in which we have no voice or representation.' She then moved from the particular to a characterisation of men in general: 'that your sex are naturally tyrannical is a truth so thoroughly established as to admit of no dispute'.[3]

The call to 'remember the ladies' was well-placed, for a few months later John Adams was appointed to the small committee responsible for drafting the Declaration of Independence. Here his wife's request was either forgotten or ignored. The affirmation that 'all men' are created equal presumably meant just that, for Thomas Jefferson, who framed the Declaration, held unambiguous and conservative views on the proper place of women: 'Were our state a pure democracy', he exclaimed, 'there would still be excluded from our deliberations women, who, to prevent deprivation of morals and ambiguity of issues, should not mix promiscuously in gatherings of men.'[4]

In France the Declaration of the Rights of Man prompted from Olympe de Gouges the lesser-known Declaration of the Rights of Woman (1791), but apart from abolishing male primogeniture the French revolution did little for women. Women had participated in revolutionary clubs and societies and sat as spectators in the galleries of the National Assembly, but in 1793 all women's political associations were outlawed. Then in 1804 the Code Napoléon categorised women as legal minors and forbade them the right to appear as civil witnesses. Wives were obliged to obey their husbands and so, among other limitations, could not own property without their husbands' consent.

In England Mary Wollstonecraft's *Vindication of the Rights of Woman* (1792) attempted to apply Enlightenment principles and adapt revolutionary declarations to women's needs. She was derided as ' a hyena in petticoats' and for about a century afterwards the issue of women's rights, as we saw in the case of Carlyle, was usually treated as little more than a source of mirth. In terms of legal rights married women were reduced almost to the level of children or lunatics as also being under the control of a legal keeper. In his *Commentaries on the Laws of England* Blackstone explained that 'by marriage, the husband and wife are one person in law: that is the very being or legal existence of the woman is suspended, or at least is incorporated and consolidated into that of the husband'.[5]

In Prussia the 1793 Civil Code, soon after being adopted by the other German states, explicitly pronounced the husband as head of the family and legal guardian of his wife. He could deny her permission to take a job or sign a contract. Similar power was exercised over unmarried daughters, for the father controlled their property and represented them in law. These provisions remained on the statute book until 1900.

An organised feminist movement first emerged in the United States of America. In 1848 the Women's Rights Convention met at Seneca Falls, New York State, and produced a Declaration of Sentiments closely modelled on the Declaration of Independence of 72 years earlier. Echoing Abigail Adams's transposition of anti-colonial arguments, the new Declaration referred to 'the repeated injuries and usurpations on the part of man towards woman' and asserted that 'We hold these truths to be self-evident . . . that all men *and women* are created equal.' Ellen du Bois has referred to the convention's need 'to borrow political legitimacy from the American revolution'.[6] This is no doubt true, for any radical movement needs all the legitimacy it can muster and it is tactically advantageous to address a society in a form of language it both understands and respects. However, there was more to it than simple expediency, for the adaptation of Jefferson's terminology could be used to assert that the

American revolution remained incomplete so long as the practices of the nation remained inconsistent with its revered and much-vaunted principles.

The earliest major challenge on this score came from the abolitionist movement, and it was in the struggle against black slavery that a number of prominent American women received their first practical political lesson. One such was Angelina Emily Grimké who found that 'the investigation of the rights of the slave has led me to a better understanding of my own'.[7] Like slaves, women were infantilised, denied full legal and property rights, allowed education only to the extent deemed appropriate to their allotted place, without the vote, and, once married, without their own surnames. Given the affinity between their causes, might not female citizenship be achieved on the coat-tails of black emancipation? This turned out to be impossible. By and large abolitionist leaders were unwilling to reciprocate the support they received from feminists. Their characteristic argument was that removing black slavery was in itself enough of a task. One major reform at a time was all that could be achieved. In 1865 the anti-slavery campaigner Wendell Phillips informed women's rights activists that 'this hour belongs to the negro'.[8] Woman's hour would have to be delayed. So it proved, much to the consternation of certain educated middle-class women who felt increasingly humiliated. 'It is an open, deliberate insult to American womanhood', argued Elizabeth Cady Stanton in 1869, 'to be cast down under the iron-heeled peasantry of the Old World and the slaves of the New'.[9] Thus the first chapter of the first feminist movement drew to a close. It provided a valuable legacy at a later date, but for the moment traditional patterns remained undisturbed.

As with black slavery, so here also, the intellectual foundations of western civilisation were delved for their anti-reform rationale. In 1820 a delegate to a franchise convention in Boston drew upon the authority of Aristotle, who had pronounced the male 'more fitted to rule than the female', for in terms of 'the faculty of deliberation' women were only one step in advance of slaves. So 'as between male and female', said Aristotle, 'this relationship of superior and inferior is permanent'.[10]

In the culture of ancient Greece women, like children, slaves and animals, were regarded as a sub-section of property. According to Hesiod, Pandora, the first woman, brought misfortune and evil into the world. In terms of mental capacity women were placed with the immature and weak as unfit to discuss important issues. Their functions were properly limited to childbirth and care of the household.

The imperatives of Antiquity and Christianity were broadly similar concerning the role of women, but Christianity had its institutional apparatus and in some instances the Churches provided powerful supports for the traditional inequalities within the family. In 1854 the United States national convention of the women's rights movement declared that 'the most determined opposition it encounters is from the clergy generally whose teachings of the Bible are intensely inimical to the equality of women with man'.[11] From the religious side we find numerous instances where the suffrage movement is denounced as atheistic in challenging the divine command of female subjection. In 1904 a contributor to *Sewanee River* declared that 'her [woman's] rightism is simply sex-atheism'.[12] A long procession of vicars, priests and preachers found biblical support, mainly in Genesis and St Paul, for their anti-suffragism. From Genesis they learnt that the Lord created woman merely that man might have company and that the wife's 'desire shall be to thy husband, and he shall rule over thee'.[13]

In all our four countries the moral tone had long been set, if not enforced, by the various Christian churches, whether predominantly Protestant, as in Great Britain and the USA, or Catholic as in France, or a mixture of both in the various German states. In France, where the feminist movement emerged comparatively late, the Roman Catholic church was particularly influential in enforcing the traditional view of women's place. In eighteenth-century Germany there were 'learned doctors of theology who denied that women had a soul'. In 1818 a writer on education noted that 'everywhere but especially in Germany, the woman's destiny has always been: wife, mother, household'.[14]

The power of tradition is nowhere more striking than when found in writers otherwise regarded as unconventional and radical extremists. In Rousseau the previously-mentioned limitation in the application of liberal doctrine is particularly apparent. Rousseau, the hero of the Jacobins, regarded by friend and foe alike as the embodiment of a revolutionary terror he did not himself witness, had published the *Social Contract* in 1762. In the same year as this appeal for popular sovereignty, Rousseau, who had abandoned his five children to the care of a foundling hospital, also published *Emile*. This work had more immediate appeal than the now more famous *Social Contract* and made Rousseau one of the most influential educational philosophers of the eighteenth century. In upper-class households in both

France and Britain attempts were made to educate young children according to the pattern he had advocated. That the title of a book on education should bear the name of a boy is already indicative of the author's notion of where educational effort should be concentrated, for the notorious political radical was decidedly traditionalist on the issue of the sexual division of labour. Here are a few of Rousseau's comments on the role of women:

> Woman is especially made for man's delight.
> She should learn to submit to injustice and to suffer the wrongs inflicted on her by her husband without complaint.
> The daughter should follow her mother's religion, the wife her husband's.
> Unable to judge for themselves they should accept the judgement of father and husband as that of the church.
> The search for abstract and speculative truths, for principles and axioms in science, for all that tends to wide generalisation, is beyond a woman's grasp; their studies should be thoroughly practical.[15]

When, in 1792, Mary Wollstonecraft sought to extend the application of revolutionary doctrine to the position of women, she particularly directed her *Vindication of the Rights of Woman* at the theories of Rousseau. Following Wollstonecraft, many modern feminists have regarded Rousseau as their arch-opponent. The ideas he was condemned for in his own time are now uncontroversial, whilst those that were then conventional are now denounced as reactionary. In 1762 Rousseau's ideas on women suffered no condemnation, for, as Susan Okin has noted: 'the case he argues is, in a qualified sense, representative of the whole Western tradition regarding women'.[16] So, we may conclude, Rousseau is no isolated misogynist. The only reason he is now singled out for condemnation is that he was unusual enough to put pen to paper, and quite exceptional in the clarity with which he did so. In fact the major opponent of women's liberation has not been this or that male chauvinist writer but rather the heavy weight of traditional practices and their supporting assumptions.

In time, as J.S. Mill noted, the habitual comes to appear natural, and nature is credited with having produced the characteristic patterns of social institutions. In consequence the inequalities within the family did not have to be defended for they were taken to be beyond human control. On the contrary, the onus of justification lay on those who wished to upset the pattern that nature had evidently ordained.

In the age of science, Social Darwinism had already been used to explain and justify the inferiority of black and colonial peoples. It was also used to ascertain the different capacities of men and women. Nascent sociology, striving hard to win recognition for its scientific credentials, played its part here.

In *The Division of Labour in Society* (1893) Emile Durkheim drew on the work of Gustave Le Bon for proof that as civilisation advances the volume of the crania in men and women increasingly differentiates to the advantage of the former. In *L'homme et les sociétés* Le Bon had noted that 'the difference which exists, for example, between the average cranium of Parisian men of the present day and that of Parisian women is almost double that observed between male and female in ancient Egypt'. This notion of increasingly differentiated functions and capacities fitted perfectly into Durkheim's general thesis, that the progressive division of labour was in fact the sign of an advancing civilisation. Durkheim noted with satisfaction that over time women's role became increasingly specialised. 'Today among cultivated people, the woman leads a completely different existence from that of the man. One might say that the two great functions of the psychic life are thus dissociated, that one of the sexes takes care of the affective functions and the other of intellectual functions'.[17]

For that other great founding 'father' of French sociology, Auguste Comte, the sexual division of labour was likewise grounded in biology. Comte felt that it had been established 'both anatomically and physiologically that, in almost the entire animal kingdom, and especially in our species, the female sex is formed for a state of essential childhood, which renders it necessarily inferior to the corresponding male organism'.[18] As for the exclusion of females from the world of politics, Comte felt it should not be a matter of regret, for it prefigured the future positivist commonwealth where politics itself would be transcended.

Herbert Spencer, the foremost sociological proponent of Social Darwinism, explained most fully how the division of labour between the sexes served the cause of social evolution. In women, he thought, intellectual development ceased earlier than in men as energy was concentrated on reproduction. Correspondingly, the more hard physical labour was monopolised by men, the better the offspring their unburdened women would produce, and the more such a society would gain in the struggle for existence. In order that evolutionary progress continue it thus appeared necessary that women be excluded from both intellectual and physical activity.

On this issue the church joined hands with sociology – a rare thrill for both – in their judgements on the inequality of the sexes. In the 1890s the Rev. Father Walsh of Troy delivered a speech at a meeting of the Albany Anti-Women's Suffrage Association. It is noteworthy that he too summoned the support of biology. 'A woman's brain', he explained, 'evolves emotion rather than intellect; and whilst this feature fits her admirably as a creature burdened with the preservation and happiness of the human species, it painfully disqualifies her for the sterner duties to be performed by the intellectual faculties. The best wife and mother and sister would make the worst legislator, judge and police.'[19]

Thus the clamour for female rights, the rights of *men*, and the vote, was taken to involve a war with nature. It was, in the words of one pamphleteer, a 'deformity of human character',[20] a failure to comply with what nature had intended.

This brings us to the core of the feminist dilemma: that God, tradition, nature, biology, science and evolution had all concurred in the creation of separate spheres for men and women. With the emergence of industrial society production increasingly moved outside the home. Paid labour and unpaid 'home work' now had their separate locales and those women left inside the home suffered a loss of economic opportunity and a narrowing of their tasks. Thus arose the familiar pattern of the wife confined to domestic concerns and the husband earning a 'family wage'. For the significant number of women in paid employment, their wages could be set at the low level commensurate with so-called 'pin money'.

The counterpart of the family wage was the family vote, by which the man who earned the family income also monopolised its political voice. This was in accord with the medieval idea that the vote properly represents an *interest*, and that not of an individual but of a group. Here experience, maturity and expertise could be regarded as the prerequisites for such a task. This is a corporate notion of representation in that the head of a designated group can formulate decisions on the other members' behalf. Women, on this argument, were not excluded from political representation, but rather enjoyed 'virtual representation' when the franchise was exercised for them by their husbands or fathers.

The more modern view is that it is an *opinion* which is to be represented. Here the only qualification is to have an opinion, and, as with the Benthamite notion of happiness, no one else has a right to formulate your own expression of it. This form of representation is thus both democratic and individualistic. The slow shift from the medieval to the modern form helps us understand one of the obstacles to the enfranchisement of women. For this to occur it was not only necessary to alter traditional attitudes concerning their role and capacities; but also to overcome the medieval corporatist idea that representation is of groups and that the male head of the household is the proper and sufficient spokesman for all its members.

In all its aspects feminism represents a challenge to such an allocation of separate spheres but the suffrage movement drives to the heart of the sexual division of labour, for it leaps the basic divide between the public and private realms into which men and women had been respectively placed.

Each challenge to traditional role-limitations produced almost simultaneously a conservative counter-movement. In the late 1830s women began to attend the meetings of popular preachers of the Prussian and Saxon Protestant churches. Eda Sagara notes that 'the orthodox cleric Hengstenberg thundered in moral outrage at "the shameful spectacle of women entering the public scene"'.[21] The law soon came to his rescue, for in 1850 the Prussian legislature decreed that women must never be admitted into any association which partook of political discussion. Similar laws also existed in Austria and some of the other German states. In this endeavour the German section of the International Workers' Association also lent a helping hand, not unsurprisingly, for female labour had often been used to undercut male wages. A discussion document of 1866 devoted rare eloquence to the issue: 'Alongside the solemn duties of the man and father in public life and the family, the woman and mother should stand for the cosiness and poetry of domestic life, bring grace and beauty to social relations and be an ennobling influence in the increase of humanity's enjoyment of life.' In the same year Coullery, a French delegate to the socialist International concurred in the view that 'the woman's place is at the domestic hearth, in the midst of her children, watching over them and instilling into them their first principles'.[22]

The more women threatened to emerge from their domestic sphere, the more charming their confinement appeared to anti-feminists. At a New York convention of 1867, one speaker waxed sentimental on how he loved 'to look upon the sweet face of a virtuous woman. I love to see her standing at her place in the family circle, with a new, clean, gingham dress on, baking warm biscuits for tea.'[23]

The exaltation of where women should be was by implication also an indication of where they should not be. We may assume that Abigail Adams's concerns were not immediately made known, for Thomas Jefferson voiced his assurance that women were contented with their lot. 'Our good ladies', he declared, 'have been too wise to wrinkle their foreheads with politics. They are contented to soothe and calm the minds of their husbands returning ruffled from political debate.'[24]

When women began to transgress their confinement the implicit became explicit. Female participation in politics would endanger society's most basic institutions, those of marriage and the family, and produce juvenile delinquency and higher divorce rates. Much of this unease is evident in a pamphlet the Liberal MP Samuel Smith delivered to the public in 1891. 'A good wife and mother', he said, 'cannot leave her home to attend clubs and public meetings, and if she does she will soon cease to be a good wife and mother.' Furthermore he feared a situation where a woman might be taken to vote by her friends while her husband was accompanied separately by colleagues of a different political persuasion. Hence 'the peace and quietness of home will be exchanged for a turbulent, excited life, out of which will spring innumerable scandals'. This, however, was far from the end of the matter. Adverse genetic consequences would ensue from a mother 'kept in a constant whirl of [political] excitement. . . . Ask any medical man', he warned, concerning the effects on the children. 'Already it is well known that a sad physical deterioration of the children is the penalty of a mother exhausting her nervous power in public life.' Great men were taken to be the children of mothers who led quiet, private lives. Enfeeblement of the race was the certain consequence of women drawing 'aside from the Sacred duties which God and nature have assigned them'. Smith ended his pamphlet in sombre fashion, presenting women's suffrage as the progenitor of 'dark days' for the Anglo-Saxon race, in which 'the splendid fabric of centuries will totter to its fall'.[25] As the First World War approached we find the prestigious voices of Lord Cromer in England and Kaiser Wilhelm II in Germany warning of the dire consequences for their respective nations if women deserted their accustomed place.[26]

As well as being for the good of society in general, women's confinement to the private sphere was simultaneously advocated for its own benefit. It was almost a privilege, for it was precisely because of their virtues that women were excluded from politics. In this variant of the white man's burden women were seen as above such sordid matters and should not be sullied with the dirty work of politics, which, like war, was better left to men. On the issue of war, the fact that men had to defend their country was frequently (particularly in Germany, where military values set the tone of prestigious society), used as a reason for confining the vote to them.

When the British parliament debated the 1891 Women's Disabilities Bill, Mr Beresford Hope, MP expressed his concern to 'protect women from being forced forward into the hurly-burly of party politics' and 'exposed to the animosities, the bickerings, and the resentments which are so unhappily inherent in the rough work of electioneering'.[27] Similarly, in 1915 Representative Clark of Florida declared that he did 'not wish to see the day come when the women of my race shall trail their skirts in the muck of partisan politics'. In surveying such writings it is noteworthy how political participation, otherwise so often designated as part of civic virtue, suddenly comes to be recategorised as sordid once the inclusion of women is suggested. One is here bound to suppose that if politics were really so rough and dirty it would have been imposed earlier on that section of the male population that traditionally did most of such work.

Exclusion from public affairs should not, we are sometimes told, be taken to imply a lack of female public influence. Several male writers pointed out that it was in the home that the most formative lessons were learned. Power in the home was the power behind the throne. In her proper place the woman, the Queen of the home, 'exercises a broader and deeper and mightier influence than she can ever exercise or hope to on the stump and in the byways of politics in this land'.[28] In this sense we can understand Mary Wollstonecraft's observation that women were 'exalted by their inferiority'.[29] One variant of this was the observation that 'so chivalrous, indeed, was the ante-bellum South that its women were granted scarcely any rights at all'.[30]

The public consequences of private, family responsibilities could also extend to the maintenance of national power and character. In an illuminating essay on women in England at the turn of the century, Mackay and Thane point out how the ideology of Englishness had been constructed in terms of masculine images. The female virtues – 'essentially domestic and maternal' – were evidently universal, English women being merely superior in their exercise. The role of

British 'surplus women' was to settle in the colonies, marry, and then 'help to keep the British Empire for the British race', thus sharing the wider female obligation to mother young men fit to give their lives for their country.[31] In this way motherhood is classified as a political task, but one that requires confinement (in both senses). It is a political activity that takes place away from the public stage. Politicisation and domestication, in this instance only, overcome their mutual exclusion and are buckled together.

It was in the home that the particular skills and capacities of women were to be put to best effect. Neglect of these responsibilities undermined the stability of family life without the partial compensation of benefiting the public sphere to which some women might aspire. Myra Bradwell, who in 1872 was refused permission to practise law in Illinois, was put back in her place with a firm lecture:

> The civil law, as well as nature herself, has always recognised a wide difference in the respective spheres and destinies of man and woman. . . . The natural and proper timidity and delicacy which belong to the female sex evidently unfits it for many of the occupations of civil life. The constitution of the family organization, which is founded in the divine ordinance, as well as in the nature of things, indicates the domestic sphere as that which properly belongs to the domain and functions of womanhood.[32]

Some women, it was known, were neither in the home nor virtuous and much unease was expressed at the prospect of them attaining political rights. If young women were to gain the suffrage, thought Samuel Smith MP, 'with this class would come in an appalling number of fallen women, whose numbers have been estimated in London as high as sixty thousand. Need I point out what canvassing these women means?'[33]

Even before the topic of brain size became an issue there had been a long-established view that women had a different mental capacity from that of men. For Jeremy Bentham, the founder of Utilitarianism, social improvement required a deeper commitment to mathematical calculation, both by individuals and more importantly by governments. Rational decisions were carefully calculated ones. Unfortunately for them, in this crucial domain of both science and ethics, women were somewhat deficient: 'The health of the female is more delicate than that of the male: in point of strength and hardiness of body, in point of quantity and quality of knowledge, in point of strength of intellectual powers, and firmness of mind, she is commonly inferior.' Furthermore, 'the female is rather more inclined than the male to superstition'. Women, it seemed, suffered 'some deficiency in point of knowledge, discernment, and comprehension',[34] and so Bentham, who later came to favour the female franchise, initially took the view that Utilitarian arithmetic was best performed by men.

The alleged difference of intellectual power also concerned a scientist of a later generation. In *The Descent of Man* (1871) Charles Darwin asserted that man attains 'a higher eminence, in whatever he takes up, than can woman – whether requiring deep thought, reason or imagination or merely the uses of the senses and hands'.[35] Here women are comprehensively eclipsed and denied even their particular sphere of superiority.

Gustave Le Bon imagined himself a scientist and was indeed one of the pioneers of crowd psychology. Although most crowds in history are likely to have been preponderantly male, such aggregations evidently descend into female characteristics. 'Among the special characteristics of crowds', thought Le Bon, 'there are several – such as impulsiveness, irritability, incapacity to reason, the absence of judgement and of the critical spirit, the exaggeration of the sentiments, and others besides – which are almost always observed in beings belonging to inferior forms of evolution – in women, savages, and children, for instance.'[36] At least, as against Darwin, we can conclude that Le Bon left women one sphere of superiority, in the exercise of the imagination.

In 1896 the historian William Lecky made almost the same point when arguing against the 'already dangerously powerful' female influence on English legislation. 'Women, and especially unmarried women, are', he explained, 'on the whole more impulsive and emotional than men . . . more subject to fanaticisms, which often acquire almost the intensity of monomania.'[37] The British House of Commons were not to be denied the benefit of such findings, for Mr Beresford Hope, MP warned them that our 'legislation would develop hysterical and spasmodic features' if a 'woman-chosen parliament' ensued. In the same debate Mr James managed to turn women's virtues against them, telling the House that 'the sympathetic element in the mental constitution of women absolutely blinded them to all logic. (Hear, hear)'.[38] In Britain the medical profession was particularly hostile to feminist causes, and a letter from a group of doctors to *The Times* in December 1908 likened suffragette behaviour to Tarantism, a dancing mania of the Middle Ages.

The Reverend Father Walsh, in a pamphlet that has already served us well, noted that 'the excessive development of the emotional in [women's] nervous system, ingrafts on the female organization, a neurotic or hysterical condition which is the source of much of the female charm when it is kept within due restraints'. However, in moments of excitement 'it is liable to explode in violent paroxysms. . . . Every woman, therefore, carries this power of irregular, illogical and incongruous action; and no one can foretell when the explosion will come.'[39]

Anti-suffrage proponents thus saw women in the situation we have seen attributed to the working classes and to blacks. Women, they said, only needed enough education for their allotted social role and so their schooling could be less academic and extensive than that of men. Through limited access to property and education, women could be politically disqualified on the same grounds as many men. The 'separate spheres' ideology kept them in their place; in a limited sense it proletarianised them. However, working-class men were disqualified by environmental circumstances rather than genetic inheritance. For women genetic factors provided the excuse to curtail their environmental possibilities.

On the issue of female education Napoleon showed himself a true heir of Rousseau and so, in that restricted sense at least, a legitimate heir of the revolution. 'What we ask of education', he said, 'is not that girls should think, but that they should believe.'[40] In like manner, Friedrich Krummacher, a neo-Pietist preacher from Bremen, was delighted with his daughters' lack of educational achievements. 'My girls', he boasted, 'have never had what they call an education. They know virtually nothing of our so-called literature, cannot speak a single foreign language; they dont know how to talk high.'[41]

Miss Dorothy Beale, who founded Cheltenham Ladies College in 1853, was concerned to provide girls with the schooling best suited to their future role. 'What', she wondered, 'seems to be the best means of training girls so that they may best perform that subordinate part in the world to which I believe they have been called?'[42] Nietzsche, more indelicately, declared that 'when a woman has scholarly inclinations there is usually something wrong with her sexuality'.[43] This was in accord with a more general view which assumed that intellectual endeavour would endanger health and fertility. Energy expended on one activity was thought to deplete the store available for another. Thus there were certain objectives which, for the sake of the species, women were encouraged to sacrifice. In 1867 Herbert Spencer had commented on the lower reproductive power of upper-class women which, he thought, 'may be reasonably attributed to the overtaxing of their brains – an overtaxing which produces a serious reaction on the physique'. Doctor Stanley Hall, the founder of academic psychology in the United States of America, recommended a less scholastic education for girls in order that the development of their reproductive capacities be safeguarded.

In the view of the prominent British psychiatrist Dr Henry Maudsley (1835–1918) female education threatened to produce a lowering of the racial stock and even an eventual disappearance of the species. 'It will have to be considered', he contended, 'whether women can scorn the delights, and live laborious days of intellectual exercise and production, without injury to their functions as the conceivers, mothers, and nurses of children.'[44] The struggle to provide mass education for boys was protracted enough. The deeper prejudices and even emotional blackmail against female education issuing from prestigious male sources render the lesser influence of women in this sphere unsurprising.

On the whole women in Protestant countries tended to gain access to public education sooner than those in Catholic ones. In the United States of America women were admitted to higher education from the 1860s, and by 1880 there were already 40 000 women, over a third of the total, enrolled as students.

In England notable advances in female education were made in the middle years of the nineteenth century. Queens' College was founded in 1848, Bedford College in 1849, North London Collegiate School in 1850 and Cheltenham Ladies College in 1853. Differences soon emerged as to the proper content of female education. We have seen that Miss Beale, founder of Cheltenham, recommended that girls' education develop its own separate path. Miss Davies of the North London Collegiate School and Miss Emily Davies, the foundress of Girton College, Cambridge in 1869, favoured identical schooling for boys and girls. In spite of the efforts of the latter, her college was not allowed to award university degrees until 1948. Without them women who became university teachers were placed in an inferior position, ineligible for full membership of the university or participation in course-planning and regulation.

Medical studies had long been a sensitive topic in discussions on female education and it took an enormous struggle before women were allowed to attend clinical lectures in a London hospital in 1877. In the following year a supplemental charter of the University of

London permitted the granting of degrees to women in all the faculties of the university. By the end of the century there were 162 women students at the four Oxford colleges, 275 at the two Cambridge colleges and 310 among the 720 students at University College, London.

In Germany in the nineteenth century, girls' schooling, when available, was predominantly directed to their future role as housewives and mothers. The churches exercised a powerful influence on this issue, and a more academic education was deemed unnecessary as women would have no opportunity to make use of it. Even those women attaining the required entry qualifications had very little chance of a university education. At the beginning of this century there were a thousand 'guest' women students at German universities, but none of them were allowed to matriculate. A small loophole was provided by the University of Zürich in German-speaking Switzerland, where women had been admitted since the 1860s. The breakthrough in Germany was made by the Grand Duke of Baden who in 1901 opened his two universities at Heidelberg and Freiberg to women. The dominant state of Prussia followed his example in 1908, the year in which the first woman university teacher was appointed, at the Commercial Academy in Mannheim. When war broke out six years later there were over four thousand female students at German universities.

In France the Falloux Law of 1850 established primary schools for girls and gave the Catholic church control over the curriculum. A general system of state secondary education for girls was introduced in the 1880s, but the pupils were only eligible for a final certificate issued by their own school rather than the state *baccalauréat* which was available for boys. University education for French women became possible during the 1880s but, as elsewhere, progress was slow. In 1913 only 10 per cent of French students were women and in 1930 there were only six women professors throughout the country.

Prejudice against female education continued, and still continues, long after legal provision was introduced. It also became a factor in the debate on female suffrage. That women should be taught something need not extend to the notion that they be taught about politics. President Woodrow Wilson had decided views on education fitting people for their proper position. Teaching politics to women was, he thought, 'about as appropriate and profitable as would be lecturing to stone-masons on the evolution of fashion in dress'.[45] By implication the latter was the proper subject of women's education.

Throughout the nineteenth and early twentieth century a suitable education was held to be one of the main qualifications for the franchise. On these grounds alone, most women were as disqualified as most men and the sexual disqualification would not have been necessary to exclude them. As with blacks in the southern United States and working-class males generally, those denied education were pronounced unfit to receive it, and could on that circular basis be exempted from full citizenship rights for not having the necessary rationality and knowledge.

We have seen that alongside education, ownership of property was a normal qualification for voting rights. Here too, women were at a disadvantage. It was well into the nineteenth century before women began to acquire legal property rights. Rather than being the owners of property they were taken to be the property of their menfolk; of either their husbands or their fathers. At the beginning of our period a married woman could not own property in her own right nor enter into a legal contract. The husband had ownership of his wife's labour and of her person as well. Property meant social standing and stability. Men voted as the agents of property. In contrast the idea of women as property long survived in the notion that they are given away in marriage by their fathers. On all such attitudes we can rely on Nietzsche being more explicit than most: 'A man who has depth, in his spirit as well as in his desires . . . can think of woman only in an *oriental* way – he must conceive of woman as a possession, as property with lock and key, as something predestined for service and attaining her fulfilment in service.'[46]

If the vote was the rightful preserve of the propertied, then until women's rights of ownership were extended their claims to political rights were considerably impaired. Inflation and widening property ownership had helped lower-class men overcome their political disqualifications, for ownership had not been *legally* denied on a class basis, as it was for women on a sex basis. Thus changes in the law were the only way this handicap could be overcome. In England a law of 1870 gave women legal control of their own earnings. This was far from being identical with full property rights, for, to take just one example, by the common law the husband possessed the property bequeathed to the wife by will after marriage if it exceeded two hundred pounds in value. A husband remained responsible for his wife's debts until the Married Women's Property Act of 1882, which enabled married women to hold property independently.

Unmarried women were usually granted property ownership and

limited political rights ahead of their married sisters. Since 1869 single English women who were ratepayers and householders were allowed to vote in municipal elections and the suffrage movement at this stage concentrated on claiming for them the same national political rights enjoyed by male property owners. The absurdity here, as Brian Harrison has pointed out, was 'a situation whereby a woman might acquire the vote before marriage, lose it on marriage, and regain it as a widow'.[47] The situation also posed a tactical dilemma. A franchise restricted to property-owning single women would be taken by opponents as an attempt to undermine and degrade marriage, for the married woman would then be singled out for political disqualification. One British MP feared that granting the vote to single women who were home-owners and ratepayers would demean those married women who were performing their 'natural' role. 'Is it any proof', he asked, 'because a woman happens to have failed . . . in the role of her own sex, that she can adequately discharge the more difficult and less congenial part of man?'[48] It seemed that if the vote was to be granted to some women it would have to be granted to all. As there were more women than men such a measure would, unprecedentedly, result in new electors outnumbering the old. Thus, according to this variant of the domino theory, a small reform would slide into a large one and so change should be avoided altogether.

In the case of single women the rationale of virtual representation by a husband clearly could not be applied. However, when one disqualification failed to have its effect, another was usually discovered. In Massachusetts in 1820 questions were raised as to why unmarried women who both owned property and paid taxes were still not allowed to vote. Surely the honourable plea of 'No taxation without representation' might be applied to them? To this, one pamphleteer replied that such women had disobeyed the biblical obligation to multiply and subdue the earth. Women not in subjection to husbands were thus to be subdued by the Bible.

In France it was not until 1907 that married women gained the legal right to full ownership and use of their wages, measures which even so could not easily be enforced, especially as the husband was still left responsible for his wife's debts. Only in 1938 did a law give legal capacity to French married women, who were now granted the right to appeal against the husband's choice of residence or his opposition to her employment.

For married women the vesting of private property-ownership in male hands was used as a justification for their own exclusion from politics. Opposition to the power of private property also came from another source, that of the socialists. For one group property appeared to be divided against them on the basis of sex; for another on that of class. Might not these separate perspectives be combined for a joint assault on the oligarchy of private property? This was precisely the fear of the Conservative MP E.P. Bouverie. In the debate on the 1871 Women's Disabilities Bill he noted that the movement for female enfranchisement aimed 'at the existing state of society and at marriage in particular. These', he concluded, 'were socialistic views.'[49]

In Germany, where the first major socialist party emerged, the 1891 Erfurt Programme called for 'universal, equal . . . and direct suffrage, with secret ballot, for all citizens. . . . without distinction as to sex', a commitment unrivalled by any other German party before the First World War. Party leader August Bebel was the author of an influential book on the woman question, *Die Frau und der Sozialismus*, and in the early years of this century a number of formidable women attached themselves to the party's cause. For many of them feminism was a sub-section of socialism. Once the latter had been attained they assumed that the demands of the former would automatically be incorporated. In Britain the Trades Union Congress had been committed to votes for women since 1884 and the Labour Party (founded in 1906) since 1912.

At the level of ideological principles we might expect the left, with its commitment to citizenship and equality, to be more pro-female suffrage than the political right, for whom the influence of tradition and the church have greater weight. In practice, however, principle was modified by particular matters of expediency. For example, feminism has usually been liberal and middle-class and the socialist Second International rejected 'bourgeois' suffrage movements financed by rich women, and whose franchise demands solely on behalf of middle-class women were likely to strengthen conservative rather than radical parties.

A related fear, particularly in France, was that women were over-influenced in a reactionary direction by the church. Louis Blanc had supported universal male suffrage in the mid-nineteenth century, but excluded women as dominated by the priests and hence inevitably conservative. Saint-Simonians supported female enfranchisement, but in the absence of strong feminist pressures the republican and radical parties limited their support to advocating educational reforms. The radical senator Georges Clemenceau believed that 'if the right to vote were given to women tomorrow, France would all of a sudden jump backwards into the middle ages'.[50]

The leaders of parliamentary socialism, insulated by elevation from the mass membership, and as yet untroubled by the responsibilities of actual power, found it easier to endorse feminist ideas than did trade union leaders engaged in actual day-to-day bargaining on the conditions of labour. Thus the two strands of the labour movement often found it difficult to coordinate on this issue. For the employers cheap female labour was a means of dividing the workforce and paying lower aggregate wages. For the male worker, female employees were competitors who undermined men's bargaining position at work and weakened their power of the purse and the traditional sexual division of labour at home. In the United States of America women workers had played a pioneering role in the first factory strikes of the 1820s and 1830s. Yet in general, as Ellen du Bois notes, 'trade unionists were particularly suspicious of black men and white women', fearing that the latter were 'ready to undersell male labour at a minute's notice.'[51] So rights battled with convenience in the labour movement as elsewhere, and radicals, as we saw with Rousseau, often shared more of the normal values of their societies than they may have cared to admit. Women, it was said, were either too uneducated or else educated in the wrong way. Sex war diverted attention from the priority of class war. As long as the vote was not divided on class lines it was said not to matter essentially if some were excluded. Writing in the *Sozialistische Monatshefte* in 1905 Edmund Fischer concluded that 'the so-called emancipation of women goes against the nature of women and of mankind as a whole. It is unnatural, and hence impossible to achieve'.[52]

Such views were not only held by men. A Women's Anti-Suffrage Association had been formed in Massachusetts. In 1889 in Britain a female anti-suffrage lobby announced its arrival with an 'Appeal Against Female Suffrage' signed by Mrs Humphrey Ward and a long list of supporters from prestigious addresses. They wanted women to have power in the community and in ethical and social matters, but not in such major affairs of state as foreign and colonial policy. 'We are convinced', they wrote, 'that the pursuit of a mere outward equality with men is for women not only vain but demoralising. It leads to a total misconception of woman's true dignity and special mission.' This, it seemed, could be performed better without the vote than with it. Furthermore, they believed no widespread female demand for the suffrage could be discerned. This point was consistently reiterated by the 'antis'. Two years later, for example, Samuel Smith MP declared that 'the advocates of women's suffrage are but a small minority of women, and they persist in pressing on their sisters a boon they do not covet'.[53] Behind this assertion lay not merely special pleading and the fact that political activism is virtually always a minority activity but also that in the nineteenth century it was common for feminists to place other priorities ahead of the franchise. Women's economic subjection in civil law, their control of their earnings, possession of their children and rights to divorce were often of greater immediate concern. In France the first feminist organisation, founded in 1866, was primarily concerned to improve female education and wages. In 1870 the female co-founder of the French 'Society for the Improvement of Women's Lot' concurred with the prevailing radical opinion that the female vote was undesirable as it would fortify the conservative parties. In the early years of this century the largest woman's organisation was the Patriotic League of Frenchwomen. By the outbreak of the First World War it claimed to have half a million members but, according to Theodor Zeldin, 'had nothing to do with the suffrage and scarcely anything with politics'.[54]

In Germany in the nineteenth century the women's movement, which was in any case legally debarred from political activity, emphasised that education should prepare women for their natural role as mothers. In Britain the inaugural meeting of the Women's National Anti-Suffrage League was held in July 1908. A year later they claimed to have nine thousand members and, thus encouraged, set up the less successful Girls' Anti-Suffrage League in 1911.

Anti-women's suffrage organisations did their utmost to find competent and articulate female speakers. Here, however, they ran up against a paradox. Through participating in the campaign, they contradicted their recommendation of female exclusion from political affairs. In arguing coherently they refuted the belief in their intellectual inferiority. Brian Harrison notes the instances when the Duchess of Atholl 'spoke so well for anti-suffragism that her audiences could not understand why, whatever she might say, such a woman should not vote'.[55]

Early feminism in the United States of America did not initially concentrate on winning the right to vote. This first gained priority in 1868 when the National Woman Suffrage Association was founded. From this time women in a number of the new western states were granted the franchise (Wyoming, 1869; Colorado, 1893; Utah, 1895; Idaho, 1896) but the federal constitutional right to vote was not attained until 1920, in line with the timing in a number of European countries, where much greater traditionalist resistance had to be overcome. As at the beginning of the movement, so also at this crucial stage, a link with the black cause was evident, for the nineteenth amendment, granting American women the vote, adapted the terminology used fifty years earlier in granting a black, male franchise.

The origins of the British women's suffrage movement may be traced back to 1866 when 1499 women signed a petition demanding that votes for women be included in the current reform bill. John Stuart Mill's amendment to that effect failed to convince the House of Commons and in 1867 the National Society for Women's Suffrage was formed. This was followed by the Women's Franchise League in 1889, the National Union of Women's Suffrage Societies in 1897 and the Pankhurst's Women's Social and Political Union in 1903. In 1870 a female suffrage bill had passed the House of Commons with a majority of 33, and between then and 1911 seven such bills passed their second readings. In 1918 British women were granted the vote at the age of 30 and in 1928 on the same terms as men; that is, at 21 years of age.

The French feminist movements founded in 1866, 1870 and 1882 did not include the attainment of voting rights among their concerns. The first to do so was the French Union for Women's Suffrage. It was founded in 1909 and claimed nine thousand members by 1914 and 100 000 in 1929. As with the other Latin countries of Europe, and Hungary and Switzerland, the political achievements of the post-First World War period passed France by. In May 1919 a proposal for women's suffrage had passed the Chamber of Deputies by the remarkable margin of 329–95, but was defeated in the Senate half a year later. There matters rested until near the end of the Second World War when, with the Radical party in decline and parliament suspended, General de Gaulle introduced the female vote by decree.

A German feminist movement had been founded in Leipzig in 1865 but a combination of disinclination for politics and legal disqualification even from forming political associations kept the suffrage question off the agenda. The legal restrictions did not apply in Hamburg, where the German Union for Women's Suffrage was formed in 1902. The collapse of monarchy and Empire in the First World War secured women the vote when the Weimar Republic was formed in 1919.

Before 1914 women had only won the vote for national elections in

New Zealand (1893), Australia (1902), Finland (1906) and Norway (1908). Within a decade 25 other states had conceded the female suffrage. The collapse of empires was a prerequisite in some instances, but anyway the *Zeitgeist* was operating with particular strength over a wide area, as the following chronology indicates.

States granting women's suffrage in national elections.
1915 Denmark, Iceland.
1917 Netherlands, Soviet Union, Finland.
1918 Sweden, Great Britain, China (six provinces), Austria, Germany, Estonia, Latvia, Poland, Lithuania, Czechoslovakia, Hungary.
1919 Rhodesia, Luxembourg, British East Africa, India.
1920 United States, Canada, Belgium.
1921 Palestine.
1922 Ireland.[56]

At this stage of our enquiry we might look back on a century-and-a-half of debate on political eligibility and ponder whether there is anything meaningful behind the sequence of political incorporation. We see that middle-class, propertied, educated men were allowed to vote before working-class men, but that the latter achieved the franchise before women. What does this indicate? Was it deemed superior to be a propertyless working-class man than to be an upper-class woman? Alternatively, does the fact that women were the last to achieve political rights indicate that

1. There was particular strength behind the notion of virtual representation and that political exclusion was not seen to be genuine when the household was represented by its male head?
    and/or
2. Discrimination on the basis of sex was in fact more entrenched than on the basis of class? Perhaps this was reinforced by the fact that the class-divide was impermanent and not always precisely apparent, whereas that between the sexes was clear and unbridgeable?
    and/or
3. Women were more fragmented, isolated, harder to organise and less organised than men; also that some feminist campaigners gave a low priority to achieving the vote?
    and/or

4. Women had more hurdles to overcome than any other enfranchised group, and some of these (separate spheres; medical
   theories) actually grew in the nineteenth century?

PART IV

9 Conclusion

The foregoing account concentrates on events and arguments that took place over seventy years ago in the United States of America, France, Germany and the United Kingdom. We have heard some of the voices of the political losers, for the franchise extensions that they opposed have now been achieved. In this conclusion we shall consider whether any of the attitudes and opinions we encountered have survived into the present day and if any of the warnings of advancing democracy may be regarded as prescient. Since, against the advice of our authors, democracy has come to be seen as a political ideal, we shall ask whether it has achieved all that its proponents hoped and expected, and whether it has run its full course now that universal suffrage is regarded as having been widely attained.

There were those who saw the British Reform Act of 1832 as a final adjustment of franchise rights and procedures. History has proved them wrong, but comparable judgements at that and later times might well be viewed as examples of wishful thinking. Those for whom further change is undesirable easily tend to attribute finality to the *status quo*. As we know, there were also conservatives who feared that reform had its own logic and that any initial extension of voting rights would exacerbate the displeasure felt and the demands made by those immediately below the line of eligibility. On this question Hegel, the Duke of Wellington and Tocqueville were correct in predicting that a movement once begun might have no termination short of universal adult suffrage.

With the granting of voting rights to all adults over the age of 18 (except the criminal and mentally ill) franchise extension is commonly regarded as having attained its fullest possible compass. What is usually ignored is that every society contains a substantial minority of people below the age of political citizenship and their relationship to the state represents a major anomaly for liberal democratic theory. A democratic state is usually presented as one that grants rights of political participation to all members of the society who will be subject to its laws. However, in Britain a child can be charged for a criminal offence at the age of 10 but is not politically adult until 18. In terms of the pre-democratic rationales outlined in Chapter 2, children are the largest category remaining under the aspect of 'virtual representation'. Just as their parents take decisions on their behalf

201

(where they shall live and go to school, when they shall go to bed, what they shall eat, wear, do, etc.) so also does the state, which decrees not only compulsory school attendance but also provision of a safety-net against parental neglect and ill-treatment. Thus it is not clear that children are unequivocally disadvantaged by not having the vote. Indeed, one could argue that they are better protected by law than are the old, the unemployed and the adult disabled who do have the vote. But on grounds of democratic theory, it is hard to see how children can be regarded as having an obligation to obey the law. For adults the act of voting may be taken to indicate consent to the outcome of an election and also to the electoral method of changing any laws or policies that they dislike. For John Locke, writing in the seventeenth century, the more passive but equally binding tacit consent was assumed merely by remaining within the territory[1] on condition that one had the right and ability to leave it. Nevertheless, not even this can be meaningfully attributed to children and so no ethical obligations can be regarded as consequent upon their remaining within a particular political jurisdiction. In Locke's opinion, children were bound only by the authority of their father: 'Tis plain then, by the Practice of Governments themselves, as well as by the Law of right Reason, that *a Child is born a Subject of no Country or Government.* He is under his Fathers Tuition and Authority, till he come to Age of Discretion; and then he is a Free-man, at liberty what Government he will put himself under; what Body Politick he will unite himself to.'[2]

Children, then, are bound by laws they have neither made nor assented to, and which, in consequence, they can be under no obligation to obey. That they compulsorily receive the protection of the law hardly alters the case in a moral sense. For Hobbes, writing in the seventeenth century, individuals are bound to obey any law which protects them, with protection defined primarily as providing order and avoiding a relapse into the anarchic state of nature. In the late twentieth century we have seen too many adverse varieties of order to be happy with the view that it alone imposes an obligation of obedience. Already in the eighteenth century Rousseau made the apposite point that 'Tranquillity is found also in dungeons; but is that enough to make them desirable places to live in?'[3] We must, then, apply to children what J.S. Mill once said of women; that their subjection provides the last major surviving instance (within liberal democracies) of the antiquated law of the strongest.

The lowering of the voting age to 18 in many instances brought it into line with the age of voluntary or compulsory military service. It thus overcame the possibility of being forced to kill and/or die for one's country before one was free to vote for it. Of course, fighting and killing may be taken as less mature acts than voting, and so justifiably made available at an earlier age. In short, the *capacity* for one is attained earlier than that for the other. However, the *obligation* of military participation is hard to justify in the absence of political rights. So also is the liability to legal punishment. In terms of coherence the ages of legal obligation and political rights ought to be made identical by raising the one or lowering the other.

Nevertheless any use of age as the sole criterion of political capacity is bound to remain somewhat arbitrary. In the few instances when children's political disqualifications are discussed the usual justifications concern the absence of rationality, experience, maturity and literacy. As for the notion that the age qualification divides those who possess these qualities from those who do not, Bob Franklin has noted that: 'As adults we pollute the environment, wage wars, create nuclear weapons, and stockpile mountains of food in Europe while people in Africa die in their tens of thousands; hardly the hall-mark of rational decision makers.'[4] Turning from ideal qualities, which clearly are not universally possessed, to minimal capacities, we may note that the basic act of political participation is not terribly demanding. John Harris points out that 'the franchise, which is perhaps the clearest and traditionally most hallowed right of citizenship, has, since universal adult suffrage, made minimum demands on the intelligence and rationality of voters. The whole apparatus of voting, whether by making an X-shaped mark on a ballot form or by pulling a lever, is designed so that a child could perform it.'[5]

As soon as one thinks of any precise qualifications for political inclusion it is evident that any actual test (beyond the present one of attaining a certain age) would bring in many children below the previous age of eligibility while disenfranchising numerous adults. If there has to be a dividing line somewhere, there will, as John Adams recognised, be problems wherever it is drawn. Clearly on any criteria of understanding or competence the use of age as the sole measure is bound to seem a blunt and inadequate instrument. Much like the imposition of one official language within a multi-lingual society, the present method of drawing the eligibility line is administratively convenient and so cheaper and easier to operate than any tests of actual individual capacity. Justifications, though, are not reasons. It is basically a matter of convention that children do not have the vote and the reason this convention endures is that it suits adults and they get away with it because children are not well placed to mount an effective challenge.

A situation much less clear-cut than the 'virtual representation' endured by children but still one of incomplete representation, is that of voters whose constituency representative is not the one of their choice. In terms of obligation they are bound to respect the result of the procedure in which they voluntarily participated, but (and here we refer only to political systems without proportional representation) it is far from clear that they are the recipients of full political representation. Those who voted for the winner got the result they wanted and plausibly indicated a certain identity of outlook with the person who became their representative; but the winner can hardly be said to represent the views and policy ideals of those who voted another way. One might say that such people have enfranchisement without representation.

Some opponents of democracy feared that a lower house based on universal suffrage would upset the balance of the constitution by which the countervailing powers of monarchical, aristocratic and popular influences were held to guarantee the survival of freedom. Comparable reasoning led to the United States Constitution stipulating the separation of powers between the legislature, the executive and the judiciary. Here we may note that two rather different principles are at work. The American theory of the separation of powers is mainly concerned with defending freedom by avoiding the aggregation of sovereignty in one unchallengeable authority. The British notion of the balanced constitution was concerned to do this also but additionally emphasised not merely separation of powers but the reciprocal influence of diverse types of power. The popular, the aristocratic and the monarchical were taken to represent different interest and outlooks. Nevertheless, throughout western democracies there has been widespread suspicion that, as the legislatures have become more democratic, real political power has moved away from the visible, public forum and towards the unseen activities of the Cabinet and the civil service. Soon after the passage of Britain's Second Reform Bill, which extended the vote to urban working-class men, Walter Bagehot pointed out that it was the Cabinet, a committee that worked wholly in secret, that was the ultimate power.[6] Writing of the United States nearly a century later, Michael Margolis noted that in the mid-1960s 'there was no longer any denying that Congress, the elected representative branch of government, had become overshadowed by the executive and its vast bureaucracy'.[7] Here we have the workings of one of democracy's paradoxes. As the vote was extended down the social scale the newly-enfranchised groups made demands on the state that led it to transcend the traditional functions of internal order, external defence and international representation and additionally take over responsibilities in the economic, welfare and educational spheres. For reasons indicated by Robert Michels and Max Weber, the consequent bureaucracies developed interests and powers which challenged and reduced those of the democratically-chosen representatives.[8]

A remnant of the belief that the franchise should be a reward for respectability and independence still exists in the exclusion from voting rights of prisoners. The exclusion of mentally-ill adults has, when discussed at all, been based on the same grounds that are applied to children: that they suffer a lack of facility for moral understanding, of the nature of obligation and of their duty to obey the law, and thus are exempt from both legal responsibility and political rights. In practice, the range of mental handicap is such that restrictions are not equally justifiable for all sufferers. In Britain the 1983 Mental Health Amendment Bill gave mentally handicapped people the right to vote, but a change the following year placed the onus on nursing staff to decide who should be enfranchised and in which constituencies. The allocation of such political responsibility to nursing staff is questionable and possibly unprecedented.

A political bonus for the educated and presumably rational lingered on in Britain until 1948 when the right of graduates to vote for their university candidate in addition to their home constituency candidate was finally abolished. In the same year the business premises qualification was also removed, the last institutional remnant of the idea that property ownership was a legitimate basis of political rights. However, aspects of the mentality that links wealth to political rights are still with us. In recent years, a vocal political cry on behalf of the presumed anguish of tax- and ratepayers has still been audible in certain areas. For example, ratepayers who were evidently outraged at having to subsidise cheap public transport were, as taxpayers, allegedly proud to finance the Falklands/Malvinas war and its prolonged and expensive aftermath. Behind all the rhetoric lay the implication that the tax/ratepayers had a right to special political consideration denied to those who did not make an equivalent financial contribution. On a pure theory of democracy all citizens would count as equal politically, simply by virtue of being members of the *polis*. Yet the rate- and taxpayers' revolt rhetoric implicitly takes some to be superior to others. Without ever saying so explicitly, it creates two levels of citizenship status based on relative contributions to public finance; a group of politically upgraded net contributors as against the downgraded net beneficiaries. Such a principle is obviously more plutocratic than democratic.

We have seen that in the nineteenth century the political rights of wealth were justified by the fear of the impoverished mass. The class divide was taken to be all-important, with the political exclusion of the poor seen as the basic means of maintaining the rights of private property. With the benefit of hindsight we can see how exaggerated this concern was. The working-class franchise certainly produced large socialist parties, but these have not inherited the future in the ways and to the extent their early supporters hoped, nor have they sought to revolutionise their societies on the occasions they have won governmental power. In western Europe, social democratic parties have sought no more than capitalism with a human face. Such parties are in the main associated with the creation and attempted defence of the welfare state and with a certain degree of public ownership, but this has never been a real threat to the basic capitalist character of the economy.

Fear of the mass has, however, continued on slightly different grounds. With the rise of the Cold War in the late 1940s, United States political science developed the notion that political apathy, to which their own country is particularly prone, was an essential feature of the democratic order. The appearance of Bolshevism and Fascism was held to demonstrate that the masses, when aroused, were more than likely to turn extremist. Thus democratic politics was redefined as a debate between pressure groups and other elites, with the people, or that part of them that cared to make the effort, confining their activities to acts of legitimation at election times. In this notion of democracy the people are allowed a role but their influence is carefully filtered and real debate – that is, the debate which is allowed to be influential – takes place at a more rarefied level.

The view that women have their own sphere and that rationality and politics are outside it is still so prevalent that it is probably unnecessary to pick any modern examples. Nevertheless, here are two from quite disparate sources. In 1983 the *Daily Telegraph*, a so-called quality newspaper and supporter of the British Conservative government, expressed an editorial opinion that 'It is not part of the values which sound Tories uphold to imagine that the wife's opinions on any subject at all command the respect or even attention of her husband.'[9] At that time Mrs Thatcher had been Prime Minister for nearly four years. Later in the decade, in Houston, Texas, Pam Postema was attempting to become the first woman umpire in major league baseball. As Marx once pointed out, in a rather different context, a crisis illuminates, and, in this instance it led Bob Knepper, pitcher with the Houston Astros baseball team, to reveal his basic beliefs: 'I believe God has ordained that there are some things women should do and some things they should not do. Umpiring is an occupation women should not be in. In God's society, woman was created in a role of sumbission (sic) to the husband. . . . I don't think a woman should be the president of the United States or a governor or mayor or police chief.'[10] Knepper is not thought to be a respected academic source but still a citizen and so a voice to be heard.

We suggested earlier that our account is a history of the losers. This now needs some qualification. The designation of 'history' could be taken to imply that the attitudes encountered are confined to the past, and the designation of our main thinkers as on the side of the losers, that the battles they fought are concluded. The main previously disqualified groups now have the vote. The unpropertied, the uneducated, the ethnic minorities and women are no longer debarred from political participation. Yet, and this is a legacy of the arguments we have been considering, all of them remain proportionally underrepresented in the parliaments and higher political echelons of the western liberal democracies. *In the 1990s western politics remains dominated by just those groups that nineteenth-century Conservatives wanted it controlled by; that is by well-off, educated, white men.* Brian Harrison concluded his studies of the anti-woman's suffrage movement with the observation that 'the difference between the Edwardian Antis and ourselves is perhaps less that anti-suffragism has vanished away in the interval than that – in its continued vitality – it no longer has the courage to articulate and intellectualise the beliefs which still so widely govern conduct'.[11] A similar point clearly also applies in respect of the other groups whose alleged political disqualifications we have discussed.

What the above situation amounts to is that as popular influence has become predominant in the legislature, so has real power been elevated almost commensurately into the executive. This, clearly, has an important bearing on our estimate of the democratic achievement.

Much of the literature and even more of our public discourse takes democracy as something which 'we' in the west have achieved. As democracy has now become the foremost badge of approval, most regimes seek to award it to themselves. Given that words have meanings attached to them by the conventions of normal usage, it is hard to find a firm standard against which to judge this appropriation. Just as a nation is a body of people who consider themselves a nation, so a democracy seems to be a society which considers itself one. As democracy has been declared an 'essentially contested concept' it is difficult to decide how any one appropriation is superior or inferior to any other. On the other hand, although there is no agreed definition of democracy, this does not mean that the word is meaningless. Each society has an understanding of what *range* of meaning specific sounds shall be taken to convey. Lack of *precise* definition does not deny the reality that there is a circumscribed range of meaning for which the term democracy is considered appropriate.

Our common understanding of democracy is that it refers to the arrangements of a political system. In 1905 A.V. Dicey noted that '"Democracy" in its stricter and older sense, in which it is generally employed by English writers, means, not a state of society, but a form of government; namely, a Constitution under which sovereign power is possessed by the numerical majority of the male citizens'.[12] Here the removal of the class barrier to political participation was the basic criterion. On this definition the United Kingdom became democratic when the vote for the lower house was granted to all men, even though it was still withheld from all women. In our time the political arrangements that go to make up western democracy are usually considered to include the following:

1. An elected, representative government.
2. An electorate consisting of almost the entire adult population.
3. Freedom to vote for any political party or person one chooses.
4. Freedoms of speech, peaceful assembly, organisation and the press.

With an explicitly stipulated institutional definition of democracy, we have criteria by which to judge which state systems are, and which are not, deserving of the label.

This approach, however, has limitations which we can explain with the help of Karl Mannheim's work *Ideology and Utopia*. Mannheim used the term 'ideology' to refer to the defence of prevailing institutions and 'utopia' for the depiction of a radical alternative.[13] Democracy has been and still can be used for both these purposes. The institutional definition lends itself to conservative purposes. From that perspective democracy in the west has been attained. We can now enjoy its blessings and watch, in an encouraging yet superior way, as other nations struggle to attain our level.

Democracy as 'utopia', nevertheless, is less static. Here we think more of democracy as a transcendent principle and so the institutions become secondary. Though remaining important they are now seen as better or worse exemplifications of the principle and though we may disagree as to which institutions are more democratic than others, surely the principle itself is not so ambiguous. It is that of the downward diffusion of power, and so the more electoral power is extended and diffused, the more democratic the system may be taken to be. Thus a political system, like that of the United Kingdom, where membership of the upper house is still largely determined by inheritance, is less democratic than one where, as in the United States of America, it is directly elected. On this 'utopian' usage, democracy denotes less a fixed institutional definition than a relative measure and so we can plausibly speak of some political systems as *more* democratic than others. In this sense western liberal democracies, rather than having implemented the full concept itself (whatever that might involve) can be said to have advanced further along the democratic road than have some other societies. In states that describe themselves as democratic we can, therefore, see them not as having inaugurated the full potential of the democratic ideal but, rather, as having attained a certain compromise with it. In fact such regimes do not seriously seek the widest *possible* implementation of democracy. Instead they suppose they have achieved the *optimal* implementation. This means that the democratic principle has to co-exist with other desired values, such as order, efficiency, expertise, liberty, national security and the rights and profits of private ownership. Though it is rarely admitted, modern liberal democracy has arrived at a *modus vivendi* with the democratic principle. Western states have not, for example, wished to extend the vote to all schoolchildren, all resident aliens, the mentally-ill and convicted prisoners. They have been reluctant to make the fullest possible use of the referendum, for this would limit parliaments' legislative powers. They have not wanted to institute economic democracy or even co-ownership in the workplace, for this would impinge on the powers of private ownership. Nor have they ever considered instituting a democratic income tax system where the required contribution would still be set by the state, but where individuals could allocate their tax between specific personally-chosen sectors. This would, no doubt, be opposed as administratively inconvenient and an impediment to even medium-term state planning but is less objectionable if one is motivated by democratic criteria alone.

In western liberal democracies the granting of votes to women has been the major franchise development of the twentieth century. For what has come to be called 'first phase feminism' political rights were the prime aim, a symbol of acceptance and a means towards further equal rights and opportunities. At the 1856 national convention of the United States women's rights movement, one resolution referred to 'the one cardinal demand for the right of the suffrage: in a democracy the symbol and guarantee of all other rights'.[14]

During the historical period we have investigated, women gained the right to own property, to keep their own wages and to vote, but they still generally earn less than men, suffer the consequences of the 'separate spheres' ideology, and are vastly under-represented in the higher echelons of political and economic power. As just one example, at the time of writing (June 1990) the United States has three women Governors (out of 50), two Senators (out of 100), and 28 members of the House of Representatives (out of 435).[15] The vote had been pursued as a means and not as an end. 'Second phase' feminism emerged in the 1960s as a result of disappointment with the consequences of the first phase. In one of the most influential works of modern feminism Kate Millett acknowledged 'the central significance of the franchise in that it aroused the greatest opposition and mobilized the greatest consciousness and effort. Yet in many ways it was the red herring of the revolution – a wasteful drain on the energy of seventeen years.' She regrets early feminism's 'failure to challenge patriarchal ideology at a sufficiently deep level, to break the conditioning process of status, temperament and role. . . . The patriarchal mentality', she believes, 'reasserted itself with great strength at the end of the first phase.'[16] It is clear from such accounts that the vote has not in itself been enough to meet the legitimate aspirations of women in terms of equal rights and real opportunities. The same is obviously true for blacks.

Our concentration on franchise rights should not be taken to imply the view that they constitute the alpha and omega of human liberation; but neither are they inconsequential. Frederick Douglass once described the psychological impact of the political exclusion of blacks in terms that can be applied equally to other groups. By disenfranchising black people, he said, 'you declare before the world that we are unfit to exercise the elective franchise, and by this means lead us to undervalue ourselves, and to feel that we have no possibilities like other men'.[17] The franchise constitutes recognition of basic human dignity and rights. How it is used or abused may vary immensely but basic legal possession provides the opportunity for moving towards fuller freedoms through constitutional means.

If we, then, take democracy as utopian in Mannheim's sense, what further steps might be taken in its direction? The first step would hardly go beyond the present at all and so would be minimally utopian on anyone's understanding of that term. It would simply bring other countries up to the level currently achieved in the most advanced instance. We do not regard our four countries as a world apart from the rest but for our present purposes they furnish a convenient frame of reference. Of them we may say that the United Kingdom seems the least democratic and the United States of America the most. Britain, having had no clear break with its feudal past, still retains an hereditary monarchy and upper house. The United States of America, the 'first new nation', has, by contrast, a directly-elected President, both houses of Congress chosen by popular election, federalism and the devolution of powers that this involves, a written constitution with a Bill of Rights, a proviso for state referenda, a Freedom of Information Act and provision for primary elections to determine whom a party candidate should be. Yet in spite of the democratic nature of their formal political arrangements, the level of real popular power and political participation in the United States has been a matter of continual unease. Participation rates in recent Presidential elections have been just over 50 per cent, 'lower than every other noncompulsory democracy in the West',[18] the level of political knowledge is very low and the society remains highly inegalitarian.

At the level of formal politics we may note that once in office United States Congressmen in practice have virtual security of tenure. In 1988, 99 per cent of incumbents of the House of Representatives were re-elected, as were 85 per cent of the Senate. Greater accountability and circulation here might be produced if, as with the British Labour party, compulsory re-selection of constituency representatives were to be introduced.

For a more thorough critique of United States' democracy, we need to turn to analyses that regard formal political institutions as necessary but still insufficient aspects of a politically healthy society. In *The Twilight of Authority*, Robert Nisbet observed both the decline of the political frame of mind and of a general sense of community. He believes that there is a 'profound distrust of the political order' and that 'the single most remarkable fact of the present time in the West is the waning of the historic political community, [and] the widening sense of the obsolescence of politics as a civilized pursuit, even as a habit of mind'.[19]

Benjamin Barber, in perhaps the most remarkable recent book on democratic theory, criticises liberal democracy from a Rousseauist perspective. For Barber liberal democracy is characterised by the theory of representation. It thus, in its very presuppositions, structures a divide between elite and mass which almost inevitably reduces the latter to a condition of apathy. Furthermore, liberal democracy puts liberalism before democracy and sees individual egoism as primary. Protection of property and privacy become the first call upon the state. In the spirit of this analysis we may note that the saying 'An Englishman's home is his castle', and the assumptions that underlie it, provide a perfect expression of this mentality. Barber finds a stark reminder of America's ideological condition in a remarkable quote from Charles Schultz, once President Nixon's director of the Bureau of the Budget and President Carter's chairman of the Council of Economic Advisors: 'Market-like arrangements . . . reduce the need for compassion, patriotism, brotherly love and cult solidarity as motivating forces behind social improvements. . . . Harnessing the "base" motive of material self-interest to promote the common good is perhaps the most important social invention mankind has achieved.'[20] With this mentality other people are feared as competitors in the controlled war of all against all and so a weak sense of community is the inevitable product. For Barber the very institutions of liberalism reduce democracy to what he terms its 'thin' variant, where politics becomes an activity of others and where citizenship is constituted solely by virtue of an individual's relationship to the government rather than by that of each to each other. Consequently most of the more than one hundred million American citizens are 'passive, apathetic, inactive, and generally uninterested in things public'.[21]

The broadening of access to institutions and the devolution of centralised powers are only part of what Barber proposes. Free institutions only provide the desired effect when they operate within an egalitarian and participatory culture. For this to occur, specialisation and the mystique of expertise have to be replaced by a self-confident public developing an understanding of the major issues that confront them.

Although Barber claims to be putting politics before economics, it seems that he considers the latter more in its institutional sense of small or large firms rather than in terms of its consequences for social stratification. Economic strength, whether inherited or achieved through market competition, is the basic determinant of class position and any recommendation of political equality has to consider its feasibility in the context of currently prevailing economic and social inequality. For some commentators absence of social equality would have no bearing on a society's democratic credentials. Rolf Dahrendorf, for example, has stipulated that 'by "democracy", however, we mean something different from Tocqueville, to wit, liberté rather than égalité, a liberal political community rather than an egalitarian society'.[22]

With this convenient reminder why should we not broaden our understanding of democracy in ways that accord with Tocqueville's definition? By now it should be clear that equality of formal political rights goes only a small way towards producing social equality. Earlier legal discriminations based on class, sex and race have been removed from western statute books and that certainly was a major step forward, but discrimination still survives through the continuation of social prejudices.

A fuller democracy requires a wider supporting culture in civil society and this will not be produced so long as the democratic mentality is considered appropriate only in the formal political sphere. As social equality is so dependent on economic equality we shall, in the first instance, look for far greater democratisation in the workplace, both in terms of the downward extension of decision-taking and in the broadening of ownership rights. The United States of America, though relatively forward in its political democracy, is less well-placed in the economic sphere. Without the support of a major party of labour, the size and strength of trades unions are unimpressive and a tradition of virulent hostility and opposition to them still persists.

West Germany is the only one of the four countries we have been considering where legal requirements for co-determination in industry exist. Their origin derives from the precise balance of forces in the immediate postwar period of allied occupation. At that time German business management was under suspicion of identification with the defeated Nazi regime, the coal and steel industries had been taken over by the occupying powers and in this situation the trade union movement was able to press for co-determination provisions that had long been included in their policy ideals. Following the creation of the Federal Republic of Germany, a law was passed in 1951 which instituted a measure of co-determination in the coal, iron and steel industries. Trades Union agitation for its extension to the rest of the economy produced partial success the following year when the government instituted a small measure of co-determination to large firms in other areas of industry. Further co-determination legislation was passed in 1972 and 1976, dealing with the establishment of works councils and the extension of co-determination at the board level to all larger companies.

The successes and failures of this situation are hard to judge, as precise causal relationships cannot be isolated. But we might note that the Federal Republic of Germany has combined high electoral participation (89 per cent in 1983 and 84 per cent in 1987), low inflation (2.3 per cent in June 1990)[23] and a low number of days lost through strike action, with being one of the world's most successful economies. Business and labour have, unsurprisingly, different attitudes to the co-determination laws. The former have feared the emergence of a situation that impairs efficiency, entrepreneurial freedom and the rights of property. Others have pointed out that the strength of the employees' side is diluted by its division into workers, salaried employees and senior executives, and that the trade union representatives have too easily identified themselves with the management.

In theory workplace participation has advantages which national political democracy cannot match. On some of the issues involved workers are likely to be much more knowledgeable than they are about national politics. On other issues (e.g. managerial investment decisions) they may be as uninformed as they are on some national issues, but here they have a motive for rapidly overcoming such lack of knowledge, for at the level of the firm they are faced with decisions which directly affect their immediate vital interests. In commenting on a study of workplace participation, Robert Lane noted that 'the "worker self-management" teams, in contrast to others, developed a sense of efficiency and "personal potency" that was not characteristic of those working under the usual hierarchical management' and that 'the distinction between exercising rights at work, daily and in an activity that forms part of one's identity, and exercising rights in politics infrequently and in an activity remote from one's self-concept, is determinative. The clear inference is that one should add to the basic right to work . . . the right to participate in the decisions affecting one's work.' What is of key significance for us is Lane's point that 'feelings of efficacy generated in the workplace were generalized to political participation'.[24]

A strengthening of the culture of democracy, then, is one of our requirements. Here we must note that those who are called upon to take political decisions obviously need to understand the questions and the issues involved in their resolution. Each political system, or level of democratisation, imposes corresponding educational requirements. Do we, then, agree with the nineteenth-century conservatives who used lack of education as a ground for political exclusion? This we can deny, for the following three reasons.

1. Opponents of franchise-extension used alleged ignorance as a justification for exclusion, rather than explicitly educational achievement as a criterion for inclusion. They gave wealth and property the dominant role. What really counted for them was the monopoly of political rights by wealthy and propertied men. Education was used basically as a cover for the defence of class privileges. In the southern states of the United States of America where explicit literary tests were applied these had nothing to do with judging educational level and everything to do with providing a veneer for racism.

2. Those using an educational rationale for political exclusion would appear more convincing if they had shown greater concern for introducing state schooling for the lower classes.

3. Political participation is in itself a form of political education. According to Benjamin Barber's neat summary, 'Politics becomes its own university, citizenship its own training ground, and participation its own tutor.'[25]

Our study has proceeded on the standard assumption that legitimate participation is possible once the franchise is granted. We now need to move a step further and note that democracy can be deeper and fuller than that which is indicated by the practice of placing a cross against a name. Meaningful understanding of, and participation in, democratic decision-taking requires a sophisticated level of political literacy. Politics, as some wit once pointed out, is mostly talk. To be part of the conversation one has to know the language. Participation, then, requires more than just the formal right; it also involves the actual means, and to an important extent these are educational.

A politically educated person would be one with the linguistic skills to formulate an argument; would have the knowledge and vocabulary of political processes; a sophisticated understanding of certain abstract terms that have ethical significance for the society; and, even more demanding than the above, an ability to understand the issues involved in policy areas of major importance – such as economics, defence and ecology – that have their own rather specialist knowledge.

This, you might think, is all very demanding, but who said a fuller democracy was the easy option? What can be suggested is not that these aims be achieved in any absolute sense but rather that they be seriously pursued. This pursuit, furthermore, is not something that should be seen as the exclusive task of the formal institutions of education – schools, colleges and universities. Rather, we should acknowledge that political education occurs, for better or worse, also through the channels of the mass media. Through these the populace are fed not just in their years of formal education but throughout their lives. In a culture seriously committed to the deepening of its democracy the press and television would raise their commitment to the presentation of public issues, broadening the understanding of the options available and outlining the possible consequences of each political choice.

At the present time this aspiration might seem implausible. Has not education become increasingly concerned with technical training rather than civic enlightenment?[26] Are not the mass media more concerned with entertainment than information? In both education and the media, the pursuit of quick profit has been given priority over the cultural quality of society. Such pressures will not abate in a hurry and, thus, any appeals based on different criteria are bound to face an uphill task. And yet, while dominant processes erode the quality of democracies, the term itself receives ever-enhanced prestige as the criterion of state respectability. With the collapse of communism in Eastern Europe and possibly even the Soviet Union itself, democracy on a world scale appears now in a situation akin to what it seemed in Europe in the 1840s, an unstoppable, ascendant force. In contrast to that time, however, all the dominant powers now claim their unequivocal allegiance to it. This allegiance is to democracy as it now is and no more. Democracy as ideology is so constituted that it depicts the western constitutional *status quo* and so suggests that nothing need be done but bask in the glow of self-satisfaction. From the viewpoint of democracy as utopia, though, current constitutional arrangements need not be taken as the final word on the subject. Political history has not come to a halt and for those committed to democratisation there remains much work to be done. Our proposals are merely brief preliminary indications of what is involved in really taking democracy seriously and are obviously not meant to provide anything approaching a comprehensive and detailed blueprint.[27] There remains no ultimate answer to the question of what democracy ought to contain. Its content will be what each generation chooses to give it, and so the dispute over the use of the word is a political battle that will continue.

Democracy, we may conclude, can still be used as a radical and subversive idea, as signifying a path along which we have ventured a little. Where it leads we cannot tell, partially because our societies do not want to and also because we may suspect that, like the horizon, democracy will recede further the closer we approach it.

Notes

PART I FACTS AND THEORIES

1 The Legislative Background

1. *Marx/Engels: Collected Works*, Vol. 6 (London, 1976), p. 356.
2. S.M. Lipset, *The First New Nation. The United States in Historical and Comparative Perspective* (New York, London, 1979), pp. 2, 21.
3. 'The Founding Fathers had not yet abandoned the classical tradition of civic humanism – the host of values transmitted from antiquity that dominated the thinking of nearly all members of the elite in the eighteenth-century Anglo-American world. . . . They still saw themselves ideally as a leisured, cosmopolitan, liberally educated gentry bound by a classical patrician code of disinterested public leadership . . . they were not modern men . . . many of them were bewildered, frightened, and awed by the emerging democratic world they had created.' Gordon S. Wood, 'The Fundamentalists and the Constitution', *The New York Review of Books*, 18 February 1988, p. 38.
4. S.M. Lipset, *The First New Nation*, p. 2.
5. A. Hamilton, J. Madison and J. Jay, *The Federalist Papers*, selected and edited by R.P. Fairfield (Garden City, New York, 1961), p. 24.
6. J.R. Pole, *The Revolution in America 1754–1788* (Stanford, 1970), p. 569.
7. C. Williamson, *American Suffrage. From Property to Democracy 1760–1860* (Princeton, NJ, 1968), pp. 136, 111 and see comments on New Jersey on p. 181.
8. Delaware, 1792; Kentucky, 1799; Maryland, 1809; Connecticut, 1818; New Jersey, 1820; Pennsylvania, 1838.
9. See R. Hofstadter, *Ten Major Issues in American Politics* (New York, 1968), p. 75.
10. D.G. Faust (ed.), *The Ideology of Slavery. Proslavery Thought in the Antebellum South, 1830–1860* (Baton Rouge and London, 1981), p. 235.
11. A.R. Myers, *Parliaments and Estates in Europe to 1789* (London, 1975), p. 29.
12. R.R. Palmer, *The Age of the Democratic Revolution. A Political History of Europe and America 1760–1800* (Princeton, NJ, 1959), p. 517 and see pp. 522–6.
13. G. Best, *The Permanent Revolution* (London, 1988), p. 174.
14. J.H. Stewart, *A Documentary Survey of the French Revolution* (Toronto, 1969), p. 572.
15. A. Cobban, *A History of Modern France*, Vol. 2 (Harmondsworth, 1962), p. 53.
16. F.M. Anderson, *The Constitutions and other Select Documents illustrative of the History of France 1789–1907* (New York, 1967), pp. 457–8.

17. P. Campbell, *French Electoral Systems and Elections 1789–1957* (London, 1958), p. 62.
18. *Marx/Engels: Selected Works*, Vol. 1 (Moscow, 1962), pp. 334, 293.
19. J.A.S. Grenville, *Europe Reshaped 1848–1878* (London, 1986), p. 117.
20. E.J. Hobsbawm, *The Age of Empire 1875–1914* (London, 1987), p. 96.
21. According to T. Zeldin, *France 1848–1945*, Vol. 1 (Oxford, 1973), p. 587.
22. A. Werth, *De Gaulle. A Political Biography* (Harmondsworth, 1965), p. 220.
23. P. Avril, *Politics in France* (Harmondsworth, 1969), p. 31. D. Pickles, *The Fifth French Republic. Institutions and Politics* (London, 1962), p. 3.
24. C.E. Schorske, *German Social Democracy 1905–1917. The Development of the Great Schism* (New York, 1972), p. 168.
25. A convenient listing of the various states and their populations is given in W.H. Bruford, *Germany in the Eighteenth Century. The Social Background of the Literary Revival* (Cambridge, 1971), pp. 333–6.
26. A. Ramm, *Germany 1789–1919* (London, 1967), p. 143.
27. Ibid., p. 197.
28. T.S. Hamerow, *The Social Foundations of German Unification 1858–1871* (Princeton, NJ, 1974), p. 297.
29. M. Weber, *From Max Weber. Essays in Sociology*, eds H.H. Gerth and C.W. Mills (London, 1961), p. 111.
30. H-U. Wehler, *The German Empire 1871–1918* (Leamington Spa and Dover, NH, 1985), p. 60.
31. See J. Schauff, 'Das Wahlsystem des Deutschen Reiches und die Zentrumspartei', in G. Riter (ed.), *Deutsche Parteien vor 1918* (Köln, 1973), p. 303.
32. R.R. Palmer, *The Age of the Democratic Revolution*, p. 144. Also see p. 143.
33. Ibid., p. 149.
34. D.G. Wright, *Democracy and Reform 1815–1885* (Burnt Mill, Harlow, 1982), p. 6.
35. E.J. Evans, *The Great Reform Act of 1832* (London and New York, 1983), p. 4.
36. N. Gash, *Politics in the Age of Peel. A Study in the Technique of Parliamentary Representation, 1830–1850* (London, New York and Toronto, 1953), p. x.
37. Ibid., p. 239. Also see F.B. Smith, *The Making of the Second Reform Bill* (Cambridge, 1986), pp. 15–20.
38. E.J. Evans, *The Great Reform Act of 1832*, p. 42.
39. Ibid., p. 30.
40. M. Bentley, *Politics Without Democracy 1815–1914. Perception and Preoccupation in British Government* (London, 1984), p. 182.
41. F.B. Smith, *The Making of the Second Reform Bill*, p. 232.
42. E.J. Feuchtwanger, *Democracy and Empire. Britain 1865–1914* (London, 1985), p. 46.
43. F.B. Smith, *The Making of the Second Reform Bill*, p. 2.
44. N. Blewett, 'The Franchise in the United Kingdom 1885–1918', *Past and Present*, 32 (1965), p. 36.

45. Quoted in ibid., p. 39.
46. See ibid., p. 46.
47. Pat Thane, 'Government and Society in England and Wales 1750–1914' in F.M.L. Thompson (ed.), *The Cambridge Social History of Great Britain 1750–1950*, Vol. 3 (Cambridge, 1990), p. 44.
48. E.J. Feuchtwanger, *Democracy and Empire*, p. 54.
49. S.M. Lipset, *Political Man* (London, 1963), pp. 78, 79.
50. S.E. Finer, *Comparative Government* (Harmondsworth, 1977), pp. 131, 62.
51. N. Mandela, *I am Prepared to Die* (London, 1984), p. 43.
52. S.E. Finer, *Comparative Government*, p. 139.
53. A. Arblaster, *Democracy* (Milton Keynes, 1987), p. 99.

2 The Case Against Democracy

1. See W. Ullmann, *A History of Political Thought: The Middle Ages* (Harmondsworth, 1965), pp. 12–13.
2. Aristotle, *The Politics* (Harmondsworth, 1962), pp. 155, 102.
3. P.E. Corcoran, 'The Limits of Democratic Theory', in G. Duncan (ed.), *Democratic Theory and Practice* (Cambridge, 1983), pp. 13, 15.
4. A. Hamilton, J. Madison and J. Jay, *The Federalist Papers*, (New York, 1961), p. 20.
5. R. Hofstadter, *Ten Major Issues in American Politics* (New York, 1968), pp. 77–8.
6. C. Williamson, *American Suffrage. From Property to Democracy. 1760–1860* (Princeton, NJ, 1968), p. 281.
7. B. Disraeli, *Selected Speeches of the late Right Honourable the Earl of Beaconsfield*, Vol. 1 (London, 1882), pp. 546–7.
8. E. Burke, *Reflections on the Revolution in France* (London, 1964), p. 121.
9. K.A. Raaflaub, 'Democracy, Oligarchy, and the Concept of the "Free Citizen" in Late Fifth-Century Athens', *Political Theory*, 11 (1983) 519. Also see p. 533.
10. However, 'a number of Swiss cantons and German cities thought themselves "democratic" in the eighteenth century'. S.R. Graubard, 'Democracy' in *Dictionary of the History of Ideas*, Vol. 1 (New York, 1973), p. 661.
11. R. Williams, *Culture and Society 1780–1950* (Harmondsworth, 1968), p. 14.
12. D.P. Crook, *American Democracy in English Politics 1815–1850* (Oxford, 1965), p. 95.
13. M. Richter, 'Toward a Concept of Political Illegitimacy. Bonapartist Dictatorship and Democratic Legitimacy', *Political Theory*, 10 (1982), p. 201.
14. B. Disraeli, *Selected Speeches*, Vol. 1, p. 625.
15. G. Stedman-Jones, *Outcast London. A Study in the Relationship between Classes in Victorian Society* (Harmondsworth, 1984), pp. 8–9.
16. See D. Morgan, *Suffragists and Liberals. The Politics of Women Suffrage in Britain* (Oxford, 1975), p. 124.

17. K.H. Porter, *A History of Suffrage in the United States* (New York, 1971), p. 248.
18. Ibid., p. 4.
19. T.S. Hamerow, *Restoration, Revolution, Reaction. Economy and Politics in Germany 1815–1871* (Princeton, NJ, 1972), p. 123.
20. T.S. Hamerow, *The Social Foundations of German Unification 1858–1871* (Princeton, NJ, 1974), p. 304.
21. E.J. Evans, *The Great Reform Act of 1832* (London and New York, 1983), pp. 2, 3.
22. T.S. Hamerow, *Social Foundations*, p. 306.
23. E. Burke, *Reflections*, pp. 53–4.
24. R. Hofstadter, *Ten Major Issues*, pp. 76–7.
25. G. Woodbridge, *The Reform Bill of 1832* (New York, 1970), p. 10. Among many such views see also the speech of the Duke of Wellington to the House of Lords on 4 October 1831, in C.K. Emden (ed.), *Selected Speeches on the Constitution*, Vol. 2 (London, 1939), p. 150.
26. Quoted in *Marx/Engels: Collected Works*, Vol. 11 (London, 1979), p. 499.
27. B. Disraeli, *Selected Speeches*, Vol. 1, pp. 543, 542.
28. A.R. Myers, *Parliaments and Estates in Europe to 1789* (London, 1975), pp. 55, 26.
29. C.B. Macpherson, *Burke* (Oxford, 1980), p. 49.
30. James Mill, *An Essay on Government* (Indianapolis, 1977), pp. 73–4.
31. C. Rossiter, *The Political Thought of the American Revolution* (New York, 1963), pp. 21, 20.
32. C.K. Emden (ed.), *Selected Speeches*, Vol. 2, p. 148. Also see B. Disraeli, *Coningsby or the New Generation* (London, 1968), p. 39.
33. G.W.F. Hegel, *Hegel's Political Writings*, ed. Z.A. Pelczynski, (Oxford, 1969), pp. 300–1.
34. A. de Tocqueville, *Democracy in America*, ed. R.D. Heffner, (New York, 1960), p. 57.
35. A. Briggs, *Victorian People* (Harmondsworth, 1982), p. 250.
36. Quoted in J. Bentham, *A Fragment on Government* (Cambridge, 1988), pp. 72–3.
37. Quoted in E. Burke, *Reflections*, p. 47. Also see p. 284.
38. J.B. Schneewind (ed.), *Mill. A Collection of Critical Essays* (London, 1969), p. 284.
39. B. Constant, *Political Writings* (Cambridge, 1988), p. 214.
40. D.G. Faust (ed.), *The Ideology of Slavery. Proslavery Thought in the Antebellum South, 1830–1860* (Baton Rouge and London, 1981), p. 176.
41. W. Bagehot, *The English Constitution* (London, 1961), pp. 265–6.
42. W.E.H. Lecky, *Democracy and Liberty*, Vol. 1 (London, New York and Bombay, 1896), pp. 108–9, 108.
43. F. Stern, *Gold and Iron. Bismarck, Bleichröder and the Building of the German Empire* (London, 1980), p. 197.
44. To raise the example of modern India, where relatively stable democracy has endured alongside about 66 per cent illiteracy, is to apply the wisdom of hindsight.

45. See E. Hobsbawm, *The Age of Empire 1875–1914* (London, 1987), p. 345.
46. T.S. Hamerow, *Social Foundations*, pp. 280, 283.
47. A. Cobban, *A History of Modern France*, Vol. 2 (Harmondsworth, 1962), p. 219.
48. These comments on French thought are based on Amy Eiholzer-Silver, 'The Movement of the Intellectuals in France under the Restoration: The Doctrinaires', University of Kent MA, 1988.
49. J.S. Mill, *Utilitarianism, Liberty, Representative Government* (London, 1962), p. 288.
50. E.J. Feuchtwanger, *Democracy and Empire. Britain 1865–1914* (London, 1985), p. 29.
51. W. Bagehot, *The English Constitution*, p. 272.
52. T.S. Hamerow, *Social Foundations*, pp. 211–12.
53. E. Sagara, *A Social History of Germany* (London, 1977), p. 281.
54. T.S. Hamerow, *Restoration, Revolution, Reaction*, p. 216.
55. A. Briggs, *Victorian People*, p. 262.
56. G. Le Bon, *The Crowd* (London, 1952), pp. 91, 92.
57. A. Briggs, *Victorian People*, p. 266.
58. W.E.H. Lecky, *Democracy and Liberty*, Vol. 1, p. 264.
59. E. Burke, *Reflections*, p. 76; Thiers quoted in A. de Tocqueville, *Selected Letters on Politics and Society*, ed. R. Boesche, (Berkeley, Los Angeles and London, 1985), p. 128.
60. J.S. Mill, *Autobiography of John Stuart Mill* (New York, 1964), p. 168.
61. A. Eiholzer-Silver, 'The Movement of the Intellectuals', p. 42; W. Bagehot, *Physics and Politics* (London, n.d.), pp. 117–18; T.S. Hamerow, *Social Foundations*, p. 164.
62. T.S. Hamerow, *Social Foundations*, p. 293.
63. J.S. Mill, *Autobiography*, p. 167.
64. W. Cobbett, *Rural Rides* (Harmondsworth, 1979), p. 81. Also see G. Stedman-Jones, *Outcast London. A Study in the Relationship between Classes in Victorian Society* (Harmondsworth, 1984), pp. 12–16.
65. P.N. Carroll and D.W. Noble, *The Free and the Unfree. A New History of the United States* (Harmondsworth, 1985), p. 128. Also see p. 240.
66. R. Hofstadter, *Ten Major Issues*, pp. 79, 80.
67. G. Stedman-Jones, *Outcast London*, pp. 128, 11, 223, 224. Also see D. Pick, *Faces of Degeneration. A European Disorder, c. 1848–c. 1914* (Cambridge, 1989), esp. pp. 165, 191 fn. 44, 201.
68. G. Le Bon, *The Crowd*, pp. 29, 207, 16.
69. J.R. Pole (ed.), *The Revolution in America 1754–1788* (Stanford, 1970), p. 568.
70. A. Cobban, *A History of Modern France*, Vol. 1 (Harmondsworth, 1963), p. 250.
71. D.G. Wright, *Democracy and Reform 1815–1885* (Burnt Mill, Harlow, 1982), p. 108.
72. Quoted in James Mill, *An Essay on Government*, p. 78.
73. R. Hofstadter, *Ten Major Issues*, p. 80.
74. K.H. Porter, *A History of Suffrage in the United States*, p. 92.
75. B. Disraeli, *Selected Speeches*, Vol. 1, pp. 554, 583.
76. B. Constant, *Political Writings*, p. 216.

77. James Mill, *An Essay on Government*, p. 76.
78. *Marx Engels: Collected Works*, Vol. 3 (London, 1975), p. 384.
79. G. Stedman-Jones, *Outcast London*, p. 335.
80. A.V. Dicey, *Law and Public Opinion in England during the Nineteenth Century* (London, 1963), p. xxxv.
81. See T. Paine, *The Rights of Man* (London, 1958), pp. 50–1, 118.
82. E.N. Anderson, *The Social and Political Conflict in Prussia. 1858–1864* (New York, 1976), p. 259.
83. Quoted in J.S. Mill, *Autobiography*, p. 183.
84. B. Constant, *Political Writings*, p. 215.
85. R. Hofstadter, *Ten Major Issues*, p. 79.
86. T.S. Hamerow, *Restoration, Revolution, Reaction*, p. 215.
87. A. Briggs, *Victorian People*, p. 250.
88. E.N. Anderson, *Social and Political Conflict in Prussia*, p. 273.
89. T.S. Hamerow, *Social Foundations*, p. 295.
90. C. Williamson, *American Suffrage*, p. 12.
91. T.S. Hamerow, *Social Foundations* p. 299. Also see ibid., pp. 294–300 and E.N. Anderson, *Social and Political Conflict in Prussia*, pp. 261–9.
92. *Marx/Engels: Collected Works*, Vol. 4 (London, 1975), p. 518.
93. S. Hall, 'The Battle for Socialist Ideas in the 1980s', in R. Miliband and J. Saville (eds), *The Socialist Register 1982* (London, 1982), p. 16.
94. K. Marx, *Capital*, Vol. 1 (Harmondsworth, 1976), p. 899.
95. Quoted in *Marx Engels: Collected Works*, Vol. 11 (London, 1979), p. 608.
96. R. Harrison (ed.), *The English Defence of the Commune* (London, 1971), p. 69.
97. B. Webb, *My Apprenticeship* (Harmondsworth, 1971), p. 202.
98. H.G. Wells, 'The Life History of Democracy', in P. Keating (ed.), *The Victorian Prophets. A Reader from Carlyle to Wells* (Glasgow, 1981), pp. 245, 264.
99. A. de Tocqueville, *Recollections* (New York, 1975), pp. 232–3.
100. T.S. Hamerow, *Restoration, Revolution, Reaction*, p. 175.
101. E.N. Anderson, *Social and Political Conflict in Prussia*, p. 271.
102. R.J. White (ed.), *The Conservative Tradition* (London, 1950), p. 225.
103. A.V. Dicey, *Law and Public Opinion*, p. 57.
104. *Marx Engels: Collected Works*, Vol. 6 (London, 1976), pp. 507–8.
105. See A.J. Mayer, *The Persistence of the Old Regime. Europe to the Great War* (London, 1981), pp. 305–29.

PART II THINKERS

3 John Adams

1. L.J. Cappon (ed.), *The Adams–Jefferson Letters* (Chapel Hill, 1959), 2 vols, Vol. 1, p. 31.
2. John Adams, *Works* in ten volumes, ed. C.F. Adams (Boston, 1850–6), Vol. X, p. 567.
3. Gordon S. Wood, *The Creation of the American Republic, 1776–1787*

(Chapel Hill, 1969), p. 568. More recently John P. Diggins wrote that Adams's '*Defence* anticipated the course of the French Revolution years before Burke's better-known reflections on that subject'. J.P. Diggins, 'Knowledge and Sorrow: Louis Hartz's Quarrel with American History', *Political Theory*, 16 (1988), p. 364.

4. A more generous evaluation is that of B. Bailyn in *The Ideological Origins of the American Revolution* (Cambridge, Mass., 1967), p. 16. Also see R.R. Palmer, *The Age of the Democratic Revolution. A Political History of Europe and America, 1760–1800* (Princeton, NJ, 1959), p. 271.
5. Z. Haraszti, *John Adams and the Prophets of Progress* (Cambridge, Mass., 1952).
6. Of most influence was Charles A. Beard's *An Economic Interpretation of the Constitution of the United States* (New York, 1913).
7. This is the main theme of J.R. Howe, Jr, *The Changing Political Thought of John Adams* (Princeton, NJ, 1966).
8. See Edmund S. Morgan, *Inventing the People. The Rise of Popular Sovereignty in England and America* (New York and London, 1988), p. 290.
9. Adams, *Works*, Vol. IV, pp. 292, 293.
10. Ibid., Vol. IX, pp. 550–1.
11. Ibid., p. 571.
12. *Adams–Jefferson Letters*, Vol. 2, p. 347.
13. T. Paine, *The Rights of Man* (London, 1958), p. 278.
14. Palmer, *Age of the Democratic Revolution*, p. 160.
15. Paine, *Rights of Man*, p. 278.
16. Adams, *Works*, Vol. VI, p. 8.
17. Ibid., p. 57. On Adams's low opinion of Paine, see Bailyn, *Ideological Origins*, pp. 288–90.
18. Adams, *Works*, Vol. VI, p. 166.
19. Ibid., p. 273.
20. Quoted in Haraszti, *John Adams and the Prophets of Progress*, p. 257.
21. Adams, *Works*, Vol. VIII, p. 265. Also see Wood, *Creation of the American Republic*, p. 571.
22. A. Koch and W. Peden (eds), *The Selected Writings of John and John Quincy Adams* (New York, 1946), pp. 59–60.
23. Adams, *Works*, Vol. VIII, p. 10.
24. Quoted in Haraszti, *John Adams and the Prophets of Progress*, p. 222.
25. Quoted ibid., p. 205.
26. Adams, *Works*, Vol. VI, p. 100.
27. Ibid., Vol. IV, p. 303.
28. Ibid., pp. 312–3.
29. F.M. Cornford (intro.), *The Republic of Plato* (Oxford, 1961), p. 281.
30. Adams, *Works*, Vol. VI, p. 90.
31. Ibid., p. 484.
32. *Adams–Jefferson Letters*, p. 357.
33. Adams, *Works*, Vol. VI, p. 288. Also see Wood, *Creation of the American Republic*, p. 569.
34. Adams, *Works*, Vol. IX, p. 216.
35. J-J. Rousseau, *The Social Contract*, Book II, Ch. XI.

36. Adams, *Works*, Vol. VI, p. 458.
37. Ibid., Vol. X, pp. 408, 409.
38. Ibid., p. 211.
39. *Selected Writings*, p. 134.
40. Quoted in Haraszti, *John Adams and the Prophets of Progress*, p. 194.
41. *Adams–Jefferson Letters*, Vol. 2, p. 358.
42. Ibid., p. 435.
43. On elections and electoral law in late eighteenth-century America, see K.H. Porter, *A History of Suffrage in the United States*, first published 1918, (New York, 1971), Ch. 1, and also C. Williamson, *American Suffrage. From Property to Democracy 1760–1860* (Princeton, NJ, 1968).
44. Adams, *Works*, Vol. IX, p. 435.
45. Ibid., p. 375.
46. Ibid., p. 378.
47. Ibid., Vol. X, p. 268.
48. Ibid., Vol. VI, pp. 8–9.
49. Ibid., p. 9.
50. Ibid., p. 280.
51. Ibid., p. 68.
52. Ibid., p. 280.
53. John Diggins notes that 'Adams not only anticipates Marx in seeing class structures as inevitable regardless of the system of government; he also goes further than Marx in insisting that power and exploitation will remain a permanent phenomenon even after property relations have been transformed, unless institutional safeguards are established.' Diggins, 'Knowledge and Sorrow', p. 365.
54. *Adams–Jefferson Letters*, Vol. 2, p. 356.
55. Adams, *Works*, Vol. IX, p. 635.
56. Wood, *Creation of the American Republic*, p. 571 and see pp. 587–92 on Adams's alienation from most American thinking.

4 G.W.F. Hegel

1. G.W.F. Hegel, *The Philosophy of History* (New York, 1956), p. 86.
2. S. Avineri, *Hegel's Theory of the Modern State* (London, 1974), p. x.
3. *Hegel's Political Writings*, intro. Z.A. Pelczynski (Oxford, 1969), p. 143.
4. Ibid., p. 190.
5. R. Plant, *Hegel* (London, 1973), p. 186.
6. G.W.F. Hegel, *Philosophy of Right* (London, Oxford, New York, 1971), para. 209. As there are many editions of *Philosophy of Right* I have followed the convention of referring to it by paragraph number.
7. J. de Maistre, *The Works of Joseph de Maistre*, ed. J. Lively (London, 1965), p. 80.
8. R. Plant, *Hegel*, p. 72.
9. G.W.F. Hegel, *Philosophy of History*, pp. 446–7. Also see G.W.F. Hegel, *Hegel: The Letters* (Bloomington, 1984), pp. 114, 123.
10. G.W.F. Hegel, *Philosophy of History*, p. 18. Modified on the contentious issue of 'the German world' according to S. Avineri, *Hegel's Theory of the Modern State*, p. 22.
11. S. Avineri, 'Hegel' in D. Miller et al., *The Blackwell Encyclopaedia of*

Political Thought (Oxford, 1987), p. 199.
12. R.L. Schacht, 'Hegel on Freedom', in A. MacIntyre (ed.), *Hegel. A Collection of Critical Essays* (Notre Dame, London, 1976), p. 326.
13. G.W.F. Hegel, *Philosophy of History*, p. 444.
14. Ibid., pp. 46–7.
15. *Hegel's Political Writings*, p. 300.
16. Ibid., p. 311.
17. G.W.F. Hegel, *Philosophy of Right*, paras 291, 297, 297a.
18. *Hegel's Political Writings*, p. 293.
19. G.W.F. Hegel, *Philosophy of Right*, para. 309.
20. *Hegel's Political Writings*, pp. 73, 257.
21. Ibid., p. 95, fn. 1.
22. G.W.F. Hegel, *Philosophy of Right*, para. 280a.
23. Ibid., para. 308.
24. G.W.F. Hegel, *Philosophy of History*, p. 48.
25. G.W.F. Hegel, *Philosophy of Right*, para. 308.
26. L. Krieger, *The German Idea of Freedom. History of a Political Tradition* (Chicago and London, 1972), p. 138.
27. G.W.F. Hegel, *Philosophy of Right*, para. 301.
28. J.P. Plamenatz, *Man and Society*, Vol. 2, (London, 1963), p. 257.
29. G.W.F. Hegel, *The Phenomenology of Mind*, quoted in C. Heiman, 'The Sources and Significance of Hegel's Corporate Doctrine' in Z.A. Pelczynski (ed.), *Hegel's Political Philosophy. Problems and Perspectives* (Cambridge, 1971), p. 117.
30. *Marx Engels: Collected Works*, Vol. 3 (London, 1975), p. 95.
31. Introduction to *Hegel's Political Writings*, p. 125.
32. *Hegel's Political Writings*, pp. 262–3.
33. G.W.F. Hegel, *Philosophy of History*, pp. 255, 252, 253, 256.
34. G.W.F. Hegel, *Philosophy of Right*, para. 308.
35. Ibid., paras 241, 317, 301.
36. Introduction to *Hegel's Political Writings*, p. 78.
37. K-H. Ilting, 'The Structure of *Hegel's Philosophy of Right*' in Z.A. Pelczynski, *Hegel's Political Philosophy*, p. 108.
38. G.W.F. Hegel, *Philosophy of Right*, paras 301, 166.
39. Ibid., para. 166a.
40. Ibid., para. 329.
41. *Hegel's Political Writings*, p. 262.
42. Ibid., p. 264.
43. Ibid., p. 88.
44. G.W.F. Hegel, *Philosophy of Right*, para. 310.
45. *Hegel's Political Writings*, p. 234.
46. G.W.F. Hegel, *Philosophy of Right*, para. 313.
47. J.F. Suter, 'Burke, Hegel and the French Revolution', in Z.A. Pelczynski, *Hegel's Political Philosophy. Problems and Perspectives*, p. 65. Also see S. Avineri, *Hegel's Theory of the Modern State*, p. 164.
48. G.W.F. Hegel, *Philosophy of History*, p. 45.
49. G.W.F. Hegel, *Philosophy of Right*, para. 317.
50. Ibid., para. 260 and addition to para. 258.

5 Alexis de Tocqueville

1. A. de Tocqueville, *Selected Letters on Politics and Society*, ed. R. Boesche (Berkeley, Los Angeles and London, 1985), p. 350.
2. See *Marx Engels: Collected Works*, Vol. 3 (London, 1975), p. 266.
3. E. Wright, 'Liberty, Equality and Clemency' in *The Times Higher Education Supplement*, 23 December 1988, p. 16.
4. A. de Tocqueville, *Selected Letters*, p. 121.
5. M. Hereth, *Alexis de Tocqueville. Threats to Freedom in Democracy* (Durham, 1988), p. 19.
6. A. de Tocqueville, *Selected Letters*, p. 253.
7. A. de Tocqueville, *Democracy in America*, ed. R.D. Heffner (New York, 1960), p. 36.
8. Ibid., pp. 36 and 26.
9. Ibid., pp. 27 and 28.
10. Ibid., p. 29.
11. Ibid., pp. 28–9 and 30.
12. A. de Tocqueville, *Journeys to England and Ireland* (New Brunswick and Oxford, 1988), p. 28.
13. A. de Tocqueville, *Democracy in America*, ed. R.D. Heffner, p. 29. Also see A. de Tocqueville, *Journeys to England and Ireland*, pp. 66–70.
14. A. de Tocqueville, *Democracy in America*, ed. R.D. Heffner, p. 29. In the conclusion to Part I Tocqueville noted that whereas 'other nations seem to have nearly reached their natural limits' the Russians and the Americans 'are still in the act of growth . . . their starting-point is different, and their courses are not the same; yet each of them seems marked out by the will of Heaven to sway the destinies of half the globe'. Ibid., p. 142.
15. A. de Tocqueville, *The Old Regime and the French Revolution* (New York, 1955), p. 135.
16. A. de Tocqueville, *The European Revolution and Correspondence with Gobineau* (Westport, Conn., 1974), p. 79. See also pp. 83, 169.
17. Ibid., p. 191.
18. D. Goldstein, *Trials of Faith. Religion and Politics in Tocqueville's Thought* (New York, Oxford, Amsterdam, 1975), p. 125.
19. A. de Tocqueville, *The European Revolution and Correspondence with Gobineau*, p. 268.
20. R. Nisbet, 'Tocqueville's Ideal Types', in A.S. Eisenstadt (ed.), *Reconsidering Tocqueville's 'Democracy in America'* (New Brunswick and London, 1988), p. 182. See also ibid., p. 196. For a contrasting view, see R. Aron, *Main Currents in Sociological Thought*, Vol. 1 (Harmondsworth, 1979), p. 232.
21. A.S. Eisenstadt (ed.), *Reconsidering Tocqueville's 'Democracy in America'*, p. 6.
22. M. Hereth, *Alexis de Tocqueville*, p. 54.
23. Ibid., p. 54.
24. A. de Tocqueville, *Democracy in America*, ed. J.P. Mayer and M. Lerner (Evanston and London, 1966), p. 383. Also see A. de Tocqueville, *Selected Letters*, pp. 56, 93, 99, 101, 102.

25. A. de Tocqueville, *Democracy in America*, ed. R.D. Heffner, p. 30.
26. M. Zetterbaum, *Tocqueville and the Problem of Democracy* (Stanford, 1967), p. 20.
27. A.S. Eisenstadt (ed.), *Reconsidering Tocqueville's 'Democracy in America'*, p. 182.
28. A. de Tocqueville, *Democracy in America*, ed. R.D. Heffner, p. 317.
29. *Marx Engels: Collected Works*, Vol. 11 (London, 1979), p. 103.
30. K. Marx, *Capital*, Vol. 1 (Harmondsworth, 1976), p. 920.
31. A. de Tocqueville, *Democracy in America*, ed. R.D. Heffner, p. 317.
32. A. de Tocqueville, *Democracy in America*, eds J.P. Mayer and M. Lerner, p. lxxxviii.
33. A. de Tocqueville, *Democracy in America*, eds R.D. Heffner, p. 36.
34. A. de Tocqueville, *On Democracy, Revolution and Society*, eds J. Stone and S. Mennell (Chicago and London, 1980), p. 131.
35. R. Nisbet in A.S. Eisenstadt (ed.), *Reconsidering Tocqueville's 'Democracy in America'*, p. 188.
36. A. de Tocqueville, *Democracy in America*, ed. R.D. Heffner, p. 32.
37. A. de Tocqueville, *Democracy in America*, eds J.P. Mayer and M. Lerner, p. 181.
38. A. de Tocqueville, *Democracy in America*, ed. R.D. Heffner, p. 107.
39. Ibid., p. 109. Also see A. de Tocqueville, *On Democracy, Revolution and Society*, pp. 121–7.
40. A. de Tocqueville, *Democracy in America*, eds J.P. Mayer and M. Lerner, p. 251.
41. Ibid., p. 329.
42. A. de Tocqueville, *Democracy in America*, ed. R.D. Heffner, p. 57.
43. A. de Tocqueville, *Democracy in America*, eds J.P. Mayer and M. Lerner, p. 406.
44. A. de Tocqueville, *Recollections* (New York, 1975), p. 42.
45. Ibid., p. 5.
46. A. de Tocqueville, *Democracy in America*, eds J.P. Mayer and M. Lerner, p. 251.
47. A. de Tocqueville, *Recollections*, p. 320.
48. A. de Tocqueville, *Democracy in America*, eds J.P. Mayer and M. Lerner, pp. 712, 713.
49. A. de Tocqueville, *Selected Letters*, pp. 115–6.
50. G.A. Kelly, 'Parnassian Liberalism in Nineteenth-Century France. Tocqueville, Renan, Flaubert', *History of Political Thought*, 8 (1987), 482.
51. A. de Tocqueville, *The Old Regime*, p. xiv.
52. D. Goldstein, *Trials of Faith*, p. 128.
53. A. de Tocqueville, *Democracy in America*, ed. R.D. Heffner, p. 30.
54. Ibid., p. 192.
55. A. de Tocqueville, *Democracy in America*, eds J.P. Mayer and M. Lerner, p. 269.
56. A. de Tocqueville, *The Old Regime*, p. 96.
57. A. de Tocqueville, *On Democracy, Revolution and Society*, p. 366.
58. See A. de Tocqueville, *Democracy in America*, ed. R.D. Heffner, p. 67.
59. See A. de Tocqueville, *Democracy in America*, eds J.P. Mayer and M. Lerner, p. 703.

60. A. de Tocqueville, *Selected Letters*, p. 121.
61. A. de Tocqueville, *Democracy in America*, ed. R.D. Heffner, p. 114.
62. Quoted in J. Lively, *The Social and Political Thought of Alexis de Tocqueville* (Oxford, 1965), p. 108. Also see pp. 114–15, 121, 122.
63. A. de Tocqueville, *Recollections*, p. 15 and also see *Selected Letters*, pp. 202, 206–8, 213.
64. A. de Tocqueville, *Recollections*, p. 94.
65. Ibid., pp. 147–8. Also see S. Drescher, *Dilemmas of Democracy. Tocqueville and Modernization* (Pittsburgh, 1968), pp. 210, 223, 227, 237.
66. E. Burke, *Reflections on the Revolution in France* (London, 1964), p. 8.
67. A. de Tocqueville, *The Old Regime*, p. xxii.
68. H. Brogan, *Tocqueville* (Bungay, Suffolk, 1973), p. 78.
69. A. de Tocqueville, *The Old Regime*, pp. xv, 115. Also see p. 168.
70. A. de Tocqueville, *The European Revolution and Correspondence with Gobineau*, p. 159.
71. A. de Tocqueville, *Selected Letters*, p. 210.
72. A. de Tocqueville, *The Old Regime*, p. 153.
73. Ibid., pp. 135, 98.
74. A. de Tocqueville, *Journeys to England and Ireland*, p. 59.
75. A. de Tocqueville, *The Old Regime*, pp. 141, 145–6.
76. S. Drescher, *Dilemmas of Democracy*, p. 68.
77. A. de Tocqueville, *Democracy in America*, ed. R.D. Heffner, p. 306.
78. Ibid., p. 57.
79. A. de Tocqueville, *On Democracy, Revolution and Society*, p. 123.
80. A. Cobban, *A History of Modern France*, Vol. 1 (Harmondsworth, 1963), p. 125; R. Aron, *Main Currents in Sociological Thought*, Vol. 1, p. 240; R. Boesche, *The Strange Liberalism of Alexis de Tocqueville* (Ithaca, New York and London, 1987), p. 265.
81. C. Strout, 'Tocqueville and Republican Religion: Revisiting "the Visitor"', *Political Theory*, 9 (1980), p. 15.
82. R. Nisbet, *The Sociological Tradition* (London, 1972), p. 130.
83. See A.S. Eisenstadt (ed.), *Reconsidering Tocqueville's 'Democracy in America'*, p. 176.

6 Thomas Carlyle

1. T. Carlyle, *Sartor Resartus* (Oxford, 1987), p. 149.
2. Ibid., p. 176.
3. Ibid., p. 179.
4. T. Carlyle, *Essays in Two Volumes*, Vol. 2 (London, 1964), p. 303.
5. T. Carlyle, *Past and Present* (Oxford, 1921), p. 197.
6. T. Carlyle, *Essays in Two Volumes*, Vol. 1 (London, 1964), p. 338.
7. T. Carlyle, *Latter-Day Pamphlets* (London, 1897), p. 44–5.
8. T. Carlyle, *Sartor Resartus*, p. 18.
9. T. Carlyle, *Essays in Two Volumes*, Vol. 1, p. 245.
10. T. Carlyle, *Past and Present*, pp. 160–1, 160.
11. T. Carlyle, *Essays in Two Volumes*, Vol. 2, p. 203.
12. T. Carlyle, *Past and Present*, pp. 231–2.
13. *Marx Engels: Collected Works*, Vol. 3 (London, 1975), p. 444.

14. T. Carlyle, *Essays in Two Volumes*, Vol. 2, p. 225.
15. T. Carlyle, *The French Revolution. A History* (London, 1891), Part One, p. 178.
16. T. Carlyle, *Past and Present*, p. 194.
17. See T. Carlyle, *Latter-Day Pamphlets*, pp. 35–6 and T. Carlyle, *Essays in Two Volumes*, Vol. 1, p. 299.
18. T. Carlyle, *On Heroes and Hero-Worship* (London, 1974), p. 264.
19. T. Carlyle, *Past and Present*, p. 244.
20. Ibid., p. 130.
21. T. Carlyle, *The French Revolution*, Part One, p. 30.
22. Ibid., p. 12. Also see p. 177.
23. Ibid., p. 115.
24. Ibid., p. 165.
25. Ibid., p. 105.
26. Ibid., Part Two, p. 248.
27. Ibid., Part Three, p. 370.
28. E. Burke, *Reflections on the Revolution in France* (London, 1964), pp. 5–6.
29. T. Carlyle, *Latter-Day Pamphlets*, pp. 32–3 and 37.
30. Ibid., p. 194.
31. Ibid., pp. 199 and 205.
32. Ibid., p. 211.
33. T. Carlyle, *Essays in Two Volumes*, Vol. 1, pp. 317, 316.
34. Ibid., pp. 301, 302.
35. Ibid., p. 311.
36. Ibid., pp. 312, 316, 337.
37. T. Carlyle, *Past and Present*, p. 226.
38. T. Carlyle, *Essays in Two Volumes*, Vol. 1, pp. 236–7.
39. T. Carlyle, *Past and Present*, p. 74.
40. T. Carlyle, *On Heroes and Hero-Worship*, p. 222.
41. T. Carlyle, *Latter-Day Pamphlets*, pp. 211 and 217.
42. Ibid., p. 209.
43. T. Carlyle, *Past and Present*, p. 62.
44. T. Carlyle, *On Heroes and Hero-Worship*, p. 168.
45. T. Carlyle, *Essays in Two Volumes*, Vol. 2, p. 220.
46. Ibid., Vol. 1, pp. 317, 316.
47. T. Carlyle, *On Heroes and Hero-Worship*, p. 284. Also see p. 241.
48. A.J. La Valley, *Carlyle and the Idea of the Modern. Studies in Carlyle's Prophetic Literature and its Relation to Blake, Nietzsche, Marx and Others* (New Haven and London, 1968), p. 268.
49. H. Trevor-Roper, 'Thomas Carlyle's Historical Philosophy', *The Times Literary Supplement*, 26 June 1981, p. 733.
50. T. Carlyle, *History of Frederick II of Prussia called Frederick the Great*, 8 vols, facsimile of 1897 edition (New York, 1969), Vol. 1, pp. 335, 337, 339.
51. Quoted in A.J. La Valley, *Carlyle and the Idea of the Modern*, p. 335.
52. Ibid., p. 214.
53. T. Carlyle, *Sartor Resartus*, p. 5.

54. *Marx Engels: Collected Works*, Vol. 10 (London, 1978), pp. 301 and 307; ibid., Vol. 4 (London, 1975), p. 579.

PART III DEMOCRACY AND DISCRIMINATION

7 'Beings of an Inferior Order': The Ideology of Black Subordination in the USA

1. C. Becker, *The Declaration of Independence. A Study in the History of Political Ideas* (New York, 1942), p. 212.
2. A.J. Hamilton, J. Madison and J. Jay, *The Federalist Papers* (Garden City, New York, 1961), p. 6.
3. G. Myrdal, *An American Dilemma. The Negro Problem and Modern Democracy* (New York, Evanston and London, 1962), p. 429.
4. Maine, Massachusetts, New Hampshire, New York, Rhode Island and Vermont never excluded blacks from voting. For the states that altered their constitutions see Chapter 1, note 8.
5. R.B. Morris, *Basic Documents in American History* (Princeton, NJ, 1956), p. 119.
6. Barrington Moore, Jr, *Social Origins of Dictatorship and Democracy* (Harmondsworth, 1969), p. 121. Also see E.D. Genovese, *The World the Slaveholders Made* (New York, 1971), p. 125 and K. Marx, *Grundrisse. Foundations of the Critique of Political Economy* (Harmondsworth, 1973), p. 513.
7. B.E. Brown, *Great American Political Thinkers*, Vol. 2 (New York, 1983), pp. 23–31.
8. See E.D. Genovese, *The World the Slaveholders Made*, pp. 152 and 156–7.
9. B.E. Brown, *Great American Political Thinkers*, Vol. 2, p. 10. T. Wicker (intro.), *Report of the National Advisory Commission on Civil Disorders* (New York, 1968), p. 236.
10. D.G. Faust, *The Ideology of Slavery. Proslavery Thought in the Antebellum South* (Baton Rouge and London, 1981), pp. 83 and 87.
11. C. Becker, *The Declaration of Independence*, p. 246.
12. D.G. Faust, *The Ideology of Slavery*, p. 89.
13. Ibid., p. 180.
14. F. Douglass, *The Frederick Douglass Papers*, ed. J.W. Blessingame, Vol. 2 (New Haven and London, 1982), pp. 14–15.
15. Aristotle, *The Politics* (Harmondsworth, 1962), p. 34.
16. D.G. Faust, *The Ideology of Slavery*, pp. 170 and 126.
17. Ibid., pp. 136 and 137.
18. Ibid., p. 151.
19. See L. Jones, *Blues People. Negro Music in White America* (New York, 1963), pp. 32–6.
20. E.D. Genovese, *Roll, Jordan, Roll. The World the Slaves Made* (New York, 1976), p. 186.
21. D.G. Faust, *The Ideology of Slavery*, p. 293. Also see E.D. Genovese, *Roll, Jordan, Roll*, pp. 75–86.

22. H. Wish (ed.), *Ante-Bellum. Writings of George Fitzhugh and Hinton Rowan Helper on Slavery* (New York, 1960), p. 71.
23. William Harper, quoted in D.G. Faust, *The Ideology of Slavery*, p. 99.
24. G. Osofsky, *The Burden of Race. A Documentary History of Negro–White Relations in America* (New York, Evanston and London, 1967), p. 315 and see pp. 316–17. Also see George Fitzhugh on the black as 'a grown-up child', in H. Wish (ed.), *Ante-Bellum*, pp. 88–9.
25. D.G. Faust, *The Ideology of Slavery*, p. 189.
26. Ibid., pp. 56, 192 and see p. 271.
27. Ibid., p. 223. Also see J.H. Van Evrie quoted in G. Osofsky, *The Burden of Race*, pp. 104–9.
28. D.G. Faust, *The Ideology of Slavery*, p. 112.
29. Ibid., pp. 121, 227, 221.
30. Ibid., p. 127.
31. Ibid., p. 130.
32. Ibid., p. 129.
33. Ibid., p. 193. See also E.D. Genovese, *Roll, Jordan, Roll*, pp. 49–70.
34. D.G. Faust, *The Ideology of Slavery*, pp. 295, 283 and 277.
35. J.B. Boles, *Black Southerners 1619–1869* (Lexington, Kentucky, 1983), p. 198. Also see G. Myrdal, *An American Dilemma*, p. 444.
36. G.M. Fredrickson, *The Black Image in the White Mind* (New York, 1971), pp. 49–50.
37. F. Douglass, *Narrative of the Life of Frederick Douglass, an American Slave* (Harmondsworth, 1986), p. 78.
38. G. Osofsky, *The Burden of Race*, p. 175.
39. Ibid., p. 171.
40. K.H. Porter, *A History of Suffrage in the United States* (New York, 1971), p. 214. Also see pp. 196–8 and G. Myrdal, *An American Dilemma*, pp. 448–51, 479–86 and 1317–19.
41. K.H. Porter, *A History of Suffrage in the United States*, p. 222.
42. M. Luther King, *Why We Can't Wait* (New York, 1964), p. 49.

8 'Exalted by Their Inferiority': On the Subjection of Women

1. G. Myrdal, *An American Dilemma. The Negro Problem and Modern Democracy* (New York, Evanston and London, 1962), p. 1075.
2. M. Wollstonecraft, *A Vindication of the Rights of Woman* (Harmondsworth, 1975), p. 100.
3. B.E. Brown, *Great American Political Thinkers* (New York, 1983), 2 vols, Vol. 2, p. 108.
4. S.M. Okin, *Women in Western Political Thought* (London, 1980), p. 249.
5. M. Wollstonecraft, op. cit., p. 249.
6. E.C. du Bois, *Feminism and Suffrage. The Emergence of an Independent Women's Movement in America 1848–1869* (Ithaca and London, 1982), p. 23.
7. Brown, *Great American Political Thinkers*, Vol. 2, p. 108.
8. Du Bois, *Feminism and Suffrage*, p. 59.
9. Ibid., p. 73.
10. Aristotle, *The Politics* (Harmondsworth, 1962), pp. 49, 50 and Okin,

Women in Western Political Thought, p. 91.

11. Du Bois, *Feminism and Suffrage*, p. 35.
12. A.S. Kraditor, *The Ideas of the Woman Suffrage Movement 1890–1920* (New York and London, 1981), p. 17. Also see Myrdal, *An American Dilemma*, p. 1074.
13. Genesis, 2:18 and 3:16. Also see I Corinthians 2:8–9; I Corinthians 14:34–5; I Timothy 2:11–14.
14. E. Sagara, *A Social History of Germany* (London, 1977), pp. 408, 410 and see p. 405.
15. J-J. Rousseau, *Emile* (London, 1964), pp. 322, 333, 340 and 349.
16. Okin, *Women in Western Political Thought*, p. 99 and see p. 102.
17. E. Durkheim, *The Division of Labour in Society* (New York and London, 1964), pp. 58, 60.
18. Quoted in Okin, *Women in Western Political Thought*, pp. 220–1. Also see J.B. Landes, *Women and the Public Sphere in the Age of the French Revolution* (Ithaca and London, 1958), pp. 177–83.
19. Kraditor, *The Ideas of the Woman Suffrage Movement*, p. 20.
20. Albert T. Bledsoe, quoted in Myrdal, *An American Dilemma*, p. 1074.
21. Sagara, *Social History of Germany*, p. 416.
22. W. Thönnessen, *The Emancipation of Women. The Rise and Decline of the Women's Suffrage Movement in German Social Democracy 1863–1933* (Glasgow, 1976), pp. 20, 22.
23. K.H. Porter, *A History of Suffrage in the United States* (New York, 1971), p. 253. Also see R. Hofstadter (ed.), *Ten Major Issues in American Politics* (New York, 1968), pp. 92–5.
24. P.N. Carroll and D.W. Noble, *The Free and the Unfree. A New History of the United States* (Harmondsworth, 1985), p. 138.
25. J. Lewis (ed.), *Before the Vote was Won: Arguments for and against Women's Suffrage* (London, 1987), pp. 430–3.
26. See B. Harrison, *Separate Spheres. The Opposition to Women's Suffrage in Britain* (London, 1978), p. 34 and R.J. Evans, *The Feminist Movement in Germany 1894–1933* (London and Beverley Hills, 1976), p. 23.
27. J. Lewis, *Before the Vote was Won*, pp. 73, 74 and see p. 431.
28. A. Kraditor, *Ideas of the Woman Suffrage Movement*, p. 26.
29. M. Wollstonecraft, *A Vindication of the Rights of Woman* (Harmondsworth, 1975), p. 145.
30. Virginius Dabney, quoted in Myrdal, *An American Dilemma*, p. 1074.
31. J. Mackay and P. Thane, 'The Englishwoman' in R. Colls and P. Dodd (eds), *Englishness. Politics and Culture 1880–1920* (London, 1986), p. 203.
32. Okin, *Women in Western Political Thought*, p. 252.
33. Lewis, *Before the Vote was Won*, p. 427.
34. J. Bentham, *Principles of Morals and Legislation* (New York, 1938), pp. 58–9.
35. W. George, *Darwin* (Glasgow, 1982), p. 74.
36. G. Le Bon, *The Crowd* (London, 1952), pp. 35–6.
37. W.E.H. Lecky, *Democracy and Liberty* (London, New York and Bombay, 1896), 2 vols, Vol. 2, p. 458.
38. Lewis, *Before the Vote was Won*, pp. 76, 79–86.

39. Kraditor, *The Ideas of the Woman Suffrage Movement*, pp. 20–1. Also see pp. 19–20.
40. R.J. Evans, *The Feminists. Women's Emancipation Movements in Europe, America and Australasia 1840–1920* (London and Sydney, 1985), p. 125.
41. Sagara, *Social History of Germany*, pp. 415–16.
42. E. Vallance, *Women in the House. A Study of Women Members of Parliament* (London, 1979), p. 5.
43. F. Nietzsche, *Beyond Good and Evil* (Harmondsworth, 1973), p. 83.
44. J. Sayers, *Biological Politics. Feminist and Anti-Feminist Perspectives* (London and New York, 1982), p. 8. On Henry Maudsley see D. Pick, *A European Disorder, c. 1848–c. 1918* (Cambridge, 1989), pp. 203–16.
45. Carroll and Noble, *The Free and the Unfree*, p. 305.
46. Nietzsche, *Beyond Good and Evil*, p. 147.
47. Harrison, *Separate Spheres*, p. 52.
48. M. Pugh, *Women's Suffrage in Britain, 1867–1928* (London, 1980), p. 9.
49. Lewis, *Before the Vote was Won*, p. 61.
50. S.C. Hause with A.R. Kenney, *Women's Suffrage and Social Politics in the French Third Republic* (Princeton, NJ, 1984), p. 16.
51. Du Bois, *Feminism and Suffrage*, pp. 113, 115.
52. Thönnessen, *Emancipation of Women*, p. 98.
53. Lewis, *Before the Vote was Won*, pp. 413, 432.
54. T. Zeldin, *France 1848–1945. Ambition and Love* (Oxford, 1979), p. 350.
55. Harrison, *Separate Spheres*, p. 113.
56. Hause and Kenney, *Women's Suffrage and Social Politics*, p. 253.

PART IV

9 Conclusion

1. See J. Locke, *Two Treatises of Government*, intro. P. Laslett (New York and London, 1965), second Treatise, para. 119.
2. Ibid., para. 118.
3. J-J. Rousseau, *The Social Contract. Discourses* (London, 1961).
4. B. Franklin, 'X marks the spot for the children', *Guardian*, 8 July 1986.
5. J. Harris, 'The Political Status of Children', in K. Graham (ed.), *Contemporary Political Philosophy. Radical Studies* (Cambridge, 1982), p. 51.
6. See W. Bagehot, *The English Constitution* (London, 1961), Ch. 1.
7. M. Margolis, 'Democracy: American Style', in G. Duncan (ed.), *Democratic Theory and Practice* (Cambridge, 1983), p. 126.
8. See R. Michels, *Political Parties. A Sociological Examination of the Oligarchical Tendencies of Modern Democracy* (New York and London, 1962) and M. Weber, *From Max Weber. Essays in Sociology*, ed. H.H. Gerth and C.W. Mills (London, 1961).
9. Quoted in *Observer*, 17 April 1983.
10. R. Hambleton, 'The American Gender Gap', *The Times Higher Education Supplement*, 12 August 1988, p. 13.
11. B. Harrison, *Separate Spheres. The Opposition to Women's Suffrage in*

Britain (London, 1978), p. 249.

12. A.V. Dicey, *Law and Public Opinion in England during the Nineteenth Century* (London, 1963), pp. 218–19.

13. 'The concept "ideology" reflects the one discovery which emerged from political conflict, namely, that ruling groups can in their thinking become so intensely interest-bound to a situation that they are simply no longer able to see certain facts which would undermine their sense of domination.'
'We regard as utopian all situationally transcendent ideas (not only wish-projections) which in any way have a transforming effect upon the existing historical-social order.' K. Mannheim, *Ideology and Utopia. An Introduction to the Sociology of Knowledge* (London, 1960), pp. 36, 185.

14. E.C. du Bois, *Feminism and Suffrage. The Emergence of an Independent Women's Movement in America 1848–1869* (Ithaca and London, 1982), p. 41.

15. According to *Observer*, 10 June 1990.

16. K. Millett, *Sexual Politics* (London, 1972), pp. 83, 85. Also see du Bois, *Feminism and Suffrage*, p. 17.

17. Du Bois, *Feminism and Suffrage*, p. 56.

18. B.R. Barber, *Strong Democracy. Participatory Politics for a New Age* (Berkeley, Los Angeles and London, 1984), p. xiii.

19. R. Nisbet, *The Twilight of Authority* (London, 1976), p. 3.

20. B.R. Barber, *Strong Democracy*, p. 172.

21. Ibid., p. 228.

22. R. Dahrendorf, *Society and Democracy in Germany* (London, 1968), pp. viii–ix.

23. From *The Independent on Sunday*, 1 July 1990. This is the last figure before the financial union of the two Germanies on 1 July 1990.

24. R.E. Lane, 'Government and Self-Esteem', *Political Theory*, 10 (1982), p. 21. Also see W.L. Adamson, 'Economic Democracy and the Expediency of Worker Participation', *Political Studies* xxxviii (1990), pp. 56–71.

25. B.R. Barber, *Strong Democracy*, p. 152.

26. See S.S. Wolin, 'Higher Education and the Politics of Knowledge', *Democracy*, 1–2 (1981), pp. 38–52.

27. For some suggested ways forward see B.R. Barber's 'unified agenda . . . for the Revitalization of Citizenship' in *Strong Democracy*, p. 307; C.B. Macpherson, *The Life and Times of Liberal Democracy* (Oxford, 1977), Ch. IV; D. Beetham, 'Beyond Liberal Democracy' in R. Miliband and J. Saville (eds), *The Socialist Register 1981* (London, 1981).

Bibliography

Adams, J., *Works*, 10 vols, ed. C.F. Adams (Boston, 1850–6).

Adamson, W.L., 'Economic Democracy and the Expediency of Worker Participation', *Political Studies*, xxxviii, (1990) 56–71.

Anderson, E.N., *The Social and Political Conflict in Prussia 1858–1864* (New York, 1976).

Anderson, F.M., *The Constitutions and other Select Documents Illustrative of the History of France 1789–1907* (New York, 1967).

Arblaster, A., *Democracy* (Milton Keynes, 1987).

Aristotle, *The Politics* (Harmondsworth, 1962).

Aron, R., *Main Currents in Sociological Thought*, Vol. 1 (Harmondsworth, 1979).

Avineri, S., 'Hegel' in D. Miller et al., *The Blackwell Encyclopaedia of Political Thought* (Oxford, 1987).

Avineri, S., *Hegel's Theory of the Modern State* (London, 1974).

Avril, P., *Politics in France* (Harmondsworth, 1969).

Bagehot, W., *The English Constitution* (London, 1961).

Bagehot, W., *Physics and Politics* (London, n.d.).

Bailyn, B., *The Ideological Origins of the American Revolution* (Cambridge, Mass., 1967).

Barber, B.R., *Strong Democracy. Participatory Politics for a New Age* (Berkeley, Los Angeles and London, 1984).

Becker, C., *The Declaration of Independence. A Study in the History of Political Ideas* (New York, 1942).

Beetham, D., 'Beyond Liberal Democracy' in R. Miliband and J. Saville (eds), *The Socialist Register, 1981* (London, 1981).

Behnken, E.M., *Thomas Carlyle. 'Calvinist Without the Theology'* (Columbia and London, 1978).

Bentham, J., *Principles of Morals and Legislation* (New York, 1965).

Bentham, J., *A Fragment on Government* (Cambridge, 1988).

Bentley, M., *Politics without Democracy 1815–1914. Perception and Preoccupation in British Government* (London, 1984).

Best, G. (ed.), *The Permanent Revolution. The French Revolution and its Legacy* (London, 1988).

Blewett, N., 'The Franchise in the United Kingdom 1885–1918' *Past and Present*, 32 (1965), 27–56.

Boesche, R.C., 'The Strange Liberalism of Alexis de Tocqueville', *History of Political Thought*, 11 (1981) 495–524.

Boesche, R.C., *The Strange Liberalism of Alexis de Tocqueville* (Ithaca, New York and London, 1987).

Boles, J.B., *Black Southerners 1619–1869* (Lexington, Ky, 1983).

Briggs, A., *Victorian People* (Harmondsworth, 1982).

Brogan, H., *Tocqueville* (Bungay, Suffolk, 1973).

Brown, B.E., *Great American Political Thinkers*, 2 vols (New York, 1983).

Bruford, W.H., *Germany in the Eighteenth Century. The Social Background of the Literary Revival* (Cambridge, 1971).

Burke, E., *Reflections on the Revolution in France* (London, 1964).

Campbell, P., *French Electoral Systems and Elections 1789–1957* (London, 1958).

Cappon, L.J. (ed.), *The Adams–Jefferson Letters*, 2 vols (Chapel Hill, 1959).

Carlyle, T., *The French Revolution. A History* (London, 1891).

Carlyle, T., *Latter-Day Pamphlets* (London, 1897).

Carlyle, T., *Past and Present* (Oxford, 1921).

Carlyle, T., *Essays in Two Volumes* (London, 1964).

Carlyle, T., *History of Frederick II of Prussia called Frederick the Great*, 8 vols, Facsimile of 1897 edition (New York, 1969).

Carlyle, T., *On Heroes and Hero Worship* (London, 1974).

Carlyle, T., *Sartor Resartus* (Oxford, 1987).

Carroll, P.N. and D.W. Noble, *The Free and the Unfree. A New History of the United States* (Harmondsworth, 1985).

Cobban, A., *A History of Modern France*, 2 vols (Harmondsworth, 1962 and 1963).

Cobbett, W., *Rural Rides* (Harmondsworth, 1979).

Cohen, C., 'On the Child's Status in the Democratic State. A Response to Mr. Schrag', *Political Theory*, 3 (1975) 458–63.

Constant, B., *Political Writings* (Cambridge, 1988).

Corcoran, P.E., 'The Limits of Democratic Theory', in G. Duncan (ed.), *Democratic Theory and Practice* (Cambridge, 1983).

Crook, D.P., *American Democracy in English Politics 1815–1850* (Oxford, 1965).

Dahrendorf, R., *Society and Democracy in Germany* (London, 1968).

Dicey, A.V., *Law and Public Opinion in England during the Nineteenth Century* (London, 1963).

Diggins, J.P., 'Knowledge and Sorrow: Louis Hartz's Quarrel with American History', *Political Theory*, 16 (1988) 355–76.

Disraeli, B., *Selected Speeches of the late Right Honourable the Earl of Beaconsfield*, ed. T.E. Kebbel, 2 vols (London, 1882).

Disraeli, B., *Coningsby or the New Generation* (London, 1968).

Douglass, F., *The Frederick Douglass Papers*, ed. J.W. Blassingame, Vol. 2 (New Haven and London, 1982).

Douglass, F., *Narrative of the Life of Frederick Douglass, an American Slave* (Harmondsworth, 1986).

Drescher, S., *Dilemmas of Democracy. Tocqueville and Modernization* (Pittsburgh, 1968).

Du Bois, E.C., *Feminism and Suffrage. The Emergence of an Independent Women's Movement in America 1848–1869* (Ithaca and London, 1982).

Duncan, G. (ed.), *Democratic Theory and Practice* (Cambridge, 1983).

Durkheim, E., *The Division of Labour in Society* (New York and London, 1964).

Eiholzer-Silver, A., 'The Movement of the Intellectuals in France under the Restoration: The Doctrinaires' (University of Kent MA, 1988).

Eisenstadt, A.S. (ed.), *Reconsidering Tocqueville's 'Democracy in America'* (New Brunswick and London, 1988).

Emden, C.K. (ed.), *Selected Speeches on the Constitution*, 2 vols (London, 1939).

Evans, E.J., *The Great Reform Act of 1832* (London and New York, 1983).

Evans, R.J., *The Feminists. Women's Emancipation Movements in Europe, America and Australia 1840–1920* (London and Sydney, 1985).

Evans, R.J., *The Feminist Movement in Germany, 1894–1933* (London and Beverly Hills, 1976).

Faust, D.G. (ed.), *The Ideology of Slavery. Proslavery Thought in the Antebellum South, 1830–1860* (Baton Rouge and London, 1981).

Feuchtwanger, E.J., *Democracy and Empire. Britain 1865–1914* (London, 1985).

Finer, S.E., *Comparative Government* (Harmondsworth, 1977).

Finley, M., *Ancient Slavery and Modern Ideology* (Harmondsworth, 1983).

Franklin, B., 'X marks the spot for the children', *Guardian*, 8 July 1986.

Franklin, B. (ed.), *The Rights of Children* (Oxford, 1986).

Fredrickson, G.M., *The Black Image in the White Mind* (New York, 1971).

Freud, S., *Civilization, Society and Religion*, Vol. 12 of The Pelican Freud Library (Harmondsworth, 1985).

Gash, N., *Politics in the Age of Peel. A study in the technique of parliamentary representation 1830–1850* (London, New York, Toronto, 1953).

Genovese, E.D., *Roll, Jordan, Roll. The World the Slaves Made* (New York, 1976).

Genovese, E.D., *The World the Slaveholders Made* (New York, 1971).

George, W., *Darwin* (Glasgow, 1982).

Goldstein, D., *Trials of Faith. Religion and Politics in Tocqueville's Thought* (New York, Oxford, Amsterdam, 1975).

Gourvish, T., and A. O'Day, *Later Victorian Britain 1867–1901* (London, 1988).

Graubard, S.R., 'Democracy in *Dictionary of the History of Ideas*, Vol. 1 (New York, 1973).

Grenville, J.A.S., *Europe Reshaped 1848–1878* (London, 1986).

Hall, S., 'The Battle for Socialist Ideas in the 1980s' in R. Miliband and J. Saville, *The Socialist Register 1982* (London, 1982).

Hambleton, R., 'The American Gender Gap', *The Times Higher Education Supplement*, 12 August 1988.

Hamerow, T.S., *The Social Foundations of German Unification 1858–1871* (Princeton, NJ, 1974).

Hamerow, T.S., *Restoration, Revolution, Reaction. Economy and Politics in Germany 1815–1871* (Princeton, NJ, 1972).

Hamilton, A., J. Madison, J. Jay, *The Federalist Papers*, selected and edited by R.P. Fairfield (Garden City, NY, 1961).

Hanham, H.J., 'The Reformed Electoral System in Great Britain, 1832–1914'. The Historical Association (London, 1983).

Haraszti, Z., *John Adams and the Prophets of Progress* (Cambridge, Mass., 1952).

Harris, J., 'The Political Status of Children' in K. Graham (ed.), *Contemporary Political Philosophy. Radical Studies* (Cambridge, 1982).

Harrison, B., *Separate Spheres. The Opposition to Women's Suffrage in Britain* (London, 1978).

Harrison, R. (ed.), *The English Defence of the Commune 1871* (London, 1971).

Hartung, F., *Deutsche Verfassungsgeschichte vom 15. Jahrhundert bis zur Gegenwart* (Stuttgart, 1950).

Hause, S.C. with A.R. Kenney, *Women's Suffrage and Social Politics in the French Third Republic* (Princeton, NJ, 1984).

Hegel, G.W.F., *Philosophy of Right* (London, Oxford, New York, 1971).

Hegel, G.W.F., *The Philosophy of History* (New York, 1956).

Hegel, G.W.F., *Hegel's Political Writings*, intro. Z.A. Pelczynski (Oxford, 1969).

Hegel, G.W.F., *Hegel: The Letters* (Bloomington, Indiana, 1984).

Heidensohn, K., 'Industrial Democracy: The German Experience', *Social and Economic Administration*, 5, (1971) 53–66.

Heiman, C., 'The Sources and Significance of Hegel's Corporate Doctrine' in Z.A. Pelczynski (ed.), *Hegel's Political Philosophy. Problems and Perspectives* (Cambridge, 1971).

Hereth, M., *Alexis de Tocqueville. Threats to Freedom in Democracy* (Durham, 1988).

Hobsbawm, E.J., *The Age of Empire 1875–1914* (London, 1987).

Hofstadter, R., *Ten Major Issues in American Politics* (New York, 1968).

Howe, J.R., Jr, *The Changing Political Thought of John Adams* (Princeton, NJ, 1966).

Ilting, K.H., 'The Structure of Hegel's Philosophy of Right', in Z.A. Pelczynski, *Hegel's Political Philosophy. Problems and Perspectives* (Cambridge, 1971).

Jones, L., *Blues People. Negro Music in White America* (New York, 1963).

Keating, P. (ed.), *The Victorian Prophets. A Reader from Carlyle to Wells* (Glasgow, 1981).

Kelly, G.A., 'Parnassian Liberalism in Nineteenth-Century France. Tocqueville, Renan, Flaubert', *History of Political Thought* 8 (1987) 475–503.

King, M.L., *Why We Can't Wait* (New York, 1964).

Koch, A., and W. Reden (eds), *The Selected Writings of John and John Quincy Adams* (New York, 1946).

Konvitz, M.R., *A Century of Civil Rights* (New York and London, 1967).

Kraditor, A.S., *The Ideas of the Woman Suffrage Movement, 1890–1920* (New York and London, 1981).

Krieger, L., *The German Idea of Freedom. History of a Political Tradition* (Chicago and London, 1972).

Lamberti, J.C., *Tocqueville and the Two Democracies* (Cambridge, Mass., and London, 1989).

Landes, J.B., *Women and the Public Sphere in the Age of the French Revolution* (Ithaca and London, 1988).

Lane, R.E., 'Government and Self-Esteem', *Political Theory*, 10, (1982) 5–31.

LaValley, A.J., *Carlyle and the Idea of the Modern. Studies in Carlyle's Prophetic Literature and its Relation to Blake, Nietzsche, Marx and Others* (New Haven and London, 1968).

Lecky, W.E.H., *Democracy and Liberty*, 2 vols (London, New York and Bombay, 1896).

LeQuesne, A., *Carlyle* (Oxford, 1982).

Levin, M. and H. Williams, 'Inherited Power and Popular Representation: a

Tension in Hegel's Political Theory', *Political Studies*, xxxv (1987) 105–15.

Levin, M., *Marx, Engels and Liberal Democracy* (London, 1989).

Lewis, J. (ed.), *Before the Vote Was Won: arguments for and against Women's Suffrage* (London, 1987).

Lipset, S.M., *Political Man* (London, 1963).

Lipset, S.M., *The First New Nation. The United States in Historical and Comparative Perspective* (New York, London, 1979).

Lively, J., *The Social and Political Thought of Alexis de Tocqueville* (Oxford, 1965).

Locke, J., *Two Treatises of Government*, intro. P. Laslett (New York and London, 1965).

MacIntyre, A. (ed.), *Hegel. A Collection of Critical Essays* (Notre Dame and London, 1976).

Mackay J. and P. Thane, 'The Englishwoman', in R. Colls and P. Dodd (eds), *Englishness. Politics and Culture 1880–1920* (London, 1986).

Macpherson, C.B., *The Life and Times of Liberal Democracy* (Oxford, 1977).

Macpherson, C.B., *Burke* (Oxford, 1980).

Maistre, J. de, *The Works of Joseph de Maistre*, ed. J. Lively (London, 1965).

Mannheim, K., *Ideology and Utopia. An Introduction to the Sociology of Knowledge* (London, 1960).

Margolis, M., 'Democracy: American Style', in G. Duncan (ed.), *Democratic Theory and Practice* (Cambridge, 1983).

Marx, K., *Grundrisse. Foundations of the Critique of Political Economy* (Harmondsworth, 1973).

Marx, K., *Capital. A Critique of Political Economy*, Vol. 1 (Harmondsworth, 1976).

Marx, K. and F. Engels, *Marx Engels: Collected Works* (London, 1975–).

Marx Engels: Selected Works, 2 vols (Moscow, 1962).

Mayer, A.J., *The Persistence of the Old Regime. Europe to the Great War* (London, 1981).

Michels, R., *Political Parties. A Sociological Examination of the Oligarchical Tendencies of Modern Democracy* (New York and London, 1962).

Mill, James, *An Essay on Government* (Indianapolis, 1977).

Mill, J.S., *Utilitarianism, Liberty, Representative Government* (London, 1962).

Mill, J.S., *Autobiography of John Stuart Mill* (New York, 1964).

Millett, K., *Sexual Politics* (London, 1972).

Morgan, D., *Suffragists and Liberals. The Politics of Woman Suffrage in Britain* (Oxford, 1975).

Morgan, E.S., *Inventing the People. The Rise of Popular Sovereignty in England and America* (New York and London, 1988).

Moore, Barrington, Jr, *Social Origins of Dictatorship and Democracy* (Harmondsworth, 1969).

Morris, R.B., *Basic Documents in American History* (Princeton, NJ, 1956).

Myers, A.R., *Parliaments and Estates in Europe to 1789* (London, 1975).

Myrdal, G., *An American Dilemma. The Negro Problem and Modern Democracy* (New York, Evanston and London, 1962).

Nietzsche, F., *Beyond Good and Evil* (Harmondsworth, 1973).

Nisbet, R., *The Sociological Tradition* (London, 1972).

Nisbet, R., 'Tocqueville's Ideal Types' in A.S. Eisenstadt (ed.), *Reconsidering Tocqueville's 'Democracy in America'* (New Brunswick and London 1988).

Nisbet, R., *The Twilight of Authority* (London, 1976).

Okin, S.M., *Women in Western Political Thought* (London, 1980).

Osofsky, G., *The Burden of Race. A Documentary History of Negro–White Relations in America* (New York, Evanston, London, 1967).

Paine, T., *The Rights of Man* (London, 1958).

Palmer, R.R., *The Age of the Democratic Revolution. A Political History of Europe and America 1760–1800* (Princeton, NJ, 1959).

Pateman, C., *Participation and Democratic Theory* (Cambridge, 1970).

Pelczynski, Z.A. (ed.), *Hegel's Political Philosophy. Problems and Perspectives* (Cambridge, 1971).

Pelczynski, Z.A., *The State and Civil Society. Studies in Hegel's Political Philosophy* (Cambridge, 1984).

Pick, D., *Faces of Degeneration. A European Disorder c. 1848–c.1918* (Cambridge, 1989).

Pickles, D., *The Fifth French Republic. Institutions and Politics* (London, 1962).

Plamenatz, J.P., *Man and Society*, 2 vols (London, 1963).

Plant, R., *Hegel* (London, 1973).

Plato, *The Republic of Plato*, intro. F.M. Cornford (Oxford, 1961).

Pole, J.R. (ed.), *The Revolution in America 1754–1788* (Stanford, 1970).

Porter, K.H., *A History of Suffrage in the United States* (New York, 1971).

Pugh, M., *Women's Suffrage in Britain. 1867–1928* (London, 1980).

Raaflaub, K.A., 'Democracy, Oligarchy and the Concept of the "Free Citizen" in Late Fifth-Century Athens', *Political Theory*, 11 (1983) 517–44.

Ramm, A., *Germany 1789–1919* (London, 1967).

Retallack, J.N., *Notables of the Right. The Conservative Party and Political Mobilization in Germany 1876–1918* (Boston, 1988).

Richter, M., 'Toward a Concept of Political Illegitimacy. Bonapartist Dictatorship and Democratic Legitimacy', *Political Theory*, 10 (1982).

Ritter, J., *Hegel and the French Revolution. Essays on the Philosophy of Right* (Cambridge, Mass., 1982).

Rossiter, C., *The Political Thought of the American Revolution* (New York, 1963).

Rousseau, J-J., *The Social Contract, Discourses* (London, 1961).

Rousseau, J-J., *Emile* (London, 1963).

Russell, B., *German Social Democracy* (London, 1965).

Sagara, E., *A Social History of Germany* (London, 1977).

Sayers, J., *Biological Politics. Feminist and Anti-Feminist Perspectives* (London and New York, 1982).

Schacht, R.L., 'Hegel on Freedom' in A. MacIntyre (ed.), *Hegel. A Collection of Critical Essays* (Notre Dame and London, 1976).

Schauff, J., 'Das Wahlsystem des Deutschen Reiches und die Zentrumspartei', in G. Ritter (ed.), *Deutsche Parteien vor 1918* (Köln, 1973).

Schneewind, J.B. (ed.), *Mill. A Collection of Critical Essays* (London, 1969).

Schorske, C.E., *German Social Democracy 1905–1917. The Development of the Great Schism* (New York, 1972).

Schrag, F., 'The Child's Status in the Democratic State', *Political Theory*, 3 (1975) 441–57.

Slater, A. (ed.), *The Correspondence of Emerson and Carlyle* (New York and London, 1964).

Smith, F.B., *The Making of the Second Reform Bill* (Cambridge, 1986).

Snell, J.C., *The Democratic Movement in Germany 1789–1914* (Chapel Hill, 1976).

Stadelmann, R., 'Deutschland und die westeuropäischen Revolutionen', in H. Böhme (ed.), *Probleme der Reichsgründungszeit* (Köln and Berlin, 1972).

Stedman-Jones, G., *Outcast London. A Study in the Relationship between Classes in Victorian Society* (Harmondsworth, 1984).

Stewart, J.H., *A Documentary Survey of the French Revolution* (Toronto, 1969).

Strout, C., 'Tocqueville and Republican Religion: Revisiting the Visitor', *Political Theory*, 9 (1980) 9–26.

Suter, J-F., 'Burke, Hegel and the French Revolution', in Z.A. Pelczynski, *Hegel's Political Philosophy. Problems and Perspectives* (Cambridge, 1971).

Thane, P., 'Government and Society in England and Wales, 1750–1914', in F.M.L. Thomson (ed.), *The Cambridge Social History of Great Britain 1750–1950*, Vol. 3 (Cambridge, 1990).

Thönnessen, W., *The Emancipation of Women. The Rise and Decline of the Women's Suffrage Movement in German Social Democracy 1863–1933* (Glasgow, 1976).

Tocqueville, A. de, *The Old Regime and the French Revolution* (New York, 1955).

Tocqueville, A. de, *Democracy in America*, ed. R.D. Heffner (New York, 1960).

Tocqueville, A. de, *Democracy in America*, ed. J.P. Mayer and M. Lerner (Evanston and London, 1966).

Tocqueville, A. de, *The European Revolution and Correspondence with Gobineau* (Westport, Conn., 1974).

Tocqueville, A. de, *Recollections* (New York, 1975).

Tocqueville, A. de, *On Democracy, Revolution and Society*, ed. J. Stone and S. Mennell (Chicago and London, 1980).

Tocqueville, A. de, *Selected Letters on Politics and Society*, ed. R. Boesche (Berkeley, Los Angeles and London, 1985).

Tocqueville, A. de, *Journeys to England and Ireland*, ed. J.P. Mayer, (New Brunswick and Oxford, 1988).

Trevor-Roper, H., 'Thomas Carlyle's historical philosophy', *Times Literary Supplement*, 26 June 1981, 731–4.

Ullmann, W., *A History of Political Thought: The Middle Ages* (Harmondsworth, 1965).

Vallance, E., *Women in the House. A Study of Women Members of Parliament* (London, 1979).

Webb, B., *My Apprenticeship* (Harmondsworth, 1971).

Weber, M., *From Max Weber, Essays in Sociology*, ed. H.H. Gerth and C.W. Mills (London, 1961).

Wehler, H-U., *The German Empire 1871–1918* (Leamington Spa and Dover, NH, 1985).

Werth, A., *De Gaulle. A Political Biography* (Harmondsworth, 1965).

White, R.J. (ed.), *The Conservative Tradition* (London, 1950).

Wicker, T. (intro.), *Report of the National Advisory Commission on Civil Disorders* (New York, 1968).

Williams, R., *Culture and Society 1780–1950* (Harmondsworth, 1968).

Williamson, C., *American Suffrage. From Property to Democracy 1760–1860* (Princeton, NJ, 1968).

Wish, H. (ed.), *Ante-Bellum. Writings of George Fitzhugh and Hinton Rowan Helper on Slavery* (New York, 1960).

Wolin, S.S., 'Higher Education and the Politics of Knowledge', *Democracy*, 1.2 (1981) 38–52.

Wollstonecraft, M., *A Vindication of the Rights of Woman* (Harmondsworth, 1975).

Wood, G.S., *The Creation of the American Republic 1776–1787* (Chapel Hill, 1969).

Wood, G.S., 'The Fundamentalists and the Constitution', *The New York Review of Books*, 18 February 1988, 33–40.

Woodbridge, G., *The Reform Bill of 1832* (New York, 1970).

Wright, D.G., *Democracy and Reform 1815–1885* (Burnt Mill, Harlow, 1982).

Wright, E., 'Liberty, Equality and Clemency', *The Times Higher Education Supplement*, 23 December 1988, 16.

Zeldin, T., *France 1848–1945*, Vol. 1 (Oxford, 1973), reprinted as *France 1848–1945 – Ambition and Love* (Oxford, 1979).

Zetterbaum, M., *Tocqueville and the Problem of Democracy* (Stanford, 1967).

Index